ORDER AND VIOLENCE

Hedley Bull

ORDER
AND
VIOLENCE

Hedley Bull
and International Relations

Edited by
J. D. B. Miller and R. J. Vincent

CLARENDON PRESS · OXFORD
1990

Oxford University Press, Walton Street, Oxford OX2 6DP

Oxford New York Toronto
Delhi Bombay Calcutta Madras Karachi
Petaling Jaya Singapore Hong Kong Tokyo
Nairobi Dar es Salaam Cape Town
Melbourne Auckland

and associated companies in
Berlin Ibadan

Oxford is a trade mark of Oxford University Press

Published in the United States
by Oxford University Press, New York

British Library Cataloguing in Publication Data

Order and violence: Hedley Bull and international
relations.
1. Foreign relations. Theories of Bull, Hedley 1932–1985
I. Miller, J. D. B. (John Donald Bruce) 1922– II.
Vincent, R. J. (Raymond John) 1943–
327.1'01
ISBN 0-19-827555-2

Library of Congress Cataloging in Publication Data

Order and violence: Hedley Bull and international relations/edited
by J. D. P. Miller and R. J. Vincent.
"Bibliography of Hedley Bull's publications" (p.)
1. International relations.   2. Bull, Hedley.   I. Miller,
J. D. B. (John Donald Bruce), 1922– .   II. Vincent, R. J., 1943– .
JX1391.068 1990   327—dc20   89-26518
ISBN 0-19-827555-2

Typeset by Pentacor Ltd, High Wycombe, Bucks.
Printed by Biddles Ltd, Guildford & King's Lynn

Preface

THIS book represents our attempt to come to grips with Hedley Bull's contribution to international relations. It deals with the big questions in the subject that preoccupied him from the time he was a young lecturer at the London School of Economics to his last appointment as Montague Burton Professor of International Relations at Oxford: the nature of international society; order in world politics; the Third World; strategic studies and arms control; the contemporary global political system; and the academic study of international relations.

We should like to acknowledge the following for their help or advice on the production of this book: Mohammad Ayoob, Henry Bosch, Colin Bull, Mary Bull, Adrian Cotter, Sir Michael Howard, Geoffrey Jukes, Klaus Knorr, Don Markwell (who prepared the bibliography), Adam Roberts, Peter Southcombe, Jack Spence, and Adam Watson. We should especially like to thank Mary Bull for her comments on the whole manuscript and her assistance with copy-editing.

J.D.B.M.
R.J.V.

Canberra and Oxford
July 1988

Contents

Notes on Contributors

ROBERT GILPIN, JR. is Dwight D. Eisenhower Professor of International Affairs at Princeton University. His most recent book is *The Political Economy of International Relations* (Princeton, 1986).

STANLEY HOFFMANN is Douglas Dillon Professor of the Civilization of France at Harvard University, and Chairman of its Center for European Studies. He is the author of several books including *Duties beyond Borders* (Syracuse, 1981).

CARSTEN HOLBRAAD was for several years Senior Research Fellow in International Relations at the Australian National University. He is the author of a number of books including *The Concert of Europe* (London, 1970). He is currently working on a project on European neo-nationalism.

T. B. MILLAR is Professor of Australian Studies at the University of London. He is the author of several books on international relations including *The Commonwealth and the United Nations* (Sydney, 1967), and has specialized in Australian defence and foreign policy.

J. D. B. MILLER is Emeritus Professor of International Relations at the Australian National University. He has written several books on international relations. His *Norman Angell and the Futility of War* was published in London in 1986.

JAMES L. RICHARDSON is Professorial Fellow in International Relations at the Australian National University. He is the author of *Germany and the Atlantic Alliance* (Cambridge, Mass., 1966), and is currently completing a study on crises in international politics.

R. J. VINCENT is Montague Burton Professor of International Relations at the London School of Economics. He is the author of *Human Rights and International Relations* (Cambridge, 1986).

1
Hedley Bull, 1932–1985

J. D. B. MILLER

HEDLEY NORMAN BULL was born in Sydney on 10 June 1932, the third child of Joseph Norman and Doris Bull. His father, who came from a family with a commercial background, was an insurance broker. His mother's maiden name of Hordern was a famous one for many years in the retail trade and the pastoral life of New South Wales. The Bull family home, first at Burwood and then at Strathfield, was a stable and conservative one. Hedley went to Fort Street High School, one of the most prominent in the New South Wales state system, where he took part in debating and dramatics. He finished with a good pass at the Leaving Certificate in 1948—including First Class Honours in history, a subject which was to inform and shape his mind, and continue to be one of his dominant interests.

From 1949 to 1952 Hedley Bull was an undergraduate in the Faculty of Arts at the University of Sydney. Initially he intended to do both arts and law, but abandoned law to concentrate on history and philosophy. In these he obtained Honours in 1952, First Class in philosophy and Second in history. He led a boisterous social life, continued with debating, launched a short-lived Sydney University Political Science Association, edited the Arts Faculty journal *Arna*, and wrote often in the student newspaper *Honi Soit*; but it was what he learnt from John Anderson that mattered most.

Anderson had been Challis Professor of Philosophy since 1927. As the foremost influence in the Faculty of Arts, he created during thirty years a following unique in Australian intellectual history. A close friend and contemporary says that 'it was in the Philosophy School at Sydney University that Hedley really came of age as a student.'[1] Bull himself wrote that 'my

---

[1] Letter from Adrian Cotter, 1 Feb. 1987.

greatest intellectual debt is to John Anderson . . . a greater man than many who are more famous . . . the impact of his mind and his example have been the deepest factors in shaping the outlook of many of us whom he taught.'[2]

It is difficult for someone who was not his student to describe Anderson's ideas and influence.[3] He was a compelling personality whose impact on students was very great; this was largely because of his views, but also because he took a keen interest in many of his students and discussed their work and ideas with them. His impact was accentuated by the fact that in the 1930s and 40s there were few external influences to affect them: Australia was relatively isolated from the outside world by depression and war, other philosophical influences were mostly ineffective, and Anderson provided the excitement of a radical alternative to conventional approaches to religion, literature, patriotism, sex, and the state, as well as being the pre-eminent philosopher of his time in Australia. Bull was fortunate in getting the best out of him.

'The best' from Anderson included an emphasis upon realism as opposed to idealism; an awareness that society and institutions were arenas for the conflict of interests rather than bodies with a monolithic purpose; a recognition that criticism was an essential feature of the intellectual life, and indispensable to enquiry; a belief in the value of traditions which embodied criticism, speculation, courage, and enquiry; and a sense of the importance of sustaining a 'position', an overall interpretation of events and social movements which enabled one to understand one's surroundings and to appreciate the significance of change; and a certain radical scepticism. All of these elements were present in Hedley Bull's thinking.

A friend and colleague has summed up what he got from Anderson:

There are occasional echoes of Anderson in Hedley's writing—his social pluralism; the life of enquiry which has its own morality; or Hedley's sustained argument in *The Control of the Arms Race* against what Anderson termed 'voluntarism'.

---

[2] Hedley Bull, *The Anarchical Society* (London, 1977), p. x.

[3] His philosophical views can be studied in John Anderson, *Studies in Empirical Philosophy* (Sydney, 1979), with comparisons in J. A. Passmore's Introductory Essay. See also A. J. Baker, *Anderson's Social Philosophy* (Sydney, 1979), and *Australian Realism: The Systematic Philosophy of John Anderson* (Cambridge, 1986), and P. H. Partridge and D. M. McCallum in the *Australian Highway*, Sept. 1958.

Much more significant, however, was Anderson's example. Much more than others of his generation, without becoming over-preoccupied with Anderson's doctrines, Hedley succeeded in drawing from his philosophical teaching a sense of the great issues, of the relevance of the classics to contemporary predicaments, of the present as a moment in history—and, above all, a capacity to discern the central elements of a problem, to think through its complexities, to arrive at a clear conclusion all the more compelling in that the argument along the way has grappled seriously with statements of the contrary position in their strongest form.[4]

Bull was awarded a Woolley Travelling Fellowship and arrived at University College, Oxford, in 1953, having intended to do the B.Phil. in philosophy. However, reading the Oxford philosophers made him reluctant to immerse himself in linguistic analysis, and he elected for the B.Phil in politics. His choice of papers did not include international relations. Amongst his teachers were H. L. A. Hart, Isaiah Berlin, K. C. Wheare, John Plamenatz, and Norman Chester. In March 1954 he married Mary Lawes, to whom he had become engaged before he left Sydney. Their honeymoon transport was provided by another Australian graduate student, R. J. L. Hawke, later Prime Minister of Australia.

After graduating from Oxford in 1955, Bull decided that he would like to teach at a British university for a few years before returning to Australia. He was offered an assistant lectureship in political philosophy at Aberdeen, and was about to accept when he was unexpectedly offered an assistant lectureship in international relations at the London School of Economics and Political Science. C. A. W. Manning, who was the Montague Burton Professor at the LSE, was pleased that the appointee had done no academic study of international relations. Since Manning had his own highly esoteric notion of what the subject was about, he may well have thought that the best sort of appointee would be someone who was unsullied by other people's ideas about it; but in appointing Bull he had chosen intellectual distinction rather than the local academic orthodoxy of other candidates, and his choice was right.

Oxford and London were receptive environments for Australians in the 1950s. Indeed, so was Britain as a whole. The

---

[4] J. L. Richardson at a commemoration of Hedley Bull, Research School of Pacific Studies, Australian National University, on 29 May 1985.

memories of wartime association were only a decade old; Australians were freely admitted into Britain and were given all the rights of employment and participation that the British themselves enjoyed. 'Commonwealth immigration' had not yet become contentious, and the effects of immigration from India, Pakistan, and the West Indies were only beginning to show themselves. The restrictions on immigration which have since become commonplace were then unimaginable. In 1955 the expansion of the British university system was just starting. The atmosphere was one of hope and activity, of opportunity and achievement. Wartime rationing had ended; the balance of payments, while greatly troublesome, was manageable; the Commonwealth of Nations looked for a time like a significant international institution, largely organized in favour of British interests. Even the Suez Crisis of 1956 (which occurred when Bull was writing on Cobden's ideas about non-intervention) failed to destroy the heady atmosphere of the time.

From 1955 onwards, Hedley Bull's task was to learn his trade in international relations while practising it. The subject had been taught at the LSE since just after World War I, and Manning, a former Oxford don, had held the Chair since 1930. A South African with a background in international law, and a brief experience of the ILO and the League of Nations in their formative years, he had a somewhat idiosyncratic view of the subject which arose partly from his background, partly from his desire to make a sharp distinction between international relations and political science, and partly from his lack of rapport with developments in the United States. Because he had not yet written a book explaining his views, it was necessary for his colleagues to attend his lectures in order to know what to discuss with the students in tutorials. This was an unusual situation for the young Bull, and his relations with Manning throughout his time at the LSE were complex; but he always admired Manning's wide view of the subject, and enjoyed the stimulation of trying to understand his themes. These were not, however, the only stimulants to be found.

Amongst Bull's colleagues the most notable was Martin Wight, the Reader in the subject, who looked somewhat aloof but was in fact highly approachable. Manning recommended that Bull attend his lectures on international theory. 'These lectures made a profound impression on me, as they did on all who heard them,' wrote Bull in 1976, after Wight's death. 'Ever since that time I have felt in the shadow of Martin Wight's thought—humbled by it, a constant borrower from it, always hoping to transcend it but never able to escape from it.'[5] To Wight, the guide to the relations between states was history, especially the history of the principal traditions of thought about those relations. Bull already had a keen interest in political philosophy. Wight showed him that there were distinctive traditions of thought—to which he gave the names Realist, Rationalist, and Revolutionist—in terms of which the debate about the theory and practice of international politics in any era could be presented and criticized. Wight himself had been a realist of sorts, his monograph on *Power Politics* (later expanded) having been a guidebook to many of us in the years immediately after World War II; but his main concern was to identify these traditions, to indicate their application, and to subdivide them so as to show their continual application. His scholarship was so remarkable, his capacity to apply the traditions so effective (he was well aware of current events, having for many years been associated with Chatham House and having broadcast and written from the San Francisco conference of 1945 for the *Observer*), that there can hardly have been a better mentor for a young man learning what to make of international relations. There was no obvious link between Wight and Anderson; but it was easy for Bull to assimilate the Wight doctrine while retaining much of what he had learnt from Anderson, who had no interest in international relations except to excoriate the Soviet Union. In particular, the habit of scepticism and of controversy, which was rather less characteristic of Wight, remained with Bull as a valuable legacy from his time in Sydney.

There were also institutional influences upon him. Occasional attendance at the Institute of Commonwealth Studies gave him acquaintance with the doyen of Australian historians, Sir Keith Hancock, and assisted with the course on Commonwealth relations which he gave at the LSE—and which produced eventually the iconoclastic and highly effective essay, 'What is

---

[5] Hedley Bull, 'Martin Wight and the theory of international relations', the second Martin Wight Memorial Lecture, in *British Journal of International Studies*, 2. 2 (July 1976), 101. For further discussion by Bull of Wight's views, see the Introductions to Martin Wight, *Systems of States*, ed. Hedley Bull (Leicester, 1977), and Martin Wight, *Power Politics*, ed. Hedley Bull and Carsten Holbraad (Harmondsworth, 1979).

the Commonwealth?'[6] Chatham House, a venue for political spokesmen and international figures, provided useful experience. In 1958 there was established the British Committee on the Theory of International Politics, financed by the Rockefeller Foundation and providing a forum for the exchange of views between such people as Sir Herbert Butterfield, Martin Wight, Michael Howard, and Geoffrey Hudson.[7] Bull became a member, and after two meetings Butterfield said to another member of the group, 'It looks as though Hedley Bull will be the ablest of us all.'[8] The committee continued for many years to be one of Bull's prime interests.

His introduction to the United States took place in September 1957 after Manning had arranged a Rockefeller Travelling Fellowship which gave him time at Harvard, Washington, Chicago, and Berkeley. This American year enabled him to meet many of the leading practitioners in the field. He was impressed by the work done on strategic questions in Harvard, in particular by Thomas Schelling and Henry Kissinger. He was disturbed by much of the behaviouralist literature which was gaining such ground at the time. In its neglect of history and philosophy, and its attempt to emulate the physical sciences, it offended against his growing conception of the subject, and was to remain an object of attack in his writings and conversation. It was the subject of his most frequently reprinted article, 'International Theory: The Case for a Classical Approach', in *World Politics* for April 1966.

The interest in strategic studies and especially in arms control which Bull developed at Harvard did not constitute an entirely new departure. In exploring the literature of international relations he had paid particular attention to writers such as Mahan who tried to place military power in the context of the international system as a whole. He was interested in war as a factor in the preservation and alteration of that system, and not, as it is so often seen, as a fortuitous or isolated phenomenon. In

---

[6] *World Politics*, 11. 4 (July 1959), 577–87.

[7] Some papers read before the committee are in Herbert Butterfield and Martin Wight, eds., *Diplomatic Investigations* (London, 1966). The book that Bull edited with Adam Watson, *The Expansion of International Society* (Oxford, 1984) was the outcome of the committee's work after Martin Wight's death.

[8] Quoted by Adam Watson at the memorial service to Hedley Bull, Oxford, 17 Oct. 1985.

1959 two events led to a concentration on military power and especially on the significance of armaments.

The first of these was abortive, though it did enable him to organize his thoughts more clearly. Philip Noel-Baker, who had been Manning's predecessor at the LSE and had done much work on disarmament, asked him to do research for a book he was planning on the Disarmament Conference of 1932. After spending some time on this, Bull gave up the task, because he disagreed with much of Noel-Baker's thinking and especially with the notion of complete disarmament as a means of attaining peace. Soon, however, he was engaged in an enterprise with much more fortunate results.

The second event was an invitation from Alastair Buchan, the Director of the newly established Institute for Strategic Studies, later the International Institute, to act as draftsman and rapporteur for a study group on arms control. In the latter part of 1959 and the early months of 1960 he worked on individual chapters, putting them before a distinguished group which included Buchan, Kenneth Younger, John Strachey, and Peter Wiles. At the IISS Conference at Oxford in September 1960 he presented the report as a whole. While it purported to be a report of what a study group had decided, it was so obviously the product of a single relentlessly analytical mind that it immediately provided him with a high reputation. Sir Michael Howard has described the occasion thus:

> I can still vividly recall the sessions where veteran disarmers, bureaucrats and warriors shook their heads over the lucid draft chapters, clear, uncompromising, sensible, in which this tall, diffident yet abrasive young man cut through half a century's emotional waffle and forced them to think again from first principles. It was this experience which first cast Hedley in the role of the *enfant terrible* of International Relations; one whose impatience with political cant and academic folly made him the delight and terror of every conference he attended.[9]

The result of these efforts was *The Control of the Arms Race*, which appeared in 1961 and was immediately recognized as an authoritative statement of what could be done to control nuclear weapons. In the United States it was hailed because it combined what was regarded as British common sense and historical

---

[9] Michael Howard at the Oxford memorial service to Hedley Bull.

judgement with the creative abstractions of such Americans as Schelling. In Britain it provided for many students an introduction to the previously uncharted territory of arms control in the nuclear age. Its success led to Bull's appointment to a Readership in 1963, at the early age of 31. His association with the IISS, over a period of 26 years, was of value to both him and it.

He spent 1963 at Princeton University, again encountering the phenomenon of American behaviouralism, but making contact with other thinkers, such as Richard Falk, who were to become important in the formulation of his own approach to the notion of international order. It was characteristic of Bull that he was less interested in the conventional than the unconventional: he knew all the arguments of the conventional theorists, and could use them with effect when he wanted to; but he found it more rewarding to bounce his ideas off those of some more extreme theorist such as Falk or Johan Galtung. The same was true of his later Indian experience: a theorist such as Rajni Kothari gave him more pleasure than those Indians who were patiently restating the latest orthodoxy from the United States or Britain. A word used to describe him by a rather serious-minded Princeton colleague is 'insouciant'. He was by now master of his trade, and could afford to enjoy it. If this meant occasionally being mischievous or abrasive towards those whose minds worked more slowly than his own, so much the worse for them.

Early in 1965, after the election of the Wilson Labour Government, Bull was offered the directorship of an Arms Control and Disarmament Research Unit to be established in the Foreign Office in London. It meant that he had to take leave from the LSE for the time being; but it offered new opportunities and he was glad to accept. The job was unlike many others in government. He was able to recruit his own staff from within and outside the Civil Service; the emphasis was on research; and the atmosphere was more that of a university department than of a government office. Initially there was some suspicion from departmental sources;

but it was not very long before they realised·that the kind of intellectual back-up the Unit provided was very valuable, not perhaps so much in dealing with the Soviets as in enabling the U.K. to 'keep its end up' with the Americans' tendency to try and 'blind us with science'. Here, of course, Hedley's approach was crucial; I think the F.O. originally thought it was getting a bunch of starry-eyed peaceniks, and though it didn't take long to disabuse them of that it perhaps took longer to persuade them that we weren't just impractical and 'academic'. This was where Hedley set the tone—the Unit's first major study set out to establish minimum limits at which deterrence would be stable, and . . . it established the Unit as practical and down-to-earth in its approach.[10]

Before long Bull was taking part in wider policy discussions than those concerned simply with arms control.

In 1966 Bull was offered a Professorship of International Relations in the Research School of Pacific Studies at the Australian National University, Canberra. The offer, which was for him alone, included joint headship of the department. He and the existing incumbent would serve two years each, turn and turn about. The offer was tempting: it involved a return to Australia, which he had always envisaged, and conditions of work which were hard to match in Britain. He did not hesitate in accepting. He arrived in Canberra in June 1967.

There followed ten years during which he settled effectively into Canberra while maintaining his contacts in Britain and the United States. He had a period at Columbia University in New York, another at Jawarhalal Nehru University in New Delhi, and a third at All Souls, Oxford. He was elected a Fellow of the Academy of the Social Sciences in Australia in 1968. He acted as Australian representative on the Council of the IISS. He served as Research Director of the Australian Institute of International Affairs from 1968 to 1973, read papers on a variety of subjects including Australian foreign policy to conferences at home and in New Zealand (such as those included in the book he edited, *Asia and the Western Pacific*), and took an active part in controversy: he was one of the signatories of a public letter before the 1972 federal elections, which recommended a vote for the Australian Labor Party. In no sense, however, was Bull a party man. The signature expressed his impatience with the absurdities of the Macmahon government, especially in foreign policy, rather than any lasting commitment to one side or the other in Australian politics.

It was in seminars in Canberra that most of the chapters of his major work, *The Anarchical Society*, were presented and discussed. Bull was highly effective at seminars and in the

---

[10] Statement by Geoffrey Jukes.

supervision of Ph.D. students. He was remorseless in criticism of what he regarded as high-flown or misguided comment, but he was highly receptive to other people's impressions of his own work, and prepared to make considerable changes if he thought they were justified. Perhaps from his experiences with Anderson, perhaps from the tutorial system at Oxford, he had acquired a genuine concern for individual graduate students. Those whom he supervised (the department had only Ph.D. students until 1975, when, largely under his guidance, it instituted a one-year course-work programme for an MA in International Relations) found him searching but sympathetic, determined that they should do well and concerned about their ideas and their circumstances. The formidable reputation for supervision which he was later to gain at Oxford was already present in the minds of his students in Canberra.

The death of Alastair Buchan in 1976 left vacant the Montague Burton Chair of International Relations at Oxford. Bull was an obvious choice for the post: the year he had spent immediately beforehand at All Souls had convinced the Oxford community of his remarkable quality and the maturity which now sat plainly upon him, in spite of the occasional outburst at some stuffy gathering. He left Canberra in 1977 for the chair and a fellowship at Balliol. It was something of a hard choice for him, and he did not give up the idea of later returning to the ANU; but the Oxford post was a challenge which he could not resist.

He was determined to build up the subject at Oxford, and to rescue it permanently from the obscurity in which it had languished for many years before Alastair Buchan had attempted to improve the situation. Although money was scarce, Bull begged and borrowed teaching resources from wherever he could find them, and managed to establish some new options and a generally wider sphere for International Relations. His own activities as a supervisor of graduate students were awesome in scope yet highly successful. He found time for substantial editing and organizing tasks. His students used words like 'magisterial' to describe him; yet much of the old mischievousness remained. Sir Michael Howard said at the commemorative service:

By the end of his life Hedley was well on the way to becoming one of those grand elder statesmen whom he used to tease when young.

Election to the British Academy came just in time for him to appreciate it. But in his case the grandeur came not from pomposity or self-importance but from a truly comprehensive vision of the world and a shrewd insight into affairs which gave his pronouncements an authoritative quality to which one listened with awe. His abrasiveness had softened into an ironical amusement, which in its silence could sometimes be more disconcerting than the direct assaults of his youth. He had achieved that most precious of all qualities, wisdom. But one still felt that there lurked, never far away, that impish desire to tease, if no longer to outrage, the bourgeois which kept him until the end of his life such a fundamentally youthful and such an endearing person.[11]

Hedley Bull died on 18 May 1985 after a long and valiant fight against the effects of cancer.

In person he was tall, slightly stooped, and inclined to portliness. He used a pipe for gestures and to emphasize points as he made them; his speech was slower than that of many academics, but the sentences were perfectly formed and felicitously expressed. He was capable of pungent language but never of obscurity. A slight Australian accent remained with him. His handwriting was uniform, concise, and sometimes difficult to read: he never learnt to use a typewriter. It was impossible to persuade him to leave a margin in which one could criticize his manuscripts or in which he could make alterations. This was not because he shunned suggestions or criticism; it may have been because he thought things out very carefully before he began to write, and had hardly any need to make corrections. He saw things very sequentially. Many of his articles begin with a series of numbered questions which he proceeds to answer in sequence, the whole forming a logical entity of impressive power. He would begin a lecture by saying that he had four or five points to make; students could number them with confidence, since the divisions between them were quite apparent, though he might not get to point five. It may well be that the penchant for order which he displayed in regard to the international system had its roots in the natural orderliness of his own mind, his impatience with irrelevancies, and his conviction that 'the big questions' needed to be answered.

Bull liked family holidays in Corfu; he enjoyed dining at All Souls, belonging to the Travellers Club, going for a solitary walk on Black Mountain in Canberra with a stick to keep off the

---

[11] Michael Howard at the Oxford memorial service to Hedley Bull.

magpies, bathing at Parsons Pleasure, and playing sedate and not very successful tennis. The good things of life attracted him, but not to excess. He could sometimes be childish; he could seem painfully shy and liable to compensate for his feelings by overstating a point for effect. He could be engagingly naïve: once he was discovered looking for Barataria in an atlas and wondering why he could not find it. He had an impish sense of humour. Sometimes in controversy he could be wounding. The Andersonian tradition of hitting hard in argument was often at variance with the American academic practice of emollient comment, of bland disapproval wrapped in flattery. Americans found his frontal attacks troublesome and tended to fear him. He was especially hard on the pompous and the propagandist. He was not a debater so much as someone who specialized in the crushing blow towards the end of the day. What was notable about him, however, in distinction from many who had gone through Anderson's hands, was that he was rarely if ever content with destructive criticism. He looked for ways out, for designs that would last, for propositions which were realistic in that they went with the grain of things, but which also pointed towards reconciliation and improvement.

2
International Society

STANLEY HOFFMANN

I WAS always an admirer of the extraordinary sweep of Hedley Bull's mind, and yet when I reviewed his work I was left with an inevitable sense of incompleteness. He accomplished so much, but there were also so many more directions in which he might have gone and in which he was beginning to go.

The most striking aspect of his work is its extraordinary unity and the coherence of his approach: the unity of method and of substance, and the consistency and continuity of his concern about international society and those contemporary issues which are decisive for the survival of an international society. However, there were also significant tensions in his work: they gave it its density, and make it particularly instructive and thought-provoking.

I

The first question to be taken up on the issue of Hedley Bull's world view is where does he belong within the study of international relations? The second concerns his unity of method and substance, to which I have already alluded; and the third concerns Bull's view of international society.

At first sight it appears to be obvious where Hedley Bull fits into the discipline of international relations. He seems to take up a position close to realism, the school of thought that looks at international relations as the politics of states in their external aspects, to quote from his own account of Martin Wight's approach.[1] Realism starts by rejecting all forms of utopianism,

This chapter was first published in slightly different form in *International Affairs*, 62. 2 (Spring 1986).

[1] Hedley Bull, 'Martin Wight and the Theory of International Relations', *British Journal of International Studies*, 2. 2 (July 1976).

as Bull himself did. His most magisterial criticism of utopianism is to be found in *The Anarchical Society*, where he disposed decisively of such concepts as world government, a new medievalism, a regional construction of the world, and revolutionary schemes for change.[2] Even in his first book, *The Control of the Arms Race*, he had been incisively critical of proposals for world disarmament.[3]

And yet things are not so simple. Unlike many destroyers of utopias and many realists—I have in mind George Kennan and Henry Kissinger—Bull never showed great enthusiasm for giving policy advice to usually indifferent princes. Many contemporary realists have been attracted to policy guidance like moths to a flame. Bull had no particular objection to scholars giving policy advice as long as it went to a morally acceptable government;[4] he himself served as an adviser to the British government on arms control matters for several years. Yet on the whole, he showed more tolerance than enthusiasm for this task. His attitude was similar to that of Raymond Aron: in the field of international relations, as indeed in political science in general, what Aron called 'wise counsel' was quite naturally derived from scholarly research, but the main purpose of scholarship was to advance knowledge.

To be sure, not all realists have felt a need to outdo the bureaucrats on their own ground (certainly Hans Morgenthau never did). But there were two other very important differences between Bull's approach and that of the realists. The first came from his distrust of the realist model of state behaviour, which lies behind the realists' prescriptions. Morgenthau was the one who put it most forcefully in the first few pages of *Politics among Nations: The Struggle for Power and Peace* (5th edn., New York, 1973): one can derive from the study of history, from the logic of interstate relations in the international milieu, and from the geopolitical position of a state, something like a rational set of rules for the conduct of its foreign policy. Instances of departure

---

[2] Hedley Bull, *The Anarchical Society: A Study of Order in World Politics* (London, 1977).

[3] Hedley Bull, *The Control of the Arms Race: Disarmament and Arms Control in the Nuclear Age* (London, 1961).

[4] In 'Strategic Studies and its Critics', *World Politics*, 20. 4 (July 1968), Bull states that being an adviser to a government is, for a scholar or a scientist, unbecoming or not depending on 'what we take the moral nature of that government and its objectives to be' (p. 599).

from such rational behaviour are treated, in the realists' works, as aberrations. Hedley Bull was no believer in the ordinary rationality of states, nor in the usefulness of developing prescriptions for rational action, because he was even more pessimistic than the realists. To them, departures from the norm are exceptions; to Hedley Bull, stupidity, folly, miscalculations, and mischief were always possible.

The second major point of difference between Bull and the realists lay in his point of departure. He did not begin his study, as the realists do, by looking at the state and its power, a concept about which he has rather little to say. (And what he does say about power is actually quite close to the realist emphasis on military power as the heart of the matter). Bull's whole body of work takes as its point of departure the group, or milieu, or 'ensemble' which states form by interacting. It is the international system, and, above all, international society. When, in his famous article attacking the so-called scientific approach, he drew up a list of important questions to be asked in the study of international politics, Bull's first question was: 'does the collectivity of sovereign states constitute a political society or system, or does it not?'[5] Similarly, in his critique of E. H. Carr's *Twenty Years' Crisis, 1919–39: An Introduction to the Study of International Relations* (2nd edn., London, 1946), written thirty years after its publication, he concluded that 'in the course of demonstrating how appeals to an overriding international society subserve the special interests of the ruling group of powers, Carr jettisons the idea of international society itself. This is the idea with which a new analysis of the problem of international relations should now begin.'[6] Bull's interest in this idea was constant. Between the late 1950s and the 1980s, American scholarship moved away from general theories towards greater specialization, and it has tended to split into two groups—the strategists and the political economists. Bull never separated his interest in strategic questions from his investigation of the nature, history, and evolution of international society.

---

[5] Hedley Bull, 'International Theory: The Case for a Classical Approach', in Klaus Knorr and James N. Rosenau, eds., *Contending Approaches to International Politics* (Princeton, 1969), 27.

[6] Hedley Bull, '*The Twenty Years' Crisis* Thirty Years On', *International Journal*, 24. 4 (Autumn 1969), 638.

II

Thus we come to what I called the unity of method and substance in Bull's work. The most fruitful way of grasping this is to start with his critique of the scientific approach to international relations theory: his rejection of 'propositions based on logical or mathematical proof, or upon strict empirical procedures of verification'.[7] He attacked the practitioners of the scientific approach for a number of reasons. In the first place, this method kept its practitioners from asking what were, according to him, the essential questions about international relations.[8] The practitioners of the scientific approach seemed to Bull like characters who, having lost a watch in the dark, look for it under a light even though they did not lose it there, just because the light happens to be there. As Bull put it himself, their method 'keeps them as remote from the substance of international politics as the inmates of a Victorian nunnery were from the study of sex'.[9] Secondly, he disliked the scientific method because he thought its practitioners were obsessed by the quest for a far greater degree of precision than the field of international relations allows. Hence his harsh critique of Karl Deutsch's 'measurements', which, according to Bull, ignored the connections between the units being measured and the significance of what was being counted. Hence also his sarcasm about the abstract model-building technique displayed by Morton Kaplan, whose models, according to Bull, were scientifically disguised versions of reality which either lacked rigour and consistency precisely because rigour and consistency are not to be found in international reality, or achieved those qualities at the cost of a complete divorce from reality. They were not like economic models, which often manage to remain not only faithful to, but capable of explaining, the way in which economic variables interact. Thirdly, Bull thought that the practitioners of the scientific method were obsessed by an urge to predict and to resolve the issues which they tackled, and he accused them of brashness. These criticisms were addressed primarily to the behaviourist school of the mid-1960s. In

---

[7] Bull, 'International Theory', p. 21.

[8] Hedley Bull, 'New Directions in the Theory of International Relations', *International Studies*, 14. 2 (Apr–June 1975), 279.

[9] Bull, 'New Directions in the Theory of International Relations', p. 26.

'International Theory' he kindly exempted from blanket condemnation such kindred souls as Raymond Aron, Kenneth Waltz, and myself. However, in his major work on *The Theory of International Relations* (Reading, Mass., 1979), Kenneth Waltz himself subsequently became a prime example of the very approach which Hedley Bull had condemned many years before. Mercifully, Hedley spared Waltz's book, which, as far as I know, he never reviewed.[10]

What was his own preference? He talked about 'a scientifically imperfect procedure of perception and intuition', which sounds remarkably like Max Weber's concept of understanding.[11] In Bull's view, in other words, beyond the causal explanation of events or of sequences of events, the social scientist still has to travel one more step and try to grasp the meaning of the whole; and this requires, above all, judgement in the construction and testing of hypotheses. Interpretation, the attempt to seize the meaning of what has been explained, is an artistic enterprise rather than a scientific one. Unlike many of his colleagues in the field, therefore, and unlike Kenneth Waltz in his last book, Bull did not begin his study of international relations with the requirements of method. (Waltz, for instance, begins by laying down a very interesting and rigorous notion of theory, and then, by applying it to international relations, manages to leave most of the substance of the field outside the straitjacket.) Bull started with the questions which were essential to him: questions about society and culture, about the place of war and the conceptions of it, about the relations between the influence of the system and the nature of the state in the determination of events, about the right of states to intervene in each other's affairs—and so on.

To begin with such questions is to realize, first, that they can only be understood by reference to the works of the political philosophers who have discussed and sharpened them. Secondly, they can only be answered comparatively across time and place: for instance, to be able to talk intelligently about what looks like

---

[10] On the basis of his remarks about game theory in 'Strategic Studies and its Critics', pp. 601–2, one can presume that he would have been equally sarcastic about current attempts by champions of 'rational choice theory' to use game theory not just 'to illustrate points that are independently arrived at', but 'in order to determine solutions' to problems of international relations.

[11] Bull, 'International Theory', p. 20.

the extraordinary amount of intervention that occurs in the present-day international system, or about the seemingly original network of contemporary transnational relations, it is useful to be able to compare the present system with past ones—something which led Hedley Bull to conclude that the amount of intervention today was not all that unusual, and that the network of transnational relations was far less original than many have claimed. Thirdly, to begin with these questions is to understand that they can only be evaluated by reference not merely to the state's power but also to the rules which states observe, and particularly to that quite special category of rules which constitutes international law.

Bull called this approach a traditional one, and it was indeed traditional if one considers that the study of the history of ideas and of diplomatic history is the very thing from which the modern scientific approach had tried to emancipate the discipline of international relations; but it was a traditional approach at the service of as rigorous an understanding of international relations as the field allows. In this way, Bull's work is very different from that of traditional international lawyers or diplomatic historians. His very concern for a systematic understanding of international relations leads him, as it had led Raymond Aron, to insist on conceptual distinctions in order to make a clear analysis possible. In *The Anarchical Society* one finds a whole forest of distinctions: between the different meanings and kinds of order in international affairs, between the different meanings of justice, between the different functions of war, between intervention and inequality, different types of balance of power, and so on.

Ultimately, Hedley Bull's work is a blend of intelligent social science and humanism. I insist on his humanism because it takes so many forms. Predominantly, it takes a Weberian form. Weber wanted the social scientist to respect and empathize with the meanings which political actors gave to their actions, just as he wanted him to be aware of and to highlight the frequent divorce between actors' intentions and the results obtained. It is because of this divorce that it is possible to talk about a system— which might be described as a net of interacting variables which often foul up the intentions of the actor—but it is because human beings are the actors and have the intentions that there is no need to look at the system in the way in which, for instance, Morton Kaplan seems to have done: as a divinity which determines the acts of the various players as if they were puppets on a string. To illustrate this point one can say, as Bull often did, that a balance of power in the international society, or the current balance of terror, can develop even though their creation or preservation was not the deliberate policy or intention of all the participants in international society. On the other hand, how this balance will turn out, how stable it will be, *will* depend to a very large extent on the participants' intentions and policies.

Humanism is also manifest in the extraordinary density of the historical knowledge of Bull's works, particularly the most recent ones—something which is not to be found in the works of many of his American colleagues. Lastly, humanism is manifest in the importance of moral concerns in Bull's works.

III

Hedley Bull's writings on ethics and international relations are more suggestive than systematic. The interest shown in ethics by specialists in international relations has increased enormously in the last ten years, as Bull himself noted. His own concern with this issue started much earlier, but even in his work an increasing emphasis on ethics can be traced in the last years of his life. His thoughts on the subject can be summarized as follows.

First, as far as the study of international relations is concerned, international society has a moral basis; indeed, Bull's concern for international society and his interest in moral conceptions are inextricably linked. The beliefs of the members of the international society cannot be reduced to their interests and strategies of power—a reduction for which Bull criticizes E. H. Carr sharply, particularly in pointing out that the famous principle *pacta sunt servanda* cannot be described merely as a cynical expression of the interests of the strong. According to Bull, the beliefs of the members of the international society influence the historical evolution of that society. Consequently, the study of international relations must address the question of moral beliefs, in particular in order to establish which beliefs represent a consensus of the members, what the substance of that consensus is, and where its limits and weak points can be found. This was a task which Bull performed rigorously in the last years of his life, both as regarded conceptions of justice in the present international system[12] and in his essay on South Africa. There, taking up the argument of South Africa's defenders, who complained that the South African government was the victim of a double standard, he argued:

there is not a world consensus against communist oppression, or oppression by military governments, or of one Asian or African ethnic group by another, comparable to that which exists against this surviving symbol of a white supremacism that all other societies in the world, to different degrees and in different ways, have repudiated over the last three decades. . . . While this should not lead us to fail to protest against . . . other [violations of human rights,] we should also recognize that it is not now possible to unite the international community on any other basis than that of a clear repudiation of white supremacism.[13]

Secondly, Bull believed that the social scientist must recognize that there can be no value-free enquiry; and, he added, if it were possible it would be of little interest—another reason for Bull's distrust of the purely scientific approach.[14] Nevertheless, while the presence of values is one thing, to smuggle them in or to peddle them explicitly is quite another. There are many warnings in Bull's work against this—against models of the future into which the writers inject their value preferences by indulging in excessive 'salvationism', and against moral preaching in writings on arms control and international justice which oversimplify highly complex moral issues and disregard some of the costs of the solutions they recommend. Indeed, Bull is critical of moral generalizations. To him they are impossible, because of the complexity of concrete situations and because of the very difficulty of the choices faced by statesmen. For instance, the avoidance of war is not always the highest imperative (Bull was writing about Munich); justice and order cannot always be reconciled; the universal promotion of human rights can be 'subversive of coexistence' because of the absence

---

[12] Hedley Bull, *Justice in International Relations*, the Hagey Lectures (Univ. of Waterloo, Ontario, 1984).

[13] Hedley Bull, 'The West and South Africa', *Daedalus*, 111. 2 (Spring 1982), 255–70, at p. 266.

[14] Bull, 'New Directions in the Theory of International Relations', p. 284.

of any substantive consensus in this field.[15] Bull was painfully aware not only of the gap between moral imperatives and political reality but also of the multiplicity of moral perspectives in the contemporary world. As he pointed out in his critiques of works by E. B. F. Midgley[16] and Michael Walzer,[17], neither natural law nor Walzer's brand of liberal individualism is acceptable as the truth: for instance, they have been rejected by revolutionaries and by absolute pacifists.

On the other hand, as early as p. 25 of *The Control of the Arms Race* we find the following statement: 'Moral judgments . . . should never be overridden or sacrificed.' The social scientists need to ask broad moral questions. These questions—about the role of the great powers, or the claims of the Third World, or the virtues of the states system—Bull always asked. He did so because he believed that moral issues were susceptible to rational investigation, and could even be settled if the parties shared the same moral premises or if the premises involved were universally held—the respect for human life, for property and the sanctity of agreements.[18] Both the multiplicity of moral alternatives and the possiblity of moral argument led Hedley Bull to demand that social scientists and philosophers dealing with moral issues in foreign affairs should try to transcend subjectivity and lay out the foundations of their positions. (This was the rationale behind his critique of Michael Walzer, whom he commended for his determination to revive just war theory, but blamed for refusing to explain his own moral theory from the ground up.) However, it must be said that Bull himself never did lay out fully the foundations of his own moral position; he also recognized that, ultimately, there is often no rational way of choosing between moral ends.[19]

The third point to be made about Hedley Bull's thoughts on ethics and international relations is that this omission did not prevent him from making explicit prescriptions (in just the same way that he would have liked a 'self-proclaimed realist' like E. H. Carr to have made out a moral case against Munich). It is

---

[15] Bull, *Justice in International Relations*, p. 13.
[16] Hedley Bull, 'Natural Law and International Relations', *British Journal of International Studies*, 5. 2 (July 1979), 171–81.
[17] Hedley Bull, 'Recapturing the Just War for Political Theory', *World Politics*, 31. 4 (July 1979), 588–99.
[18] Bull, 'Natural Law and International Relations', p. 180.
[19] Ibid., p. 181.

not surprising to find two sources behind Bull's own explicit prescriptions: the natural law tradition, and the values of the West. Natural law, 'a doctrine which proclaims that rules are valid among all mankind quite irrespective of the social and cultural facts of the time', he found particularly interesting, 'now that there exists a global international society that has clearly outgrown its originally European social or cultural base, . . . and doubts may be entertained as to whether any genuinely universal society or culture has yet taken its place'.[20] It was the values of the West which he invoked in his argument for 'some degree of commitment to the cause of individual rights on a world scale',[21] as well as in his condemnation of South Africa and of Western, primarily American, arguments for supporting the white regime there.[22] It is natural law, tempered by his awareness of the limits and fragility of consensus in the realm of justice, which informs his recommendations about the concept of justice we should embrace in the present international system. Taken together, Bull's writings show that he heeded his own advice about the need to go beyond the language of the sociology of moral belief to that of morals—to that of rights and duties.

IV

We now come to his view of international society. Here is where Hedley Bull's originality lies: it is *society* rather than *system* which he, virtually alone among contemporary theorists of international affairs, stresses and studies. *System* means contact between states and the impact of one state on another; *society* means (in Bull's words) common interests and values, common rules and institutions. His point of departure is what has sometimes been called the Grotian approach. More will be said about this below. Here we find one of the differences between Bull and Aron or Waltz: unlike him, they start with the international system. A second feature of Bull's originality, a consequence of his emphasis on society over system, is his theory of change, which is very different from that of Waltz or Robert Gilpin. Gilpin attributes change in international affairs to the rise and fall of hegemonic powers; Waltz sees change as

---

[20] Bull, 'Natural Law and International Relations', p. 171.
[21] Bull, *Justice in International Relations*, p. 13.
[22] Bull, 'The West and South Africa', pp. 269–70.

the result of shifts in the distribution of power between states, leading from a bipolar to a multipolar system, or vice versa. In contrast, Bull is interested in the cultural change which produces a different perception of common interests in a context of coexistence and co-operation. He is, in other words, emphasizing the passage from a mere system to a society, or from a narrower society to one that includes many more members. He is also interested in the effects of major upheavals like the Reformation, the French Revolution, and the Russian Revolution, which introduced drastically new beliefs and rules into the international society.

What was the origin of Bull's concern for the international society? It seems to have started with his dissatisfaction with alternative approaches. Bull rejected a purely Hobbesian view of international affairs as a state of war, or a struggle of all against all. He refuted Hobbes by using some of Hobbes's own arguments, so as to explain why the state of war between nations was more bearable than the state of war between individuals, and why there was therefore no need for a universal Leviathan (the state's ability to protect the industry of its subjects, the lesser vulnerability of the state compared to the naked individual because of its greater power, the unevenness of states compared to the puny equality of individuals in the state of nature).[23] Moreover—unlike the Hobbesians—Bull denied that it was only the existence of central state power which could make possible the emergence of a society, or could prevent its collapse or disintegration; anarchy *is* compatible with society, because the state is not the only reason for obeying rules in society. In one of his first published essays on the British commonwealth of nations, he noted the incompatibility of theories of Realpolitik with the reality of a group of states whose mutual relations were not inherently antagonistic.[24]

On the other hand, Bull also rejects what he considers to be Kant's universalism and cosmopolitanism, and he criticizes Kant for inconsistency[25]—although, in my opinion, he misreads Kant, who was much less cosmopolitan and universalist in his writings on international affairs than Bull suggests. Kant never

---

[23] Hedley Bull, 'Society and Anarchy in International Relations', in Herbert Butterfield and Martin Wight, eds., *Diplomatic Investigations* (London, 1966), 35–50.

[24] Hedley Bull, 'What is the Commonwealth?', *World Politics*, 11. 4 (July 1959).

[25] Bull, 'Society and Anarchy', pp. 48 ff.; *The Anarchical Society*, p. 262.

advocated a world state or government, after all, and Bull failed to distinguish here between two conceptions which Michael Walzer, for instance, separates carefully: cosmopolitanism, which tries to overcome the barriers to the unity of mankind set by the existence of nations and by national borders; and what Walzer calls the 'legalist paradigm', which looks at international relations as a society of states with mutual rights and duties, a conception which is not only similar to Bull's but actually quite close to Kant's.

The second source of Bull's view of international society is his intellectual sympathy for historical authors whose work stressed society even at a time when (as he recognized) reality was really more like a jungle than a society—the theologians and international lawyers of the sixteenth and seventeenth centuries, particularly Grotius. Clearly there is a parallel between these men, writing at a time when, amidst considerable strife and chaos, a radically new system was being created out of the disintegration of the medieval one, and today's expansion of the international system into the first truly global one.

Bull's approach to the study of international society is marked by one important tension, which gives rise to a number of unanswered questions. This is the tension between his realism and his emphasis on the rules and institutions which dampen anarchy—international law, the balance of power, even war as a means of preserving a balance, the role of the great powers with their special responsibilities to international society, the rule of non-intervention. He also emphasizes the community of culture that makes international society possible and requires, if not ideological homogeneity, at least the toleration of ideological differences. In other words, he stresses elements which, taken to an extreme, cause him to appear perilously close to the construction of Hans Kelsen, which he himself criticizes. Kelsen analysed international law both as the product of a system in which states interact in pursuit of their separate interests, and as the product of an organized society which collectively delegates functions to its members for the enforcement of the common good. In one of his very last works, on international justice, Hedley Bull wrote about 'the concept of a world common good' and about the need, 'in the absence of a supranational world authority, . . . for particular states to seek as wide a consensus as possible, and on this basis to act as local agents of a world common good'. In the next sentence, however, we are reminded that 'states are notoriously self-serving in their policies, and rightly suspected when they purport to act on behalf of the international community as a whole'; such a pretence can be 'in fact a menace to international order'.[26] The same oscillation can be found in some of his writings about questions of military security: in *The Control of the Arms Race*, Bull's concern, he tells us, is not national security but international security, the security of the society of states as a whole—a concept which I myself, with a view of international relations a little more Hobbesian and less Grotian than Bull's, have always found difficult to understand, since in the matter of security 'international society' consists of members who distrust one another and spend most of their time if not actually attacking each other then at least protecting themselves from attack.

Bull's own kind of realism, however, was never left far behind. He always managed to correct his Grotian inclinations by an infusion of what he called Oppenheim's pluralism. As a reader of Oppenheim, Bull had commented on the inadequacy of a domestic model for the understanding of the nature of international law or international society; and he stressed the role war plays as an ordinary instrument of state policy rather than as a crime condemned by international society or a sanction enforcing that society's principles. Bull had commented that the adherence of states to international law does not mean that they respect it. He had expressed his scepticism about what he called 'the neo-idealist fashions' of today—the recent tendency of some American scholars to depreciate the continuing importance of force in international affairs and to celebrate the emergence of a transnational society.[27] Bull was aware of the fact that in the period following the First World War the revival of Grotianism had led to a utopian attempt to reform the international milieu into a society in which war would be banned unless it was an exercise of collective security—an effort that may have been detrimental to the placing of limits on the conduct of war (Bull cites such cases as the Italian invasion of Abyssinia, the Nuremberg trials, and the Korean war).[28]

[26] Bull, *Justice in International Relations*, p. 14.
[27] Hedley Bull, 'Civilian Power Europe: A Contradiction in Terms?', *Journal of Common Market Studies*, 21. 1–2 (Sept.–Dec. 1982), at pp. 150–1.
[28] Hedley Bull, 'The Grotian Conception of International Society', in Butterfield and Wight, eds., *Diplomatic Investigations*, pp. 51–73.

The questions that Hedley Bull left unanswered are of two kinds. In the first place they have to do with the delicate balance between Kelsen, or Grotius, and Oppenheim, or Hobbes—the distinction between society and system, which Bull never expounded systematically. He showed that anarchy was compatible with society; but how much society, as it were, is likely to flourish in an anarchical structure? Conversely, could the factors of society ever hope to overcome the antagonisms which are built into and grow out of an anarchical structure?

Bull's own work laid stress on the emergence of a universal international society, a society previously dominated by Western states and gradually extended, first to non-Western states which accepted European values, and then to all the new states which emerged from decolonization after the Second World War. This expansion raised a question which Bull had only begun to address in his most recent work: can one have a universal society without a common cultural framework, with a cosmopolitan ideal that is only an ideal—indeed, one that is not even shared by all the cultural systems? Bull's final answer was yes, so long as there are still common interests.

The second kind of question which Hedly Bull left unexplored, and which is sorely missed, concerns the distinction, not in theory but in international reality, between different types of international society, in the way in which Martin Wight had distinguished different kinds of states-systems. From the point of view of the international order (and this was always Hedley Bull's), there must be a difference between an international society endowed with a common culture and one whose only cement is provided by the (perhaps very short-lived) common interests of its members. From that same point of view, much depends on the kind of culture which underlies a given international society, on the nature of its values, and on how broad or deep the culture is. These are questions which Bull had only begun to address in his writings about the present-day international system.

V

The three aspects of Hedley Bull's work on current international politics that will be taken up here are, first, Bull's analysis of the nature of the contemporary world scene; secondly, Bull and the nuclear conundrum; and thirdly, Bull's writings on the super-powers and the power balance.

Bull's analysis of the nature of the contemporary world scene is extremely rich; but it is marked by considerable ambivalence and unresolved tension. The question he asked was, what is the degree of society present today? His reply is complex and ambiguous.[29] He produces considerable evidence to show that there has been a dangerous weakening of the elements of society in the current system. He lists the following factors. First, obviously, there is the superpower conflict. Surprisingly enough, this is the factor Bull writes least about, perhaps because he believed his American colleagues were writing about almost nothing else; there is particularly little in his work about the ideological aspects of the superpower conflict. In the second place, Bull finds that the balance of power has been preserved, but, in contrast to that of the nineteenth century, it continues without a common culture as its basis. Thirdly, in addition to the balance of power there is now mutual nuclear deterrence; but Bull finds it extremely fragile, for reasons to be mentioned below.

The fourth factor in the weakening of current society that Bull discusses, particularly in his most recent work, is the 'revolt against the West', the positions taken by the developing nations. This revolt he sees as triply dangerous. It is dangerous, first, because it entails a partial repudiation of the pre-existing rules and institutions of international society. He mentions practices by Third World states which violate the principle of diplomatic immunity; he refers also to multiple interventions by some of these states in the affairs of others, as if the barriers against intervention existed against intrusions by the West only. In his 1983 lectures on justice at the University of Waterloo, he added that many countries of the Third World repudiate the Western view that the rights which states enjoy in international law must be compatible with their obligations to the international community. The revolt against the West is dangerous, secondly, because it results from and contributes to the increasing cultural heterogeneity of international society. In a conference on international relations held in April 1968 at Bellagio—the

---

[29] This analysis is derived from his essays in Hedley Bull and Adam Watson, eds., *The Expansion of International Society* (Oxford, 1984), and in Hedley Bull, ed., *Intervention in World Politics* (Oxford, 1984).

conference attended by Aron and Morgenthau where Hedley Bull complained about the primitive character of Hans Morgenthau's theory—he remarked that we were now living in a worldwide international system that had 'outrun its cultural basis'. In his lectures on justice he gave as examples of increasing cultural heterogeneity the differences between Western and Third World conceptions of self-determination, human rights, and economic justice. Lastly, the revolt against the West is dangerous because it increases what might be called structural heterogeneity, on two levels. On the one hand, as he pointed out, many of the new states are states by courtesy only. And at the level of the system, the demands of the Third World aim at attaining not only greater racial, economic, and cultural equality, but also a redistribution of power, which, according to Bull, raises insoluble issues, particularly in the military realm where the need for order (he had in mind the need to preserve the world from further nuclear proliferation) must sometimes supersede demands for justice.[30]

Ultimately, however, Bull's reply to this question—what is the degree of international society today—is reasonably optimistic. Here again, several factors must be listed. First, the attractiveness of war as an instrument of policy has diminished, at least between the superpowers. Secondly, the superpowers themselves have set up various arrangements in order to preserve peace, although these arrangements—which include the Non-Proliferation Treaty of 1968—are not always in strict conformity with justice. Third come the many influences which reinforce the norm of non-intervention. Bull deemed these forces more powerful than the opposite forces which weaken it, and he presented them as a mixture of external power factors, domestic ones, and ideological or cultural beliefs. However, many of the factors which deter intervention are themselves ambiguous, because they are also facets of the revolt against the West: many barriers against intervention were set up by anticolonialist actors, by the revolt against racism, by the demands for greater economic justice. This ambiguity complicates the problem.

The fourth factor to mention, according to Bull, is the gradual acceptance by the non-Western states of the basic elements of

[30] Bull, *Justice in International Relations*, pp. 10–11.

international society, despite all the breaches of it which I have mentioned above. Bull thought that such essential ingredients of international society as the principle of state sovereignty, international law, and international organization were being accepted, in theory and practice, by the non-Western states. He also gave to their demands for greater power and greater justice a reformist rather than a revolutionary interpretation. Fifthly, in his lectures at the University of Waterloo he talked about an emerging consensus on certain common notions of distributive justice—despite the lack of agreement on who should be the distributor, the principles of distribution, and any theory of the concept of distributive justice in international relations. This emerging consensus may also have been one of the aspects of the contemporary cultural change which Bull saw as a positive factor: it would bring the different cultures which today coexist closer together. Lastly, he stressed his belief that it is possible for an international society to exist without a common culture, so long as there is a solid network of common interests; he pointed out that one should not identify, and confuse, present-day international society with the quite exceptional one of the nineteenth century. (One cannot fail to be struck once again here by the importance Bull attached to values and beliefs, as opposed to 'rules of the game' and what American theorists call 'international regimes', in his account of the components of present-day society.)

This balanced analysis raised the question of the forces and directions of change in the current international system. Bull answered this in two ways. Analytically, his answer is somewhat ambivalent. On the one hand, he sees no evidence of the world moving 'beyond the states system'. In *The Anarchical Society*, he asserts that the states-system is neither in decline, nor obsolete, nor dysfunctional. In his opinion, none of the schemes which have been presented for its reform are likely to be realized. On the other hand, he detects the beginning of a 'wider world political system of which the states system is only part';[31] but having given us this tantalizing glimpse, he proceeds to remove it from our sight by attempting to prove that what many scholars have presented as entirely new and beyond the states-system—

[31] Bull, *The Anarchical Society*, pp. 276 ff.

for instance, non-state actors and transnational society—either is not new at all, or is really only the states-system (or, rather, one dominant state, the United States) in disguise.

The second part of Bull's answer to the problem of contemporary change lies in his prescriptions. At the end of *The Anarchical Society*, he recognizes that the book constitutes an 'implicit defence of the states system', in particular a defence of the principle of state sovereignty as the best contemporary way of protecting human beings against forcible external interference. Yet Bull was clearly aware of the need for change beyond the status quo, and in a number of directions. Most important of these was his plea for a broadening of the consensus on common interests among states in a way that would include the countries of the Third World. The need to take into account the demands of the 'have nots' was the one positive element he had found in the work of E. H. Carr. Bull's recommendations on justice in international relations showed his desire to satisfy the legitimate demands of the developing countries without in any way giving up essential Western values. This is why he insisted that the recognition of the rights of states should be kept subject to and limited by the rights of the international community, and why he emphasized the importance of what he called a profound change in the perception of justice in international law: 'the rights and benefits to which justice has to be done in the international community are not simply those of states and nations, but those of individual persons throughout the world as a whole'.[32] Indeed, the most striking prescriptions in his most recent work concern the need to develop the cosmopolitan elements in the present world culture, not only as they affect the rights of individuals, but with reference to the new conception of a common good for the human species. In both these domains he was aware of the broad range of disagreements between states—especially on human rights questions—and of the absence of any consensus on the means and institutions for stemming 'the dangers of nuclear war, disequilibrium between population and resources, or environmental deterioration'. Nevertheless he tried to suggest ways of moving in this direction, which might be called, if not 'beyond and after the states system', at least a 'states system plus', a states-system within a wider one that

---

[32] Bull, *Justice in International Relations*, p. 12.

borrowed elements from the 'domestic model'. Society would thus be sought not only within the (anarchical) states-system, but beyond.

Ultimately, in this part of his work we find one tension that could also be detected in the work of E. H. Carr: a tension between Bull's awareness of the special importance of the great powers because of their evident stake in preserving international society (a stake which he thought greater than that of other powers), and his awareness of their inadequacy in a global international system in which they cannot fulfil their traditional functions alone any more—for two reasons: because of the greater capacity of smaller powers to resist, and because of the greater potency of ideologies of resistance and of international equality. Like Carr, Bull resolves this tension by an argument in support of much broader definition by the great powers of their own interests—and of the common interest.

One of the main perils threatening the human species is the nuclear predicament. Hedley Bull's work on arms control is of considerable importance to students of international affairs. First, it was planted firmly in a political context, unlike, for instance, the contribution of Thomas Schelling. Like Schelling, Hedley Bull emphasized the unity of strategic doctrine and of arms control; but unlike him, Bull also believed in the unity of all military policies (whether strategic or arms control) and foreign policy. Secondly, the political context Bull had in mind was never just the superpower rivalry with which his American colleagues are obsessed. Bull tried to analyse the possible contribution arms control might make to international society as a whole, since contemporary society rests to such a large extent on a recognition of common interests. It is always from this point of view that Bull asserted that superpower arms control alone was inadequate.[33] Thirdly, although he thought it far more realistic than disarmament, Bull remained extremely sceptical about the value of arms control as a panacea. For him, it could become one, perhaps, but only if states had arms control as their central objective (and most of the time they do not) or if states behaved entirely rationally. But, once again, he greeted

---

[33] Cf. Hedley Bull, 'Arms Control: A Stocktaking and Prospectus', in *Problems of Modern Strategy*, pt. 2, Adelphi Papers, 55 (Mar. 1969), 11–20.

the concept of 'the rational action of a kind of strategic man' with derision, on the grounds that it was good only for 'formal theorizing'. Strategic man, he wrote, is ' a man who on further acquaintance reveals himself as a university professor of unusual intellectual subtlety'.[34]

What were his main contributions to the study of arms control? They may not appear deeply original today, but they certainly were in 1961. Along with Aron's, his was the main non-American voice in the early—and still the best—chorus of 'nuclear theorists'. In the first place, Bull very soon became aware of the conditions for the stability of nuclear deterrence, and of the risks of destabilization. As early as 1961, in *The Control of the Arms Race*, he had defined the conditions of stability as the absence of any capacity for a disarming first strike and the absence of any capability to defend one's population and one's industries. Destabilization could therefore result both from weapons of increasing accuracy and payload—Bull was disturbed by the appearance of multiple independently targeted re-entry vehicles (MIRV)—and from the development of anti-ballistic missiles or strategic defences in general. Many years ago, Bull reviewed the arguments which had been presented, particularly by the late Donald Brennan, in favour of strategic defences.[35] He analysed them with great fairness: he sympathized with the doubts Brennan and Dyson had expressed about the 'rationality models' that underlie deterrence theory. But ultimately he rejected their case: he thought that defences would lead to a dangerous escalation of the arms race, largely because of the countermeasures which each side would obviously be eager to take in order to restore the supremacy of the offensive.

Bull's second contribution to the study of arms control was his awareness of the fragility of arms control as a basis for international order. At the end of his life he seemed to be more optimistic about the stability of nuclear deterrence, in spite of the fact that the theoretical vulnerability of land-based missiles was growing—something which was driving so many Americans crazy. He thought that countermeasures could make these missiles less vulnerable, and that stability could survive the vulnerability of one element of the triad of sea-based, land-

---

[34] Bull, *The Control of the Arms Race*, p. 48.
[35] Hedley Bull, 'The Scope for Soviet–American Agreement', in *Soviet–American Relations and World Order*, Adelphi Papers, 65 (Feb. 1970), 1–15.

based, and air-based nuclear systems. Bull wrote that stable deterrence did not depend on or require the doctrine of mutual assured destruction. He thus acknowledged the possibility of what McGeorge Bundy would later call existential deterrence: a condition in which the nuclear powers deter each other from the use of nuclear weapons whatever their strategic doctrine may be.[36] Nevertheless, Bull believed that strategic nuclear deterrence could never serve as a satisfactory foundation of international order, for a whole series of reasons. First, deterrence concentrates on a set of *means*, whereas the important question for Hedley Bull concerned states' *ends*. Secondly, it focuses attention on military issues when the important issue in avoiding war is the management and control of political crises. Thirdly, deterrence deals with the prevention of war but leaves out of discussion what states should do if deterrence fails and war breaks out. Fourthly, deterrence is based on that assumption of rationality which Bull always distrusted. Fifthly, strategic nuclear deterrence is an intensely bipolar phenomenon in a world in which nuclear weapons are spreading. Sixth and lastly, a point which Bull made in passing with his usual discretion: peace based on nuclear deterrence alone is 'morally disreputable'.[37] It is the same awareness of fragility which made Bull sceptical about the scenarios—so often favoured by American scholars—of limited nuclear war used to compensate for Western conventional inferiority.

Bull's own recommendations in the nuclear realm were conspicuous for their realism. He could be scathingly critical of pleas for unilateral disarmament or for complete and general disarmament. He was sceptical—more, perhaps, than I would be—about the prospects of comprehensive arms control agreements; he showed more sympathy for unilateral and parallel restraints, and he thought partial agreements more probable. He was aware of the impossibility of distinguishing offensive from defensive weapons; and he did not think it was possible to distinguish between weapons on the basis of the different missions assigned to them, since each weapon system is capable of performing a whole variety of missions. He realized that many weapons systems, including anti-ballistic missiles and multiple

---

[36] Hedley Bull, 'Future Conditions of Strategic Deterrence', in *The Future of Strategic Deterrence*, pt. 1, Adelphi Papers, 160 (Aug. 1980), 13–23.

[37] Bull, 'Future Conditions of Strategic Deterrence', p. 16.

independent warheads, could be both stabilizing and destabilizing. All these points contributed to his doubts about the
chances of comprehensive negotiated arms control. Such
negotiations, Bull noted, had actually generated new increases
in armaments.

Nevertheless, Bull did not give up on the subject of arms
control. He had his own prescriptions. He did not think states
needed to put the threshold for mutual assured destruction as
high as they did. In other words, it did not make much sense for the
superpowers to have (as they now do) something like 10,000
strategic nuclear warheads each. But he was aware of the fact
that if the threshold was set too low, the risks incurred in case of
a violation—or, put another way, the incentive to attempt to
disarm the adversary by a first strike—would increase corre-
spondingly. He was hesitant about the best formula for arms
control. In 1969, before the first large-scale superpower
agreements, he suggested the superpowers should try to limit
the numbers of deployed launch vehicles; in 1979, after the
mixed record of the SALT process, he wrote that the formula of
parity in numbers of deployed launch vehicles followed by
reductions was unsatisfactory. He wanted nuclear weapons to
serve only to deter from the use of other nuclear weapons—a
position which anticipated the stand taken by McGeorge Bundy,
George Kennan, Robert McNamara, and George Ball, among
others, against any first use of nuclear weapons in case of a
conventional attack. (Bull himself doubted, however, whether
the conventional capabilities of NATO would allow it to adopt
such a doctrine.) Finally, he advocated much greater urgency in
the task of preventing nuclear proliferation, and he blamed the
superpowers' 'high posture', their constant escalation of their
nuclear arms race, for encouraging third parties to become
nuclear states.

Two interesting tensions are to be found in Bull's work on the
subject of the balance of power in the present-day international
system. The first of these is a tension between two modes of
international society.[38] In the first mode, society can be, as he
put it, 'contrived' or deliberately arranged. In this respect Bull
pointed to the role of the great powers: they form a club which

---

[38] Bull, *The Anarchical Society*, ch. 5 (see esp. p. 104).

has special rights and duties and performs important functions even in the conflictual bipolar world of today. Bull stuck to this notion, largely because of his remarkably non-Manichean view of the contemporary international system. He emphasized the set of 'rules of the game' developed by the superpowers in the 1960s and expanded during the period of *détente* of the 1970s, which he greeted as a period of progress. But in the second mode, society can be more 'fortuitous'. In this perspective, Bull's emphasis was on a rather more mechanical and contentious balancing of power than the agreements between the superpowers or their observance of mutual respect for each other's spheres of local preponderance. For Bull, the balancing of power was a necessity for the survival of international society; and this conviction led him to repeat frequently an interesting argument, which enraged many Americans. According to Bull, in the world of today only the Soviet Union is capable of balancing the power of the United States. Bull used this argument to explain, or perhaps explain away, the Soviet military build-up.[39]

There was another tension in Bull's work on the balance of power: a tension between two approaches to universal society. At one point Bull depicted universal society as resting on a single culture. In the 1968 Bellagio conference, he pointed out that the United States was providing the only basis for the new global society, because American culture had spread through most of the world. He wondered whether the removal of this common basis would not be disastrous, since it could lead either to the risk of Soviet hegemony or to the multiplication of troublesome and potentially nuclear powers. But at a later stage he thought that the universal society which had been formed through the extension of membership to the nations emancipated from colonialism, and which was characterized by the revolt against the West, could only survive by accommodating all the different cultures which exist in it today—even if this kind of compromise provided a much weaker common basis than that which European culture had constituted for the international society of previous centuries.

It appears to me that Bull made one attempt to reconcile these divergent notions: in his plea for a West European entity capable

---

[39] Cf. Hedley Bull, 'A View from Abroad: Consistency under Pressure', *Foreign Affairs* (issue on *America and the World 1978*), 57. 3 (1979), 445–6.

of providing its own defence system. It is one of the paradoxes of recent years that non-Europeans have often been more militantly in favour of a European entity than the Europeans themselves. Bull's rather belated but spectacular conversion to 'Europeanism' was a way of achieving a synthesis of his different concerns. First, he saw in the European entity an answer to a problem which he saw as increasingly pressing: the need to balance the power of a United States which in recent years had repudiated *détente* and appeared to be seeking superiority or even hegemony. Secondly, a European entity was needed to balance the power of the Soviet Union, which had not repudiated *détente* and whose policy Bull interpreted as probably defensive in its inspiration, but which would remain defensive in action only as long as there was a strong Western guard. Clearly, Bull had become deeply disillusioned with both superpowers. Already in 1980 he had denounced them as ill-fitted to the role which great powers had traditionally played—the United States because of its peculiar past and its tendency to proselytize its own vision; the United States and the Soviet Union together because of their instinctive belief that the menace of superior power can be cancelled by virtuous intentions. Both superpowers seemed to him to be insufficiently dependent on the world economy, and plagued by what he called the domestic self-absorption of very large societies.[40] If neither one nor both together could claim to be regarded as trustees for mankind, maybe Europe could.

Bull believed that Europe had a special link with the Third World, largely because of the combination of a colonial past and a sense of guilt about that colonialism. He thought that Europe was uniquely qualified to conduct in the Third World the policy of accommodation which, according to him, the Reagan administration had abandoned and repudiated. Bull also believed that the Europeans would not follow Mr Reagan's America in a policy of 'constructive engagement'—for instance, appeasement of South Africa—which he deemed strategically as well as morally wrong and attributed to cold war obsessions and oversimplification in Washington. Finally, he thought that the construction of a European political and military entity was vital for West European dignity.

[40] Hedley Bull, 'The Great Irresponsibles? The United States, the Soviet Union and World Order', *International Journal*, 35. 3 (Summer 1980), 437–47.

In other words, the West European undertaking seemed to Bull to represent the choice of universalism over 'Americanism' in culture, and of a mixed policy combining balance (between the major powers) and deliberate contrivance (in the relations with the Third World) in international society. Bull's objective was still to strengthen that society: Western Europe, he thought, was the area where the greatest recognition of the need for international society was to be found; and he wished Western Europe to become a great power so as to prevent the rift in the superpower club from becoming irreparable. But, once again, the only thing missing has been the capacity and the will of the Europeans to play such an ambitious role.

VI

In *The Control of the Arms Race* Bull had written that 'the world is very much more complicated than the arguments' he had presented, and that 'the destinies of nations are not determined by simple choices of the soul.'[41] But Hedley Bull's work has illuminated these complications in a way which is unique and original precisely because of the rich tension and dialogue between the Grotian elements of his work and the more pluralistic, conflictual views; the choices of this particular soul were never simple, but always generous and wise. This is why his disappearance at a tragically early age is such a serious loss for all students of international relations. In such a small number of years he has given us at least three reasons for admiring his achievements and continuing his effort. He provided us with the first comprehensive defence and illustration of arms control in an age dominated by the nuclear threat. He gave us the most panoramic and incisive analysis of the rules, institutions, and prospects of the 'anarchical society' constituted by the modern states-system. And he showed that one can recognize 'the limits of rigour and precision' and be 'on guard against their misuse' without ever 'abandoning rigour and precision in favor' of sloppiness or stridency.[42] His was a highly civilized voice, in which scepticism and hope were admirably balanced. There are few such voices left.

[41] Bull, *The Control of the Arms Race*, p. 212.
[42] Bull, 'Strategic Studies and its Critics', p. 602.

3

Order in International Politics

R. J. VINCENT

THE international anarchy, the coexistence of independent political communities, if not in a state of nature then certainly in the absence of a common government, Hedley Bull took to be the central fact of international life and the starting-point for theorizing about it.[1] Then the central theoretical task was to decide how it was that order could obtain in this anarchy: what was order, how was it maintained in international politics; and was order in world politics as a whole best sustained by the society of sovereign states or by some other political arrangement?[2] It is possible to see in the recurrence of these questions in Hedley Bull's work the remarkable unity and coherence which Stanley Hoffmann draws our attention to in his chapter, so that matters as diverse as the objectives of arms control, the sophistication of Australian foreign policy, the superpower balance, reform in South Africa, the relaunch of Europe, and the rise of the Third World, can all be interpreted from the standpoint of the maintenance of international order. Unlike John Rawls, for whom justice is the first virtue of social institutions,[3] or Thomas Hobbes, who is (in Bull's own arguably idiosyncratic interpretation) 'a true philosopher of peace',[4] Hedley Bull takes the pre-eminent problem (of international

The author would like to thank Mary Bull, Don Markwell, Bruce Miller, James Richardson, and Adam Roberts for their comments on earlier drafts.

[1] See e.g. Hedley Bull, 'Society and Anarchy in International Relations', in Herbert Butterfield and Martin Wight, eds., *Diplomatic Investigations* (London, 1966), 35.

[2] These questions provide the structure for Hedley Bull, *The Anarchical Society: A Study of Order in World Politics* (London, 1977).

[3] See John Rawls, *A Theory of Justice* (Oxford, 1971), 3.

[4] Hedley Bull, 'Hobbes and the International Anarchy', *Social Research*, **48. 4** (Winter 1981), 738.

relations, at any rate, if not of all politics) to be 'that of identifying and strengthening the foundation of . . . order'.[5]

Why this priority given to order in international relations? Partly perhaps because of the unprecedentedly grave threat of disorder in contemporary international politics, which was the subject of Hedley Bull's first book, *The Control of the Arms Race*.[6] But it was partly too the result of the tradition of thought within which Hedley Bull located himself. 'Nineteenth century thought', he said in an early paper which set out the intellectual concerns that were his for the rest of his life, 'had regarded both the existence of international society and its further consolidation as entirely consistent with the continuation of international anarchy'.[7] And he went on to argue that the rejection of the international anarchy itself that was associated with the particular brand of liberal progressivism that produced the Covenant of the League of Nations was a retreat from the wisdom of the nineteenth century rather than an advance on it.

In seeking to vindicate the wisdom, in this respect, of the nineteenth century, Hedley Bull interposed the idea of international society between, on the one hand, the Hobbesian rejection of the possibility of a society of states (because states existed together in a state of nature which was a state of war) and, on the other hand, the Kantian view of a cosmopolitan or world society of individuals (which was, at the same time, a more fundamental fact than inter*national* society, and a productive fiction foretelling the end of mere inter-state society).

Hobbes's account of the state of nature as a state of war was rejected as a characterization of international relations on three grounds. Its assertion that in the state of nature there could be no industry, or agriculture, or navigation, or trade, or other refinements of living, was false: trade, the activity 'most characteristic of international relationships as a whole',[8] gave evidence of the robustness of each of these items supposedly excluded by the international state of nature. Second, its assertion that notions of right and wrong had no place in the

---

[5] Hedley Bull, '*The Twenty Years' Crisis* Thirty Years On', *International Journal*, 24. 4 (Autumn 1969), 637.

[6] Hedley Bull, *The Control of the Arms Race: Disarmament and Arms Control in the Nuclear Age* (London, 1961).

[7] Hedley Bull, 'Society and Anarchy', p. 36.

[8] Ibid., p. 42.

international state of nature was observably untrue: states recognized the existence and authority of legal and moral rules; they criticized each other's conduct in terms of them; and they showed their attention to them even in the breach by making excuses for their infraction. Third, the assertion that the international state of nature was a state of war was not true without considerable qualification, and, in any event, it was possible to regard war as much as an institution of a working international society as an item of evidence for its non-existence.

On the other side of the *via media* of international society from Hobbes was Kant, who along with other 'revolutionists' generally got shorter shrift from Hedley Bull than did Hobbes and the 'realists'.[9] The argument from the desirability of perpetual peace to the establishment of a universal state was not necessarily a foolish one, but it had to take account of the two central bastions defending international society against it: the preservation of the liberty of states; and the provision that the international anarchy makes for order as well as for liberty by not seeking to hold disparate communities within a single political authority.

There were, however, strains within the international society camp, as well as between it and the Hobbesians and the Kantians. If it was reasonable to take Grotius as the standard-bearer of the international society camp, then notice had also to be taken of certain recalcitrant followers such as Vattel and the nineteenth-century positivists. These writers might agree on the answer to the central question in international relations—is there an international society?—but disagree on the nature of that society. Hedley Bull contrasted Grotius with Oppenheim in this regard, finding between them disagreement on the extent to which war was governable by international law, on the sources of international law, and on the membership of international society.[10] Grotius, the 'solidarist', made international law apply to each aspect of war—the reason for which it was undertaken as well as the manner in which it was conducted. He had as the

---

[9] The source of Bull's thought here was Martin Wight; see Hedley Bull, 'Martin Wight and the Theory of International Relations', *British Journal of International Studies*, 2. 2 (July 1976).

[10] Hedley Bull, 'The Grotian Conception of International Society' in Butterfield and Wight, eds., *Diplomatic Investigations*.

source of international law not merely the codified practice of states but also, and more importantly, the precepts of right reason distilled in natural law. And he had as members of international society not merely states, but also individual human beings. Oppenheim, the 'pluralist', was less sanguine about the reign of law in international society: war was inevitable, let us seek only to regulate its conduct; the sources of law should be confined, realistically, only to what states could be deemed to have agreed; and let not the purposes of individuals obstruct the maintenance of peace and security among states. So the strain was between Grotius (Lauterpacht and the naturalists) pulling towards the revolutionists, and Oppenheim (Vattel and the positivists) pulling towards the realists.

It is tempting to try to place Hedley Bull in this gallery of thinkers on international relations, despite the crudity of the enterprise that he might have disparaged. There was the occasional, even frequent, alignment with the realists, usually to vanquish some foolish utopian or to expose some rationalizing hypocrisy.[11] There was the much rarer excursion with the revolutionists, especially when they presented a powerful and coherent alternative to positivism and allowed a snipe at his realist companions.[12] But Hedley Bull stood four-square in the Grotian or rationalist tradition, towards its pluralist extremity in the early writing on Hobbes and on Grotius himself, more towards the solidarist extremity in the later writing on the expansion of international society.

We may observe this swing at work in Hedley Bull's discussion of order which is the subject of this chapter. The structure follows his: what is order; what are the institutions that maintain it and what is the evidence for its existence in contemporary international politics; what alternative arrangements might be made for the maintenance of world order and in terms of what other values might international relations be considered. Finally, we might ask, as he did of other thinkers, what his legacy is and what work he has left us to do.

---

[11] The discussion of disarmament in *The Control of the Arms Race* illustrates both these aspects.

[12] See e.g. the discussion of E. B. F. Midgley's work in 'Natural Law and International Relations', *British Journal of International Studies*, 5. 2 (July 1979).

Hedley Bull was a great definer. He wrote his undergraduate dissertation at Sydney University on 'Definition' and he never got out of the habit. It was not least in the making of clear distinctions and in setting out 'the problem' with as much clarity as the subject allowed (and usually in three, and later five, points) that his contribution to the academic study of international relations consisted. In deciding between 'order' and 'justice' we could make some progress by understanding the distinction between the concepts themselves. Coming to terms with the nature of international relations was assisted by first understanding the difference between a system and a society. The quality of the discussion of arms control was dependent on a tough-minded distinction between arms control and disarmament. It may even be the case that Hedley Bull's genius for making distinctions that went to the heart of a subject-matter constituted the essence of his contribution to international relations.

He began his discussion of order in international relations with a definition of order in social life generally.[13] Order denoted a particular kind of social pattern, a pattern drawn so as to facilitate the achievement of certain purposes, among which he isolated three as fundamental: the security of life against violence; the sanctity of promises; and the stability of possession. It was not possible precisely to specify the extent to which these purposes needed to be provided for if social order were to obtain, but their achievement in some degree was elementary, primary, and universal. It was *elementary* because such achievement was constitutive of society; it was *primary* in that other social goals presupposed their achievement; and it was *universal* because no society was to be found that did not allow for their achievement.

It was possible to observe the achievement of these purposes taking place at three levels of world politics: that of the state; that of the society of states; and that of world society. It was Hedley Bull's chief concern to show how order obtained at the second level—that of the society of states. And he did this by seeing the goal of limitation of violence represented by such

[13] The source for the remarks here about definition is *The Anarchical Society*, ch. 1.

rules as those associated with the just war tradition; by seeing the goal of keeping promises represented by the principle *pacta sunt servanda*; and the goal of stabilizing possession represented by the recognition by states of each others' sovereignty. But he was also interested in the emergence in practice of a more inclusive world political system. And this interest was not merely a positive one in what was actually happening but also a normative one in what ought to happen. In a tantalizingly brief passage in *The Anarchical Society*[14] he argues that this more inclusive order 'among mankind as a whole' is something more fundamental and morally prior to order among states: more fundamental because its units are ultimately individuals and not any artificial construction among them; morally prior because it is the purposes of those individuals which should inform the activities of states and the theoreticians and practitioners of order among them.

I call this passage tantalizingly brief because in it Hedley Bull took a moral position. This was rare. For while he often argued that values should be at the centre of our subject-matter as something to study, he himself was reluctant ever to assert that this or that value should have moral priority, unless it was the value of enquiry itself which he said was subversive of all other values.[15] The taking of a self-conscious moral stance was very unusual. It was not, however, absent altogether. It is there in his attitude to the morality of war in *The Control of the Arms Race*, and more obviously in the comprehensive attitude he took up towards justice in international society in his later writing, to which I shall later return.

This moral scepticism was a feature of *The Anarchical Society* itself. Bull was well aware that a study of order in international politics would be taken as a tract in defence of it, and he took pains to detach himself from advocacy of the value of order above other values. It was not to be assumed that order was a desirable goal, he wrote in the Introduction, still less an overriding one. A study of justice might yield some very different perspectives from those turned up by the enquiry into order. No general priority was to be asserted for the value of order over that of justice or, indeed, of any other value. He

---

[14] Ibid., p. 22.
[15] See e.g. Hedley Bull, 'International Relations as an Academic Pursuit', *Australian Outlook*, 26. 3 (Dec. 1972), 264–5; *The Anarchical Society*, p. xv.

would deal first with the logic of international order, and then, he hoped, in a companion volume with that of international justice.

It may be, however, that in trying to detach himself in this way from the value of order Hedley Bull protested too much. And this is the first objection to his conception of order—that the claim he made to detachment was not in the end a successful one. The second objection is the politically specific version of the first one, that the exponent of order in social life in general is in practice a defender of particular orders. And the third objection is not to Hedley Bull's politics, but to his social science; to order not as a defence of the interests of a particular class of states or of any particular class, but as a useful notion in political and social theory.

Hedley Bull wrote within a tradition of thought about political order going back, as he acknowledged, to H. L. A. Hart, his teacher at Oxford, and beyond him to Hume, Hobbes, and ultimately to the Stoics.[16] It is the tradition which begins the discussion of political order with the conditions which are necessary for social coexistence. In Herbert Hart's account of the 'minimum content of Natural Law', so long as certain simple truisms about human nature and the world in which people live hold good, there are certain rules of conduct which any social organization must contain if it is to be viable.[17] Because of human vulnerability, there must be rules restricting the use of violence. Because of limited resources, there must be some minimal form of the institution of property, in order that resources can be won from the environment. And so on. This 'if–then' mode of thought seems to be detached enough from an ethical point of view. It seems merely to state what is necessary for social life, not whether or not it is desirable. But if it isolates purposes whose achievement in some degree is *prerequisite* to the enjoyment of any other social values, there does seem to be built in a general presumption in favour of order. This does not mean that a claim to justice may not override it in a particular case; but even then, presumably, it is a claim for the realignment of the

---

[16] See H. L. A. Hart, *The Concept of Law* (London, 1961), 189–95; David Hume, *Treatise of Human Nature*, Bk. III pt. 2; Thomas Hobbes, *Leviathan*, chs. 14 and 15; for the Stoics see S. I. Benn and R. S. Peters, *Social Principles and the Democratic State* (London, 1959), 27.

[17] Hart, *The Concept of Law*, pp. 186–95.

order rather than for its replacement with a system organized
with some other value in mind—for what sustains the system is
attention in some degree to the purposes of order. The move,
for example, from a dynastic to a popular basis for sovereignty
may be defended according to a principle of justice, but it is still
sovereignty which is taken to be the basis for order. For this
reason, Hedley Bull's bending over backwards to escape from
attaching himself to the value of order might have been
overdone, as he himself seemed to recognize when he dealt with
justice later in *The Anarchical Society* and in the lectures on
justice given at the University of Waterloo which will be
discussed below.

The second objection to Bull's conception of order is that
associated with the writings on international politics of E. H.
Carr: order is the doctrine of satisfied powers. Bull dealt with
this kind of objection, at least in its cruder version, in his own
discussion of Carr's *The Twenty Years' Crisis*.[18] In that book, Bull
reminded us, Carr had argued that doctrines of peace and
international harmony (to which *The Anarchical Society* might in
some respects be assimilated) had no absolute validity, but had
to be viewed in the light of the 'sociology of knowledge'. The
sanctity of treaties, the primacy of peace, and the obligations of
the League Covenant reflected, as Hitler said they did, the
special interests of Britain and France. Bull thought the
difficulty with this line of argument (powerful though it might be
in unmasking pretension, and used in that role not least by Bull
himself) was that its relativism denied all independent validity to
moral argument, and that its instrumentalism made all law and
morality merely the tool of the ruling group. He was reluctant to
accept relativism as a knock-down argument against any morality,
and he argued emphatically that to assert and deny, 'as ordinary
men do who are not afflicted by philosophical doubt',[19] the
existence of rights and duties was crucial to providing a moral
basis for foreign policy. On the question of instrumentalism he
merely noted the utility of rules to groups other than the ruling
one. The principle *pacta sunt servanda* (which Bull noted Carr
singling out for a special criticism, and to which he replied with
a special defence) might be upheld by particular powers at

---

[18] Bull, '*The Twenty Years' Crisis* Thirty Years On'.
[19] Ibid., p. 629. For a discussion of relativism in relation to human rights see Bull,
'The Universality of Human Rights', *Millennium*, 8.2 (Autumn 1979).

particular times for their own reasons, but it did not derive simply from the interests of those powers, but from the interests of all states in social coexistence.

There is an analogy here with Burke's defence of the privileges of aristocrats.[20] The aristocracy had a special interest in the existing distribution of property because they were the chief beneficiaries of it. But in safeguarding their particular interests they promoted the interests of all owners of property by defending the institution in which they shared. This was Hedley Bull's defence of the privileges of the international aristocracy, the great powers, and the reason for his sympathetic consideration of the notion that they were 'great responsibles' as well as great powers. He did not, in this respect, abandon his scepticism about self-serving doctrine, but he had more time for the practical problems of those saddled with power and responsibility for policy than for those who, having neither, enjoyed the luxury of criticizing both. I never heard Hedley Bull express a view about A. J. P. Taylor's fascinating book, *The Trouble-Makers*,[21] which dealt with the tradition of dissent from British foreign policy, but I would expect him to have admired not dissent *per se*, but dissent which was expressed with coherence and intellectual *élan*, and which had an eye to the possibility of itself becoming policy: Richard Cobden rather than E. D. Morel.[22]

If this was a conservative viewpoint, it was conservatism of a thoroughly unideological kind. A letter Bull wrote to John Strachey after the publication of *The Control of the Arms Race* is more revealing of this than anything which has appeared in print:

It may be that I am not as anti-Establishment as anti the anti-Establishment. But the view I tried to express in my book was a kind of political quietism bordering on nihilism. I exposed the humbug of governments, including our own, about disarmament; said the issues in the cold war were trivial; said it was a struggle of right and right in which neither side was morally different from the other; distributed no

---

[20] See R. J. Vincent, 'Edmund Burke and the Theory of International Relations', *Review of International Studies*, 10. 2 (Apr. 1984).

[21] A. J. P. Taylor, *The Trouble-Makers* (London, 1957).

[22] Bull himself wrote a paper which was never published on 'Richard Cobden and International Relations'. It was, I understand, delivered at a Cumberland Lodge Conference of the LSE at the time of the Suez Crisis in 1956.

praise or blame; argued that the balance of power was a precarious and uncertain source of security . . . There is not a word in the book to suggest I prefer the West to the East, which I do not do with any conviction, except as a matter of personal convenience; as far as I know it may well be best in the long run that the Russians should complete their civilizing mission. My political position is really less 'sound' or respectable than that of any self-respecting communist.[23]

He later wrote of the same book that there was not 'so far as I am aware, anything in my book that exalts the particular values of Britain or the West. It could equally have been taken as advice to the Soviet Union or Egypt.'[24] This 'political quietism bordering on nihilism' is open to the charge, from a practical point of view, that it leaves the political arena to the ideologues and has nothing constructive to contribute to it. More seriously still, it may be said that such a stance is one that is always shifting according to the ground taken by others and has no autonomous authority. But as an analytical device, it was, in the hands of so formidable an exponent as Hedley Bull, a richly rewarding scholarly instrument subverting all doctrine except the doctrine of scepticism itself.

This leads to the third objection to Bull's notion of order, which questions its utility as a constructive concept in the study of political science. There are three aspects to this objection. The first is the claim that the conception of order is redundant because what it does is merely to turn what the structural-functionalist sociologists dealt with as functional prerequisites for the existence of society into a different language. Against this it can be argued that Bull's language was (perfectly legitimately) that of political enquiry, appropriate to looking at society from the point of view of political order and seeking to assemble a conception of minimum order. The second aspect is the criticism of Bull's conception of order for failing to be clear about whether its proclaimed purposes were empirical generalizations (no society was to be found that did not in some degree observe the principle *pacta sunt servanda*) or logical requirements (if you want society then you must honour promises). Bull presented his definition in the former form: 'all societies seek to ensure that life will be in some measure secure against violence',

[23] Letter to John Strachey, 19 Dec. 1961, Hedley Bull Papers.
[24] Letters to Terry Schaich, 30 Nov. 1970, Hedley Bull Papers.

and so on.[25] But he also acknowledged that what he was dealing with was the 'empirical equivalent' of natural law theory, which dealt with what was mandatory for all people.[26] Then he left it at that, merely saying that it was not his intention to revive the central tenets of natural law thinking itself.[27] It is of course true that if something is a logical requirement for the existence of society then no society would be found without it, but the separation of what ought to be from what is here might have been done more systematically. In this respect, it is ironically apposite to turn Hedley Bull's criticism of others against himself (a point noted also in this book by Stanley Hoffmann and James Richardson). In concluding a review of Michael Walzer's *Just and Unjust Wars* which praised its attempt to recapture the just war for political theory, he nevertheless called for the establishment of foundations to anchor opinions.[28] The foundations of his own opinions might themselves be said to have been neglected, since he relied so much on the trenchant criticism of others as a starting point for his own thought.

This leads to the third aspect, which is the allegation that Bull's purposes are not in fact generalizations derived from observation of the practice of international, or any other, society, but are the hypostatized preferences of someone writing within the political tradition that was uncovered earlier. This leads back to the objection, already noted, about the reality of the detachment of the author from his subject. A reply to it might take one or both of two forms: one, as already suggested, is to acknowledge that what is being defended is in fact a general priority given to the value of order, and to work this priority out; a second is to acknowledge that there is more empirical work to be done on the question whether values which are held in one tradition to be unproblematically universal are in fact universally practised and acknowledged.

None of this is to suggest that Hedley Bull got order wrong and that we should return to the drawing-board. It was his treatment of the subject that turned the discussion of order in

---

[25] Bull, *The Anarchical Society*, pp. 4–5.

[26] Ibid., p. 6.

[27] Ibid., p. 7. For a penetrating criticism of Bull's treatment here see Mervyn Frost, *Towards a Normative Theory of International Relations* (Cambridge, 1986), 131–7.

[28] Hedley Bull, 'Recapturing the Just War for Political Theory', *World Politics*, 31. 4 (July 1979), 599.

international politics into a rigorous enquiry and away from its use merely as a slogan (as in 'law and order') or as a hold-all concept (as, in many uses, in 'world order'). What have been suggested here are some difficulties with the notion that warrant further thought and research. More of this will be said in the conclusion to the chapter.

II

It is appropriate now to deal with Bull's second question: how is order maintained in international politics? He thought that this order existed. It was part of the historical record of international relations, and could be identified in contemporary world politics. It had roots in the actual practice of states and not just in ideas about their relations. That it might be a precarious and imperfect order did not mean that it did not exist. The evidence for its existence lay in the common interest of all states in the achievement of the elementary goals of social life, in the rules that they established to that end, and in their participation in common institutions—conceived in the anthropological sense as recurrent patterns of activity. Two particular institutions might be used here to illustrate both how order is maintained in international politics, and how Bull characteristically considered the subject: they are the balance of power and international law. In his discussion of power Bull revealed the pull of the Grotian in the 'pluralist' direction; in his discussion of international law he revealed the pressure the other way towards 'solidarism'.

Hedley Bull did not innovate in the theory of the balance of power. His discussion of it did not pioneer the application of systems analysis to international politics as did that of Morton Kaplan, whose work Bull took seriously and even admired.[29] He started with Vattel's definition of the balance as 'a state of affairs such that no one power is in a position where it is preponderant and can lay down the law to others'.[30] Then he produced a series of magisterial distinctions which have been reproduced ever since in undergraduate essays on the subject: between a simple and a complex balance; between general and local balances; between dominant and subordinate balances; between

---

[29] Morton Kaplan, *System and Process in International Politics* (New York, 1957).
[30] Bull, *The Anarchical Society*, p. 101.

subjective and objective balances; and between fortuitous and contrived balances.[31]

These distinctions dealt with much of the theory of the subject, but Bull's chief concern in *The Anarchical Society* was to illustrate the functions of the balance of power in relation to the maintenance of international order. There were, he said, three such functions in the modern states-system: the prevention of the transformation of the system into a universal empire; the protection of the independence of states; and the provision of conditions in which other institutions of international order were capable of operation. In this last sense the balance of power was *constitutive* of international order in the same way as the three primary goals of order in general were constitutive of society. These functions were not, however, perfectly harmonious one with the other, all pulling together in the direction of international order. Equilibrium in the system as a whole had often been maintained by sacrificing the independence of a part of the system; and the institutions of order such as international law that were in general dependent on the maintenance of a balance of power were often violated by the working of the machinery of the balance itself.

One central part of this machinery was war, and, in a striking passage, Bull identified its integral role:

From the point of view of the international system, the single mechanism or field of forces which states constitute together by virtue of their interaction with one another, war appears as a basic determinant of the shape the system assumes at any one time. It is war and the threat of war that help to determine whether particular states survive or are eliminated, whether they rise or decline, whether their frontiers remain the same or are changed, whether their peoples are ruled by one government or another, whether disputes are settled or drag on, and which way they are settled, whether there is a balance of power in the international system, or one state becomes preponderant. War and the threat of war are not the only determinants of the shape of the international system; but they are so basic that even the terms we use to describe the system—great powers and small powers, alliances and spheres of influence, balances of power and hegemony—are scarcely intelligible except in relation to war and the threat of war.[32]

The centrality of war, however, did not mean the banishment

[31] Bull, *The Anarchical Society*, pp. 101–6.
[32] Ibid., p. 187.

of international order. War itself might be interpreted as an institution of international society, the *ultima ratio* not only of kings but also of the system itself, because through it challenges to the balance of power were met when lesser means had failed. In the fulfilment of this function the great powers had a special part. One of their defining characteristics was that they were in the front rank in terms of military strength, and in a system ordered by might they had special rights and duties both in regard to the management of the balance between themselves and to the laying down of the law to others. The management of the balance between themselves involved such institutions as those associated with the avoidance and limitation of crises and of wars. Such institutions as tacit and open agreements as to spheres of influence, and the joint ordering of affairs outside the neighbourhoods of the great powers so that their global interests were accommodated ahead of local preoccupations, were characteristic of great power arrangements made for the management of lesser powers.

By making use of these institutions great powers simplified the pattern of international politics and made it in some degree predictable. But the power differential itself provided, at least potentially, some degree of order by making possible the unilateral exploitation of preponderance. Bull distinguished between three forms of this preponderance: 'dominance', which was characterized by the habitual use of force by a great power against the lesser states comprising its hinterland (for example, the USA in relation to Central America and the Caribbean from the late nineteenth century to 1933); 'primacy', which denoted leadership freely conceded by the lesser states but which was achieved without coercion and with 'no more than the ordinary disregard for norms of sovereignty' (for example, Britain's relationship with the Old Dominions until the end of the Second World War); and 'hegemony', in which a great power does resort to force in its hinterland but does this occasionally and with reluctance, preferring to rely on other instruments of authority (for example, the post-war relationship between the Soviet Union and the countries of Eastern Europe).[33]

The order that is achieved by means such as these Bull

---

[33] Ibid., pp. 214–19. These ideas were first tried out in 'World Order and the Super Powers' in Carsten Holbraad, ed., *Super Powers and World Order* (Canberra, 1971).

recognized as being precarious and at times hardly perceptible. Still less was he disposed to see, as some did, in the pattern of contemporary great-power politics, an emerging condominium or concert among them such that they sought jointly to manage the international order. His style of argument with regard to the institution of the balance of power was more to present it as the best arrangement that states had been able to make in the circumstances than to celebrate it as a high achievement of Western civilization. Thus he wrote in *The Control of the Arms Race*:

If—like the critics of the balance of power, from Richard Cobden to President Wilson to the present supporters of unilateral disarmament —we contrast the security provided by a military balance with that provided by some imagined political system that might arise in the long run . . . we shall be very conscious of its shortcomings. If we examine the present military balance alongside our image of a just and liberal world government, or total disarmament, or free trade and universal brotherhood, or the Roman peace, we must be impressed with its dangers. But if we examine it alongside the alternatives to it that exist now, the alternatives that we by our action or inaction can bring about, we must form a very different impression. The alternative to a stable balance of military power is a preponderance of power, which is very much more dangerous. The choice with which governments are in fact confronted is not that between opting for the present structure of the world, and opting for some other stucture, but between attempting to maintain a balance of power, and failing to do so.[34]

In this spirit he wrote also about nuclear deterrence, which he took pains to distinguish from the balance of power, but then pointed to the functions it fulfilled in contemporary international politics that were analogous to the historical role of the balance of power.[35]

There are two difficulties with Bull's treatment of the balance of power that will be dealt with here; the first concerning what it left out, the second concerning what it built in.

What is left out of the discussion of the practice of power politics, especially in the treatment of the unilateral exploitation of preponderance, was the economic dimension. The spectrum from dominance through hegemony to primacy which Bull dealt with by referring to the kind of coercion associated with the use of force might have been reproduced using economic indicators.

[34] Bull, *The Control of the Arms Race*, p. 39.
[35] Bull, *The Anarchical Society*, ch. 5.

The discussion of hegemony associated with 'neorealism' in the United States[36] (in which camp Bull once placed himself, in response to an anxious enquiry from an American graduate student about where he stood), which was fundamentally about political economy, was not one that Bull actually joined. This may have reflected merely his entrenched disdain for whatever was the latest fashion; but his own discussion of hegemony, which dwelt on the relations of the superpowers with the states in their spheres of influence, might have been deepened and broadened by the inclusion of economic aspects. Bull noted that it was clear that 'the United States prefers to rely upon economic forms of pressure'[37] than on the use of force to police its sphere of influence, but that was all. The neglect is interesting given Bull's comprehensive mandate in *The Anarchical Society*, and the existence of a classical literature on political economy, notably in the books on imperialism, and his remark that was noted earlier that trade is perhaps the most characteristic of international relationships. And it is a gap (whose existence he came to acknowledge) that could be filled without doing violence to his method.

What Bull's discussion of the balance of power built in was the notion that it was possible to spell out its functions in relation to international order and to identify actors who played roles in its maintenance. These sociological notions of function and role recur throughout his analysis of how order is maintained in international society, and while he specifically disclaimed any association with the structural-functional mode of analysis in sociology which, he said, asserted the primacy of the whole over its parts in accounting for whatever occurs within it,[38] there is an inescapable element of this in his discussion. For the international system itself was defined as being framed 'when two or more states have sufficient contact between them, and have sufficient impact on one another's decisions, to cause them to behave—at least in some measure—as parts of a whole'.[39] Constructing this whole was the grand enterprise that Bull embarked on when he wrote *The Anarchical Society*, and the

[36] See e.g. Robert O. Keohane, *After Hegemony* (Princeton, 1984); and Robert O. Keohane, ed., *Neorealism and its Critics* (Columbia, 1986).

[37] Bull, *The Anarchical Society*, p. 217.

[38] Ibid., p. 127.

[39] Ibid., pp. 9–10. This 'holism' is one of the targets for Roy E. Jones's attack on the English School published in the *Review of International Studies*, 7 (1981). James Richardson deals with this article in his discussion below.

bricks and mortar were provided by the identification of institutions and actors which had functions and roles within it. The teleological element is in this enterprise unavoidable.

To show that this is more than merely a pedantic difficulty we might conclude this discussion of the balance of power by returning to Vattel. Consider the situation in which one power does threaten to become preponderant, and the remainder, not wishing the law to be laid down to them, take up arms against it, and are successful. The outcome is then interpreted from the point of view of the theory of the balance of power as a vindication of its precepts. But what of the theory available to the vanquished state? It is more likely to suppose the rhetoric of the successful to be a version of 'victor's justice' than to be satisfied that the system had somehow disinterestedly survived, that the wheels of international order had turned to its own unavoidable disadvantage. And if it determines as a result to fight more vigorously against the erstwhile victors the next time, and if it should on that occasion succeed—it could then produce its own version of the theory of balance, which might appear to the new vanquished as 'victor's justice'. Hence the precariousness of order in a situation in which international society is, owing to the continuing vitality of the separate sovereigns, insufficiently solidarist to produce an agreed version of the fundamental rules that will be acknowledged even by those directly the victims of the 'operation of the system'. This 'sub-system dominance' permanently threatens the survival of the system. The realist in Bull knew this, producing the scepticism which reminded him at every point of the fragility of international order, and which held in check the rationalist proclamation of society amidst anarchy.

One of the chief evidences for the existence of this society was international law: 'the body of rules which bind states and other agents in world politics in their relations with one another and is considered to have the status of law'.[40] The function of international law in relation to international order, according to Bull, was not itself to produce it, as some progressivist thought asserted, but to identify the constitutive principle of the political organization of humankind—the society of states; then to state the basic rules of coexistence between them; and then to

---

[40] Bull, *The Anarchical Society*, p. 127.

provide a language in which their formal relations could be carried on.

This was an important function, but it was not fundamental in the sense that the function fulfilled by the balance of power was fundamental. For this reason the imperatives of balance often undermined those of international law—by, for example, requiring from time to time preventive war, or failure to respond to aggression, or intervention, support for none of which was to be found in the textbooks on international law. This fact was one giving to international law its peculiar character and was a basic limitation on its contribution to international order. So changes within the domain of international law—its widening scope, or its access to different sources, or its admission of other subjects—could not themselves deliver a more solidarist international order, but only reflect the provision of one by other social forces.

The interest in international law, then, was not for what it was, but for what it signified. It provided evidence for the existence of society, not the reason for its existence. It was in this regard a very useful instrument for Bull, locating society like a miner's lamp locating gas: *ubi societas ibi jus est*. Hence the importance of the question of international law in the discussion of *The Expansion of International Society*.[41] A central theme in the expansion of the rules and institutions of what had been European international society to the whole of the globe was, for Bull and Adam Watson, the revolt against Western dominance. Their chief research question in regard to contemporary international politics was what could be described as 'social' about the relations between states that were coexisting after this revolt as religiously, ideologically, and culturally divided groups. For this quest, international law was an indispensable guide. Each aspect of the revolt against Western dominance—the struggle for equal sovereignty, the anti-colonial struggle, the struggle for racial equality, the struggle for economic justice, and the struggle for cultural liberation—was given legal expression. The struggle for equal sovereignty and against extraterritorial jurisdiction was ended typically by treaties obliterating the privilege. The anti-colonial struggle, carried forward in international society at the United Nations, led to

---

[41] Hedley Bull and Adam Watson, eds., *The Expansion of International Society* (Oxford, 1984).

resolutions of the General Assembly (such as the famous
Resolution 1514 of 1960) giving evidence of a rapidly solidifying
customary law, and was incorporated as the principle of self-
determination in the two human rights covenants which came
into force in 1976. The struggle for racial equality has given rise
to conventions sponsored by the United Nations against the
crime of apartheid and more generally against any kind of racial
discrimination. The struggle for economic justice has led to
such resolutions as the 1974 Charter of the Economic Rights
and Duties of States. And the struggle for cultural liberation has
found expression in non-Western contributions to the human
rights instruments that have been produced by the international
community since the Second World War, such as the attention
given to the rights of 'peoples' in the Banjul Charter on human
rights in Africa.

Not all international lawyers would admit these developments
as 'hard' international law, and there is considerable debate
about their status. But from the point of view of establishing the
continuing vitality of international society, even after the
successful assault on Western dominance, the debate itself can
be appropriated as evidence of the civilized conversation
associated with the existence of a society.

International law, hard or soft, is not itself the vehicle for
pulling international society in a solidarist direction. It merely
follows the path taken by more fundamental political, economic,
and cultural determinants. Law for Hedley Bull, rather like Sir
Alfred Zimmern's rendering of law for the classical Greek, was
'the formulation of the will of the community . . . an external
manifestation of its continuing life'.[42] But however brilliantly it
illuminates this continuity it does not itself provide it. And this is
the weakness of the pull of international law in a solidarist
direction: it is a cart, not a horse.

III

If Hedley Bull saw the first function of international law to be
the identification of the society of states as the mode of political
organization on a global scale, he conceded that certain

---

[42] See Sir Alfred Zimmern, 'International Law and Social Consciousness', *Transactions of the Grotius Society*, 20 (1934), 27–8.

international lawyers saw in the same material the common law of mankind in an early stage of its development.[43] He accepted that other ways of organizing world politics were conceivable, that some of them might in principle be desirable from a moral point of view, and that his discussion of order in world politics would be incomplete without an examination of them. He reviewed, therefore, arrangements that would mean change within the states-system—a disarmed world, or a world of ideological solidarity; and other arrangements that would mean movement beyond the states-system—'a new mediaevalism' in which political authority was scattered at a number of levels of government, or world government where authority was gathered at the centre.

What he was chiefly interested in, in regard to the question of the survival of the states-system, was whether it was true to say that it was obsolescent. He isolated three versions of the doctrine of obsolescence:[44] the notion that the states-system could no longer provide peace and security, if it ever had done; the idea that it could not provide for the more demanding goals of economic and social justice; and the argument that the system was inconsistent with the achievement of ecological equilibrium on the globe.

On the question of the provision of world peace and security, Bull accepted that war was endemic, that the international system was to some extent 'a war-system', but he did not go on from there to argue for the abolition of the system. This was so for three reasons. First, it was a facile account of the causes of war that confined itself to the structure of the system in explaining conflict. In this regard, other kinds of political arrangement might be equally prone to conflict and war. Second, the states-system which played host to war did not thereby shut out some minimal approximation to order, because the division of political authority between several sovereigns (as we have seen earlier) might be less dangerous to the maintenance of order in a divided community than, say, any attempt at the establishment of central authority. Third, there was the possibility of reform within the system, which made the

[43] See e.g. C. Wilfred Jenks, *The Common Law of Mankind* (London, 1958).
[44] The target in much of what Bull wrote on this subject was Richard Falk of Princeton. See Falk's *This Endangered Planet* (New York, 1969), and *A Study of Future Worlds* (New York, 1975).

doctrinaire insistence on its abolition if war itself was to be removed seem rather extravagant.

Having established this threefold rebuttal of the argument for the obsolescence of the system of states as one that provided for peace and security, Bull turned it with equal effect on the arguments about economic and social justice and ecological equilibrium. There was no reason to find the cause of these substantial difficulties at the level of the states-system. There were good reasons to think that the states-system played some role in ameliorating them; and then there was the possibility of reform in the states-system, such that a task it now coped with sketchily if at all need not always be neglected.

Indeed, reform in the states-system, though not necessarily *of* it, was argued by Bull to be crucial to the survival of international society. For if the consensus that sustained such society as obtained in contemporary international politics was to endure, not only did the great powers have to be satisfied, in some degree, that their interests were met by it, but also the lesser powers had to be brought along by a quite radical redistribution of wealth and power in the system. And between the great and the small, Bull went on to argue, the element of a common culture had to be deepened and enriched in order to provide the soil in which common values and institutions might take firm root.[45]

If all this amounted to what Bull conceded it was in the conclusion to *The Anarchical Society*—an implicit defence of the states-system[46]—it was also a classical statement of the rationalist or Grotian position on world order. Against the realist deniers of international society, and the revolutionary destroyers of it, Bull argued that order in world politics was dependent on the survival of international society, such that if the element of society in contemporary international politics were under threat the task would be to entrench it rather than to abandon it in favour of some other arrangement. But making world order, in this way, the achievement of *international* society was a provisional conclusion which had constantly to be reassessed in the light of developments in the direction of a genuinely global polity.

[45] Bull, *The Anarchical Society*, pp. 315–17.
[46] The defence is much more explicit in 'The State's Positive Role in World Affairs', *Daedalus*, 108. 4 (Fall 1979).

At the conclusion of *The Anarchical Society*, not only did Bull concede the extent to which it defended the states-system, he also seemed to acknowledge the general priority of order over other values (that was dealt with above) as a conclusion he was reluctant to reach. But this did not mean justice conceding to order in any particular instance, and in any event he was hesitant to be dogmatic about this until the companion study on justice was completed.

He began this task in earnest for the Hagey Lectures at the University of Waterloo in Canada in 1983–4.[47] There was nothing new to be found there about the definition of justice. He began, as he had begun his earlier discussion of 'Order vs. Justice in International Politics' (reprinted from *Political Studies* in *The Anarchical Society*) with the Aristotelian categories of general and particular justice; justice as fairness, justice as conformity to rules opposed to mere arbitrariness, treating like cases equally and unlike cases unequally; and arithmetical justice (equality of rights) compared to proportionate justice (discrimination according to circumstance). In the earlier work he had also distinguished usefully between international or interstate justice, individual or human justice, and cosmopolitan or world justice. But in the Hagey Lectures he anchored the discussion of justice firmly in the revolt of the Third World against the dominance of the Western powers, arguing that this was what had 'placed the issue of justice high on the agenda of world politics'.[48]

Those themes of Third World revolt that were dealt with in the previous section from the viewpoint of international law he treated as a catalogue of demands for justice, putting together a magisterial moral brief for the Third World in its struggle for emancipation. He showed how these demands took Western moral premises as their point of departure: the demand for equal sovereignty came from the doctrine of the equality of states associated with Vattel; the demand for national self-determination from the bourgeois revolutions of the eighteenth century and the Russian revolution in the twentieth; the demand for racial equality from the Western conception of human rights applying equally to everyone, regardless of race among other

---

[47] Hedley Bull, *Justice in International Relations*, the Hagey Lectures (Univ. of Waterloo, Ontario, 1984).

[48] Ibid., p. 1.

things; the demand for economic assistance from a Western sense of moral obligation to relieve poverty; and the demand for cultural liberation from European notions of the centrality of the factor of cultural difference in informing self-determination.

But the real interest of Bull's discussion of these demands was his demonstration of how those speaking for the Third World had driven them into territory no longer necessarily carrying the expectation of a sympathetic reception amongst liberal opinion in the West. Sovereign equality became absolute sovereignty asserted over economic as well as political assets. Self-determination was raised up on collectivist principles in which the traditional Western derivation from the rights of individuals was lost to sight. Racial equality as a principle aimed only at the target of white supremacy lost its universal appeal. The demand for economic justice became a principle of pay-back aimed at erstwhile colonial power, but did not entail the application of a principle of distributive justice within the new states. And the idea of cultural liberation, if it meant the rediscovery of ancient indigenous values, did not necessarily qualify as 'liberation' according to a classical Western rendering of that notion.

So the departure from minimum order involved not merely buying into an argument about what was just and due within a liberal interpretation of justice and duty, but also into a debate between cultures about what justice was. Bull's response to this was not to throw up his hands, but steadily to set out the concepts about justice in international relations that we ought to embrace: a notion of the rights of the international community setting limits to the egotism of states; receptivity to the rights of individuals as well as of states and nations; the spelling out of a notion of a world common good; and a new prominence to questions of distributive justice in relation to allocation between states as well as within them.

In reference to the theme of this chapter, however, and also to Hedley Bull's own work, the most important question is the compatibility of order and justice. He did argue that justice was only achievable within the context of order. And he did show that international society was generally inhospitable to notions of justice, even of interstate justice which did not involve any radical reordering of the planet. But he also suggested that there was no a priori reason why they should be incompatible and that there was a degree of mutual dependence between them such that an order sustainable over time enhanced its chances of longevity if it took account of considerations of justice, and justice was an end worth achieving only if an order obtained in which to enjoy it.

The difficulties arose in practice when the working of the institutions of order seemed to require an affront to justice, such as in the famous case (Poland) of the extinction of the independence of a small state in order to preserve the balance between the great. When choices had to be made in this kind of context, Bull suggested, conservatives opt for minimum order, lest more exaggerated claims bring down the whole enterprise, while revolutionaries require liberty or death, and liberals are reluctant to concede that a choice has to be made. He himself did not sign up with any of these groups, but retreated to the level of generality in admitting (as he had not done in his defining chapter) that there was 'a sense in which' order was prior to other goals. But this did not settle the question of priority. 'The question of order *versus* justice', he said in an uncharacteristically cant phrase 'will always be considered by the parties concerned in relation to the merits of a particular case.'[49]

We have given reasons earlier why the logic of Bull's argument did seem to require a general presumption in favour of order—rather like, in international law, the general presumption in favour of governments in a situation of civil war until the insurgents have shown themselves to be successful belligerents. We may note three more points about Bull's discussion of justice, before moving on to the conclusion. In the first place, it is interesting that he took the Third World to be the chief standard-bearer for the argument for justice in contemporary international politics: not dissidents, or dispossessed nations, or the global proletariat, or the 'fourth world' of poorest nations, or that other 'fourth world' which is sometimes represented as the voiceless masses within Third World states without a part in the international conversation about justice. The reason for this may

---

[49] Bull, *The Anarchical Society*, p. 97. His treatment of the particular case of South Africa is interesting both for its suggestion that that case is a microcosm of the issue of order versus justice in the world as a whole, and for its liberal rejection of the standard arguments for the need for collaboration between the West and South Africa. See 'The West and South Africa', *Daedalus*, 111. 2 (Spring 1982).

be a combination of realism and romanticism: it was actually the
Third World that was putting forward the most general
argument for justice in international politics from a plausible
position of disadvantage; and it was appealing to place that
argument in the context of the achievements of the past
disadvantaged, and notably the third estate of the French
revolution from which the Third World tag was derived.[50]

Second, Hedley Bull's account of the demands for justice of
the Third World gives them a coherence and persuasiveness
which they have seldom enjoyed in the practice of international
politics. It may be, in this regard, that Hedley Bull's search for
the classic statement of something, its most trenchant defence (a
disposition he attributed to and maybe learned from Martin
Wight) caused him in this case to produce it himself.

Third, it is striking that while Bull's writing never lost that
cool and dispassionate temper which seemed to give it a special
authority, his mood on order is that of *The Control of the Arms
Race*—iconoclastic, dismissive, tough-minded, ruthless; while
his mood on justice, at least in the Hagey Lectures, is humane,
large-minded, constructive, and optimistic. Realism and rationalism were yoked together in his nature.

IV

In conclusion I propose to deal with the following questions:

1. What remains to be said about the issue of priority as
   between order and other values?
2. What was the essence of Hedley Bull's defence of
   rationalism against realism and revolutionism?
3. What legacy has he left us, particularly from the point of
   · view of the lines of further thought that his work suggests?

The priority assigned to order, and within that value to the
wishes of the great powers, which it is possible to extract from
Bull's work, might be interpreted not as rather crude conservatism—political partisanship bored Hedley Bull—but as the
minimalist endorsement of the doctrine that authority must
reside somewhere if order is to obtain anywhere. The great
powers were burdened by responsibility as much as benefited by

---

[50] For Hedley Bull's own treatment of the idea of the Third World see 'The Third
World and International Society', *The Year Book of World Affairs*, 33 (1979).

power, and theirs was a role that had to be played. Those who were not burdened by responsibility had the luxury of criticizing those who were from a position in which they themselves were not being tested. Distaste for this position explains Bull's remark in the letter noted above about being anti the anti-establishment. His own position was, in the universality of its critical disposition, deeply unideological, and with the subtraction of the religious commitment might be compared to Augustine's 'For what doth it matter in respect of this short and transitory life, under whose dominion a mortal man doth live as long as he be not compelled to acts of impiety or injustice?'[51]

Order in contemporary international politics was best sustained by the fortification of the institutions of international society. Against the realist deniers of international society, and the revolutionist destroyers of it, Bull defended the middle way, but borrowed arguments from each extreme to use against the other. Thus the realist denial of international society on the ground that international politics was mediated by power alone was exposed by asking the idealist question about what power was for. And the revolutionist wish to transcend international society was exposed by asking the realist question about the outcome of similar aspirations in the past. Bull admired the willingness of the extreme positions to ask uncompromising questions, and to recognize that sometimes hard choices had to be made, but he used these techniques in defence of moderation: a position he sometimes found dull, but rarely deserted.

His intellectual legacy is simply that of one who has done fundamental work in his subject. On almost every page of *The Anarchical Society* it is possible to find a foundation on which further work could build. Indeed, as James Richardson points out in his chapter, he was an excavator and foundation-builder: the superstructure was left for others. And his openness of mind makes him accessible to diverse approaches.[52]

To take a number of items, almost at random, which provide the foundations for further work, it is not now possible to think about the nature of international society without familiarity with

[51] St Augustine, *City of God* (London, 1945), Bk.v, ch. 17.
[52] See e.g. Richard Ashley's fascinating paper given at the British International Studies Association Conference at Aberystwyth in 1987 on 'Hedley Bull and the Anarchy *problématique*'. See also James Der Derian's *On Diplomacy* (Oxford, 1986), for a work taking Bull in what he regarded as an unfamiliar but provocative direction.

Bull's discussion (just as he himself observed the study of international conflict is no longer conceivable without the preface of Kenneth Waltz's three images); nor could the elements of international order be dealt with sensibly except by reference to the tradition that he systematized; the distinctions which he makes in relation to the nature of unilateral preponderance await rebuttal by an exhaustive and systematic study; the discussion of justice in international politics has been given its syntax by the Hagey Lectures; and the idea of a cosmopolitan culture and its relation to international order is considerably under-researched and awaits its authoritative exponent (his own planned book on the revolt against Western dominance, the companion to *The Expansion of International Society*, would have taken this further).

As to the legacy of Bull's intellectual style, it can be reduced to four maxims: ask the big questions and get the big picture; be sceptical about every generalization, including this one; hold up every fashion to the mirror of history; and (as he said at the end of *The Anarchical Society* in a way that confirmed for his detractors their view of his 'anti-intellectualism', but in my view reveals his intellectual integrity) acknowledge the extent to which we are in the dark rather than pretending that we can see the light.

4

The Third World

J. D. B. MILLER

HEDLEY BULL was concerned about the appearance on the international scene of so many new states after World War II. His sense of order was aroused by the thought of what these states might do. Moreover, his experience in India, and his contact with stimulating people like Ali Mazrui, caused him to ask questions about the direction in which the Third World might be heading, and what were the responsibilities of the West towards it. Two matters specifically aroused his interest. One was the effect of the new states upon international society: he could estimate, without too much trouble, their effect upon the international system, but his queries were essentially about the relatively fragile society which he and Martin Wight believed to exist, and which, I shall suggest, may not be able to bear all the weight he gave it. The other was how persuasive and how effective were their demands for international justice in such matters as anti-colonialism, anti-racism, and the New International Economic Order; here I shall argue that 'justice' is more of a political than a legal or ethical concept in the world of states.

I

Society and justice are 'inextricably mixed', as Stanley Hoffmann observes in his chapter. In Bull's last years they occupied his mind to a considerable extent, especially the question of justice. His was an unusual case of a scholar who, in some respects, grew more radical in opinion as he grew older: his readiness to accept the justice of certain Third World claims after an earlier period of scepticism was paralleled by his increasing doubts about the wisdom of US policy in international affairs in general, his belief that Western Europe should attend to its own defence rather than rely upon American nuclear strength, and his contempt for Mrs Thatcher's treatment of the British universities. The radicalism was selective, and buttressed by a concern for established institutions and a dislike of left-wing nostrums. So far as the Third World was concerned, it was combined with a full awareness of the empty rhetoric of which so many Third World politicians and propagandists were capable.

His writings about the Third World are listed in the Bibliography. Here I shall begin with an unpublished seminar paper of 1968. From then on, the significant publications include his contribution to the 1972 Hunter and Reilly book, *Development Today*; his *Dyason House Paper* of 1976; his 1979 contribution to the *Year Book of World Affairs*; his piece on the State in *Daedalus*, 1979; the *Quadrant* article of 1980; his article, 'The Revolt against the West' in the Rajan and Ganguly volume of 1981 commemorating our former colleague, Sisir Gupta; his 1983 article on 'Intervention in the Third World'; the 1983 lectures at the University of Waterloo, Ontario, entitled *Justice in International Relations*: his contributions to the volume which he edited in 1984 with Adam Watson, *The Expansion of International Society*; and the volume on *Intervention in World Politics* which he edited in 1984. His writings on the Third World thus extend over a considerable period; but I do not think that his opinions changed substantially during that time, except that they became rather more benign.

These writings show his great interest in historical change, and reveal doubts, which he never quelled, about whether the Third World would ultimately accept Western ways, including what he regarded as the Western view of international society. The article in the Gupta volume, in which he quotes a letter from Gupta to considerable effect, is especially interesting in this regard. He seems never to have been sure whether the cultural element in the concept of international society was so strong as to require that states which adhered to it should have a European background: he was encouraged by some aspects of Third World behaviour and disturbed by others. The Iranian revolution, with its slide backwards from modernity, gave him much to think about. At the same time, he was impressed by the extent to which advances in technology, especially in communications, made modernization difficult for Third World states to avoid; and his general conclusion appears to have been that participation in international society might be just as difficult to avoid.

The writings also show his overall humanity and his sense of a moral duty to those persons and nations in need, combined with irritation and impatience at the pretentiousness, hypocrisy, and special pleading of much Third World rhetoric. They show that he would have liked to see a greater concern for mankind as a whole in both Western and Third World states' policies. His natural hardheadedness caused him to qualify this by the realization that the state, inner-directed and self-centred as it was, remained the vehicle through which mankind, including mankind in the Third World, expressed itself in international terms.

II

In tackling Bull's views on how the Third World states fitted into international society, it is important to know how he viewed that society. I shall take as a starting-point his paper, 'Afro-Asian States and the Western International Order: A Statement of the Problem', which he presented on 5 August 1968 to a conference organized by the Department of International Relations in the Research School of Pacific Studies at the Australian National University. This paper was possibly his first exploration of the question, though it had clearly been in his mind for some time. He had previously (in *Diplomatic Investigations*) considered the question of international society, but not in the context of the Third World.

The basis for an international order or society, he wrote, as opposed to an international system,

presupposes a group of states . . . [which] conceive themselves to be bound by rules limiting them in their relations with each other. They do not always obey these rules or agree on their interpretation, but their behaviour is marked by a sense of responsibility or accountability to each other, an assumption of the need to justify or explain what they are doing by reference to principles that are held in common, even when what they are doing is trampling upon the rights and interests of other states, as those states see them.

He reinforced this latter point by saying that

most experience of relations among European states, even at its most violent and treacherous, has been accompanied by the invocation of a common identity (Christendom, Europe, civilisation) and the appeal to principles held in common in virtue of that identity (the natural law, canon law, treaty and customary law, the law of civilised peoples). It may even be argued that statesmen who take as their guide the theories of Machiavelli, Hobbes and Hegel, which explicitly deny any moral limitation on states in their relations with one another, are providing justifications in terms of common principles of a sort: in claiming reason of state or the national interest as the only appropriate measure of state policy they are providing an explanation to the world at large as to why they are disregarding international moral or legal standards in the way that they are doing. They are recognising that there is a moral question to which they need to provide an answer.

In the 1968 paper which I have been quoting, Bull did not make any significant distinction between international *society* and the international *system*. The two looked very much the same. But by the time he came to write *The Anarchical Society*, they had become separated. The distinction is to be found on pages 9–16 of that book. To summarize a fairly complex set of definitions, the system is that which exists in the view of someone to whom states are the basic units—the constellation of states throughout the world which have some sort of contact with one another. The society is, in effect, the states with a particular purpose— those within the system which subscribe to the principles and practices which Bull describes in the 1968 paper as 'a developed structure of rules and principles, deriving from a sense of common interests and values and imposing itself upon the habits and institutions of member states. If in this structure of rules there is one principle that is basic, it is mutual recognition of sovereignty.'

Before considering the application of Bull's idea of international society to the Third World, it is important to consider how valid that idea is in itself, that is, to ask how realistic it was when applied to the international system before the Third World became a significant element in international affairs.[1]

The 'leading conceptions of international order', which Bull assumed to be 'as they were in 1914', call for some examination. There is difficulty in agreeing that a society exists, and is capable

---

[1] See Adam Watson, 'Hedley Bull, State Systems and International Societies', *Review of International Studies*, 13. 2 (Apr. 1987), for a helpful account of discussions about the concept.

of functioning, if the rules are frequently broken and if their interpretation is disputed. It is hard to believe that states hold principles in common when they 'trample upon the rights and interests of others'. To say that the followers of Machiavelli, Hobbes, and Hegel are really following the principles against which they offend is little more than to say with Rochefoucauld that hypocrisy is the tribute which vice pays to virtue. It is vice just the same. Expressing oneself thus is not to follow or to hold principles of virtue; it is merely to acknowledge that others hold them, and that it is prudent to recognize the fact while not holding them oneself. To base 'society' on such a tenuous connection is not much basis at all. The society which Bull postulates was able to accommodate Lenin, Stalin, and Hitler in varying degrees, if one extends his date of 1914 to 1945, when the Eurocentric international system finally fell apart; it is difficult to believe that these leaders shared whatever principles were involved,or that they thought the notion of an international society worth having. It can be argued that by the time the Third World appeared on the scene, the principles had already been stretched to the limit.

This particular criticism seems to me reasonable in respect of Bull's 1968 formulation; but it may not be held so effective as comment on his thinking of a decade later. In the second chapter of *The Anarchical Society*, which asks 'does order exist in world politics?', he appears to agree that the principles of international society can be stretched to the limit, though he does not see this as a reason for regarding them as ineffective. He sees the 'idea' of international society as having a basis in reality that 'is sometimes precarious but has at no stage disappeared'. Great wars strain its credibility, ideological conflicts lead to its denial, and it is forced to go underground when contending states treat each other as outside the pale. Nevertheless, it survives and is available as a basis when peace or *détente* occurs again. Even so, it is to be seen as 'no more than one of the basic elements at work in modern international politics'; it is a real element, 'but the elements of a state of war and of transnational loyalties and divisions are real also, and to reify the first element, or to speak as if it annulled the second and third, is an illusion'.[2]

---

[2] Hedley Bull, *The Anarchical Society* (London, 1977), 42 and 51.

Such statements suggest that the connection between states within an international society can be tenuous indeed, and that the society can, as it were, be suspended at times, while other elements in the world take over. The concept as expressed in *The Anarchical Society* is thus rather more realistic than when it was presented in 1968; but one is entitled to recognize that this further element of realism does rather diminish the claim of international society to be either universal or persistent: it becomes more partial and peripatetic, and can be held to be largely present or largely absent, depending on the current state of the international system. This makes the question of the inclusion of the Third World even more difficult to settle.

Bull did assume that the society was still in existence when the Afro-Asian states (as it was reasonable to describe them in 1968) made their appearance. His view on whether they accepted or rejected 'the Western conception of international order' was a cautious one. He did not think they agreed on any accepted doctrine of their own, and therefore rejected the notion that extremists like Nkrumah, Mao, or Sukarno might be representative of them. It was not enough to show that they broke the rules in order to say that they rejected them: 'the breaking of rules does not necessarily indicate a failure to accept their validity.' Their extreme rhetoric was confined to a few leaders, and their occasional abuse of diplomatic procedure could probably be regarded as 'a resort of the impotent'. Though they were charged with a disregard for international law, what they really wanted was *change* in the law relating to colonialism, neo-colonialism, and international welfare, not a destruction of international law as such. In their operations at the United Nations they had simply reversed the order of priority in the UN charter, putting their emphasis upon 'international and cosmopolitan justice' rather than upon 'peace and security among states'. Overall, especially in relation to international law, he thought there was 'some element of common principle, or some prospect of its emergence'. Afro-Asian states could thus be regarded as members, or perhaps prospective members, of international society.

III

Bull saw the principles of international society as expressed 'in international morality and custom, in the working of the system of diplomatic representation, in the activity of claiming rights and duties under international law, in the principles of the balance of power, in the intermittent assumption by the great powers of responsibility for the management of international politics, and in universal international organisations'. This overlaps with Martin Wight's enumeration of 'the institutions of international society' as 'diplomacy, alliances, guarantees, war and neutrality'.[3] Neither list includes any mention of an indispensable part of international society, which has considerable significance for all countries, certainly for those of the Third World—the network of economic connections involved in international trade and investment, with the rules and understandings which enable these connections to operate effectively. Their relevance to Bull's views on the Third World and international society is that they have provided many of the 'common interests' which, in later writings, he regarded as important if Third World states were to be regarded as members of society.

The growth of the international economy—to a considerable extent a nineteenth-century bourgeois achievement, and hailed as such by Marx and Engels in *The Communist Manifesto*—made it essential to have rules, so that ships could sail safely, cargoes be delivered, contracts be observed, debts be paid, letters get to their destinations, funds be transferable from country to country, and money be invested in firms and governments in foreign countries. The establishment of such rules and practices was so substantial in its effects that many nineteenth-century thinkers believed that the world was converting itself into a great commercial republic, transcending the protectionist efforts of states; people like Norman Angell continued with the same belief up to World War I. Certainly, the commercial world of the late nineteenth century looked more like a society, as understood in domestic terms, than did the system of states.

The commercial society was not one of universal agreement. The rules, as understood, included harsh treatment for some, as with the British and French treatment of Egyptian finances in the 1870s, and the establishment of the treaty ports in China. There was also negotiation in difficult cases. By 1918 the British Corporation of Foreign Bondholders had been concerned in the

---

[3] Martin Wight, *Power Politics*, ed. Hedley Bull and Carsten Holbraad (Harmondsworth, 1979), 111.

settlement of foreign public debts amounting to about a thousand million pounds. Negotiation could not always solve the problem: the Council of this Corporation reported in 1918, 'the external debt of Honduras enters upon its forty-sixth year of total default.'[4] This situation, not unlike that which prevailed in the 1980s in respect of the debts of a number of Latin American countries, emphasizes the extent to which both governments and private bodies were and are involved in the system. The 'world society' so much hailed in recent years by transnationalist theorists of international relations—and which aroused Bull's interest because of the suggestion behind it that the sovereign state had reached its apogee and might become obsolescent— was already in existence when Marx and Engels were writing their manifesto. It was in fact the principal feature of international relations between the Franco-Prussian War and World War I. There was a widespread belief in Western Europe and North America that the requirements of civilized intercourse— the kind of criterion which Bull saw as amongst the principles of international society—demanded that economic defaulters be dealt with, natural resources be exploited for the good of mankind, vestiges of barbarism and excessive nationalism be curbed in the interests of commerce, and contracts be observed —even if this meant such acts as the British bombardment of Alexandria in 1882, and the Anglo-German blockade of Venezuela in 1902.

One does not need to deny that the rules of the society favoured the major powers and their investors in order to recognize that these rules were important to others too. The peasant proprietor and the indentured worker in a colonial export industry such as sugar, rubber, tea, or coffee depended on these rules as much as the capitalist financing the industry; without them his livelihood would be lost. Countries like Canada and Australia, which benefited in their infrastructure from the loans and investment provided by Europe (as distinct from those countries which wasted them, such as Egypt and Honduras) gained greatly from the rules: they got capital because the rules provided some security, and there was competition between lenders; and they obtained income from selling their produce in the expanding markets of Europe. Even

---

[4] C. Delisle Burns, *International Politics* (London, 1920), 81.

if a country's domestic arrangements were in disarray, as with China, it gained from the orderliness of revenue collection forced upon it by foreigners, from the increase in exports which the treaty port system produced, and from the access to modernization which the imposition of such a system necessarily entailed. Nationalist resentment was, of course, stimulated, and had its outcome later in the period of decolonization and of retreat from the privileged position of the European powers in areas of informal empire, such as Argentina and Egypt; but the gains made in the meantime were genuine.

There is no need to labour the point. It is one which people either accept or reject, depending on their overall political inclinations. What is indisputable is that the extension of European trade and investment following the Industrial Revolution reinforced the system of commercial rules and practices which had existed in embryo for centuries, and that increasing interdependence, while more profitable to some than others, benefited all in the sense that not only did incomes increase but modernization was spread more widely. Steamships, telegraphs, railways, water supply systems, public health measures, and increasing specialization in production were amongst the bases on which modern international society established itself.

The Third World countries of today were, in a sense, members of international society—or of *an* international society, that created by economic interdepedence, even if it was not the same as Bull's—before they became independent. They had rights and duties, obeyed rules and sometimes rebelled against them (as with the Indian national movement's symbolic protests against Britain's enforcement of free trade in the interests of the Lancashire cotton industry), benefited from trade and investment, and owed much of their infrastructure to the willingness of international bondholders to trust them. Their membership may have been passive so far as exchanges between governments were concerned, since their own negotiators were provided by imperial powers; but their businessmen, politicians, and officials gained practical experience of how the system of international trade and finance worked, what perils and opportunities there were in commodity trade, what kinds of incentives might attract foreign investment, and the like. After independence they built on this foundation in compiling the arguments to use at such forums as UNCTAD. Independence did not, however, materially

alter their day-to-day participation in the international
society created by interdependence—lopsided as that interdependence may have been, with more dependence for them
and more independence for the Western powers than they
might have liked. When they became active rather than passive
members of international society, their political status changed,
but their economic interests remained much the same. Yet
economic interdependence had given them a more continuous
and profitable participation in international society than any
amount of adherence to diplomatic protocol or involvement in
the balance of power might have provided.[5]

It is thus a basic criticism of Bull's account of international
society that it does not include a strong economic component,
involving on the one hand rules about trade, navigation, and
investment, and on the other the kinds of common interests
which these activities generate. He omitted important elements
of the societal relationship in which Third World states stood
and still stand in relation to the West.

IV

Similarly, and again with some relevance to the position of
Third World states once they gained independence, there is
little or no mention in Bull's description of traditional international society of how small and weak states fared in it. They
must have been members, if it was not to be regarded as merely
another version of the Concert of Europe; yet it could hardly be
maintained that in the eighteenth and nineteenth centuries their
formal diplomatic equality was given any more than nodding
recognition. At times of great moment for the rearrangement of
the international system and for the establishment, rejection, or
reinforcement of rules and practices—such as the Congress of
Vienna in 1815 or the Paris Peace Conference in 1919—there
is little record of their having been treated as other than
nuisances and subordinates. Henry Kissinger has made it clear
that Europe was to be re-made at the Congress of Vienna after
Metternich's design, with very few associates participating in
the process.[6] Harold Nicolson's diary in *Peacemaking 1919*[7] has

---

[5] I have elaborated the point at greater length in 'Interdependence and a World
Society', ch. 7 of *The World of States* (London and New York, 1981).

[6] Henry Kissinger, *A World Restored* (London, 1957), *passim.*

[7] (London, 1933).

the representative of one small country after another flitting into the ante-rooms or the presence of the leaders of the Great Powers, and then flitting out again, usually in despair. If there was an international society, what part was played in it by countries in the Balkans and Latin America? To what extent did they help to make the rules? To what extent were they expected to obey them? Were they to be regarded as formally passive, like Europe's colonies?

The nearest Bull comes to answering these questions (which his interest in Toussaint L'Ouverture shows that he may have regarded as important) is in his chapter, 'The Emergence of a Universal International Society', in *The Expansion of International Society*. This deals, however, much more with the partial and hesitant acceptance of non-European states into the European version of international society than with the status accorded within that society to minor European states and those which had been established abroad by European colonization, as in Latin America. There is a sentence in the Introduction to the volume which promises an examination of the issue. It reads: 'The idea that states, even within the European system, were equal in rights did not emerge until the middle of the eighteenth century, and only then to receive a setback in the nineteenth when the great powers in forming the European Concert put forward claims for special responsibilities for maintaining order, and corresponding rights that small powers did not have.'[8] The matter is not taken further; and we are left with the assumption, present in Bull's 1968 paper, that supervision of the international society by the major powers, rather than the formal equality which is often regarded as one of its main features, was the driving force of international society. Small states were there to look on, to be overborne when strategic necessity required it, to be made the subjects of informal empire, to be allowed to attend conferences and congresses, but not to make the rules or enforce them. Their sovereignty was something to be disregarded if it suited the major powers.

To what extent this description encompasses that of a society is a matter of opinion. It is certainly a description of a system or an order; whether a society, either as described by Bull in abstract terms, or as understood by sociologists, operates in this

---

[8] Hedley Bull and Adam Watson, eds., *The Expansion of International Society* (Oxford, 1984), 7.

way is a matter of opinion. Bull is open to the charge that his society, so-called, is merely an association of major powers for their own purposes, a sort of ideological projection of the Concert of Europe, even of the Holy Alliance; one which, in historical terms, habitually gave only lip-service to sovereignty and the notion of diplomatic equality. If this is the case, then the complaints voiced from the Balkans and Latin America at the Congress of Vienna, the Hague Conferences, the Paris Peace Conference, and the League of Nations had substance: if there was an international society, and if it involved equality between sovereign states, why were they not listened to?

The answer is probably the same as it would be in domestic terms, that the weak are finally subject to the domination of the strong, but that at times it may be inconvenient or counter-productive for the strong to coerce the weak, so that the weak occasionally achieve their objectives. In the case of Bull's international society, the opinions of the weak could normally be ignored, since the interests of the strong were mostly concerned with one another. The weak might be the cause of dispute between the strong, as was Venezuela between the United States and Britain in 1895, or Morocco between Britain, France, and Germany in 1905–6, 1908–9, and 1911. This gave them no more status than the ball has in the game between opposing football teams; there was no pretence of their equality or autonomy, except to the extent that it suited the propaganda of one side or the other.

If this was so, then it should have been relatively easy to contain Third World states after World War II within the international society in the same way as such states as Greece, Portugal, Argentina, and Denmark had been contained within the old. If it had been possible to include these, along with Liberia, Abyssinia, and Siam, not to speak of Japan, why should it be especially difficult to include Egypt, Nigeria, Indonesia, and the rest? The answer may lie in differences of cultural background, which is where Bull tended to locate it; but a more plausible answer lies simply in numbers: there were so many more small states to be accommodated once decolonization had begun; some of the new states were not small at all; and they showed much more willingness to join together in concerted activity. The small states which belonged to the League of Nations had begun to do this on non-security matters in the late

1930s, with little effect because of their lack of numbers, their dependence on the major powers, and the gathering storm which overwhelmed Europe in 1939.

A second conclusion is that the conditions which made the Third World states more successful in asserting their point of view than small states had been before World War II were due as much to the lessened power and significance of the West European states—which were no longer able to behave as they had been used to doing, as was shown at Suez in 1956—as to any special characteristic of the new states, apart perhaps from their numbers.

One may also remark that a 'society' which cannot accommodate increased numbers—especially when those numbers comprise states which in economic and cultural terms have, in their period of political dependence, been influenced by the original members of the society—does not have much that is societal about it. If its strength rests on power, then it is a power arrangement, better characterized as a system or an order than as a society in which the members can be expected to have reciprocal rights and duties, and in which the sense of belonging is held to be of major importance.

V

Given these criticisms of Bull's approach to the notion of international society, what is left of it? Was he asking the right question when he said that there was a problem about the incorporation into international society of the Third World; or was there no question to answer, because he was wrong about how international society was constituted?

In a sense, he was not asking the right question, or at any rate not framing it in the right terms. His international society looks at times like a straw man, a front for the interests of the major powers, or, rather, for the system of the time. It does not distort the realities of international politics so much as give them the wrong name. During the period when he believed that international society existed in its ideal form—let us say, from the end of the eighteenth century to the start of World War I—it was much tougher in terms of the exercise of power, much less co-operative in political terms, and much more extensive in its economic interdependence than he seemed prepared to admit.

It also contained more in the way of dissidence from its smaller and weaker members.

If one revises his picture of international society so as to include these attributes, then it could be expected to cope more effectively with an expansion of the number of states, and to provide them with more societal status, than his question would suggest. It is not that one needs to assert the same degree of power for the European states after World War II as they had possessed before it; this would be absurd. It is simply that, if there was an international society based on their practices, these must have been practices (and principles?) sufficiently broad and elastic to accommodate the ebullient new nationalisms. Moreover, the new states were not 'new' in the sense of having appeared new-born on the international scene like helpless infants; rather, they had been born ready-made like Minerva from the head of Jupiter, well aware of their place in the international economy and often (so far as the former British and French dependencies were concerned) fully aware of the political circumstances in which they would have to operate. Nobody can say that India or the Ivory Coast appeared on the international scene without bureaucrats and politicians attuned to what that scene might produce—perhaps as well attuned as their counterparts in Britain and France, who may not themselves have seen all the possibilities.

Bull's question may have been framed in the wrong terms, since the society to which it applied was rather different in operation from that which he postulated, and since the Third World states, which he put forward as potential members, were already passive members which had not previously possessed independent voices, though they had clearly had interests within the international system. Yet his question was still worth asking, so long as we remember that it was not about the international *system* (which has obviously changed, though more because it is no longer Eurocentric than because of its increase in numbers), but about the *social spirit* pervading the system, which gives it the aspect of a society. To what extent, in other words, is there now the sense of a society in the international system, especially so far as its majority of Third World members is concerned?

To answer, we need to note how the system itself has changed since 1945. It is no longer a system comprising three, four, or five roughly equal European powers, plus the US and Japan, as the principal actors. It is now one in which all other actors are subsidiary to the two superpowers. In effect, there are three tiers in terms of power: the superpowers on top; below them such countries as Japan, France, West Germany, China, and Britain; and below them again the Third World and various other minor states. The second tier cannot outface the superpowers in military terms, but cannot easily be overborne by them. The lowest tier is subject to frequent manipulation and intervention by the superpowers.

The two superpowers have been flagrant in their interference in smaller states' affairs, claiming on behalf of the free world and the Communist commonwealth respectively the right to do as they thought fit. Each has acted as it wished towards minor states (not all from the Third World) in which it thought the other might be interested. Iran, Hungary, Czechoslovakia, Grenada, Nicaragua, Afghanistan, Cuba, and others are cases in which the superpowers have shown a contempt for sovereignty and a conviction that the international system was there for the two top dogs to manage or to quarrel over. If one takes the case of Afghanistan, neither superpower can be regarded as having observed anything like the rules, practices, and principles of international society which Bull laid down: the sense of a society often appears to be quite lacking in Soviet and American policy.

To say this is not to deny that some sort of international society exists; it is only to assert that Bull's attempt to confine it to the practices and principles of the eighteenth and nineteenth centuries was perhaps impossible. It is still the case that an international society exists in economic terms and that the operation of diplomatic institutions—chosen by both Bull and Wight as vital to the notion of a society—now goes well beyond that which occurred in the eighteenth and nineteenth centuries, especially in the expansion of multilateral diplomacy. If the sense of a society is lacking from the utterances and actions of the superpowers, it is certainly present amongst many other states. The term 'the international community', which I take to be the equivalent, in current diplomatic parlance, of Bull's and Wight's 'international society', is frequently used by the representatives of the smaller West European states, by the second-tier states (though more guardedly, because they may wish to stand well with one or other of the superpowers), and to a great extent by Third World states. The idea that there is a universal society of states, in which certain rules and principles ought to be observed, is customary amongst all states which do not have pressing security objectives which make the need for alliance with other powers, and the exercise of military strength, their prime concern.

To this extent there *is* a sense of society within the international system; but the difference between this situation and the one postulated by Bull is that the leading states within the current international system (the superpowers) do not subscribe to the notion of an international society in which both of them would have rights and obligations. In ideological terms, they do not see themselves as belonging to the same society. Their activities within the international system are essentially antagonistic. Each would wish to construct international society in its own image; each would regard as defective an international society in which the other was a full participant. They can operate within the same system, since the system treats tension and hostility as constants; but they do not appear to be able to share the sense of a society, except in rhetorical terms, as when the Soviet Union pronounces the need for peaceful 'co-existence' and the US drops hints about '*détente*'.

Perhaps the best way to see the current situation is to regard the system as containing *two* international societies, one headed by the Soviet Union and the other by the United States. The Soviet one consists of the countries of Eastern Europe; the states abroad which depend on the Soviet Union, such as Cuba and Vietnam; potentially China, if it should see the error of its ways; and those Third World states which, like India, are sceptical of American intentions, or, like Libya, habitually attack the United States. Any state which co-operates with the Soviet Union is eligible for this society, the principles of which do not need to be more than anti-American, except in the case of Communist states, which must respect 'Socialist internationalism'. The American society consists of the allies of the United States, in Europe, Asia, and the Pacific; of Israel; and of such Third World states as profess capitalism, such as Singapore. It has little ideological content, except for anti-Communism. The countries of Latin America are potentially members of either society.

Is this a travesty? If so, it is no more of a travesty than to maintain that a universal international society has persisted, and to ask whether the Third World can be regarded as eligible to form part of it. I turn now to the performance of the Third World in respect of the concept of an international society of which its states are members.

VI

Most Third World states do act as if there were such a society in existence, and they wished to be in it. There are aspects of their international behaviour that strongly suggest this.

In the first place, they have shown a whole-hearted, perhaps over-zealous, adoption of the existing diplomatic system in its bilateral aspects—largely for reasons of prestige and domestic political obligation, since jobs are of the greatest importance in the politics of new states, and there is glamour as well as money in a diplomatic career. It cannot be said that this rush for diplomacy has been particularly beneficial to the states which have undertaken it, largely because their opportunities for making a significant impact upon the major states of the top and middle tiers in the international system have not been great. They have had very little to offer. Third World states have perhaps had most success in the capitals of their former colonial masters: this has certainly been true of the francophone African states, though probably less so of the former British colonies, once the initial British euphoria had worn off.[9] However one takes these situations, it remains true that Third World countries have engaged in bilateral diplomacy as far as their capacity to pay for missions abroad would allow.

Secondly, and perhaps most importantly, Third World states have enlarged multilateral diplomacy to an extent never previously achieved. The United Nations and the UN system have provided weak, poor, and inexperienced states with the opportunity to express themselves on a world stage, to group together for voting purposes, to represent themselves as part of the conscience of mankind, and to pretend to more importance than they actually possessed. The General Assembly of the UN and the corresponding institutions of the specialized agencies act as distorting mirrors of the realities of international politics: giving the Maldive Islands the same vote and say as the US or

---

[9] For a time, certainly, the society to which official British opinion hoped ex-colonies would primarily belong was the Commonwealth of Nations.

the Soviet Union means that there is little or no correspondence between what is said in these bodies and what takes place outside. New states are encouraged to substitute oratory for performance, committee work for decision, decision-making for results. It is true that these exercises in replacing reality by fantasy are also carried out by the major powers, within a variety of their relationships, including alliances; but the difference in the case of small, new, and weak states is that once the charade is over, they do not have an acceptable reality to fall back on. Their reality is so far removed from the conventions of the debating chamber that there is often no connection. For the major powers, acceptable reality exists in the shape of their economic strength and political connections with others of like capacity.

It may well be that Third World countries' expectations of a working international society or community have been heightened by the unrealistic character of much multilateral diplomacy, especially at the UN, to which they have devoted so much attention. Two US Permanent Representatives to the UN in the 1970s attest to their concentration upon it. According to Daniel Moynihan:

the United States has still not learned multilateral diplomacy, partly because we are quite an old country . . . whereas that's the only diplomacy most of them know. They came into the world [recently], and in a sense they are more modern than we. The world they entered into as entities was a world of party systems, these caucuses. You have the Soviet bloc, they vote their way, and you have the nonaligned, and they vote their way; and the Western nations, they vote their way. It works rather like parties in a parliament.

His successor, William Scranton, said:

an idea which I advocated to Washington often was that the U.N. should be handled differently than our bilateral foreign policy. I preached . . . that multilateral diplomacy was already more significant than we realised. None of the developed nations are prepared for this at all, either psychologically or organisationally.[10]

To both men, there was a genuine difference between the way in which Third World diplomats handled their bilateral contacts,

---

[10] Linda M. Fasulo, *Representing America: Experiences of U.S. Diplomats at the U.N.* (New York, 1985), 207–8, 216.

and the way in which they operated as elements in a Third World coalition on the floor of the Assembly.

In effect, these Third World representatives were acting as if the two kinds of diplomacy represented two worlds: one, a world of relaxed connections between country and country, in which representatives understood each other, and rhetoric was not needed because the discussions were about day-to-day matters of importance but not of symbolic significance; and the other, a world in which solidarity was required in order to express basic urges and cloudy generalities, and in which one's country would be judged by the stand one took. It is the latter which has provided much of the discussion of whether the Third World is basically anti-Western.

Multilateral diplomacy has flourished for Third World countries at several other levels. They include that of intra-caucus agreement (as between the African states or the Arab states); that of agreement between caucuses (as when Arab, African, Caribbean, Latin American, Pacific, and other groups have to agree between themselves about overall tactics in the General Assembly, UNCTAD, and other such situations); that of the non-aligned movement; that of the Muslim states; and a variety of regional operations, of which ASEAN and the connections between groups of Latin America states are examples. The second of these is where the activities at various levels become merged: the so-called Group of 77 (now greatly enlarged in number) operates as a coalition of caucuses, its strategy for the agenda being decided in advance by an executive Group of 27. (At the IMF and World Bank a Group of 24 performs a similar function.)[11]

The Third World organizations are not the only case of selective multilateral diplomacy: the Warsaw Pact countries have theirs, and the NATO/OECD arrangements ensure that Western states have ample opportunity to co-ordinate policies where this seems important to them. There is a difference, however, in the degree of importance assigned to the centralized multilateral diplomacy of the UN by these various groups. It matters much less to the Western countries than to those of the Third World. It is difficult to assess the motives of the Warsaw

[11] See Karl P. Sauvant, *The Group of 77* (New York, 1981), for details of how the Third World operates at the UN.

Pact states; but their actions suggest no great interest in the UN
except as a place where points can be scored against the United
States—an activity in which they are happy to co-operate with
the Third World coalition, since questions of colonialism, neo-
colonialism, racism, and economic exploitation can easily be
turned against the US and its allies, whereas it is known that the
Soviet Union and its associates are not prepared to accept any
relevance to themselves.

For the Third World countries, passing resolutions at the UN
is to a great extent a substitute for action. It is an occasion for
oratory of a kind which sounds good to political groups at home
and to like-minded states in similar situations to one's own.
Since there are now so few colonies, anti-colonialism is no
longer of major significance in the choice of topics; but
resolutions against South Africa (the requirement of the
Africans) and against Israel (that of the Arabs) are perennial,
while neo-colonialism as a target easily fits into the general
demand for mandatory transfers of resources from the West to
the Third World.

It is desirable to see this latter demand in perspective. It
troubled Bull, because he thought that, for the Third World
countries, 'it reflects the priority they give to overcoming their
dependence or vulnerability.' He saw it as a 'demand for the
redistribution of power'. 'As Third World countries grow
stronger in relation to the Western countries,' he wrote, 'the
latter will become relatively weaker.' He linked the demand for
greater economic power with a demand for greater military
power, notably in regard to nuclear weapons.[12]

These are forebodings; but do the facts of international life
justify them? As things stand, the Third World countries exhibit
more disarray than unity, and the disarray appears to be
increasing. Individual Third World countries may aspire to
nuclear strength, but there is no general movement of Third
World states towards a nuclear posture: what is credible and
affordable for the Argentinas and Indias may be quite unattainable and undesired by the Fijis and the Sierra Leones, not to
speak of the Nigerias and Indonesias. If greater military power is
desired in many Third World countries, it is for local use in

[12] These points are made on pp. 10–11 of *Justice in International Relations*, the Hagey
Lectures (Univ. of Waterloo, Ontario, 1984), as well as elsewhere.

local situations, not for any major war against the West. The long-drawn-out, ineffectual, and debilitating war between Iran and Iraq was probably a better indication of how military power would be used than any notion of either a concerted Third World defiance of the West or a grand alliance with the Soviet Union or China. These alternative possibilities cannot be dismissed out of hand—depending on the time-scale, a variety of military coalitions is always conceivable, though these conditions may not be feasible at the moment—but they are inherently improbable in the circumstances in which the Third World countries find themselves.

Even less likely is the prospect of any concerted action in the economic sphere which might force the Western countries to bind themselves to continued subventions of resources, sufficient to change the nature of Third World economies. The amounts needed to make any major structural impact upon more that a few countries—and those not the Indias or Indonesias or Nigerias—would be immense, and well beyond anything which taxation could extract from Western electorates, or those electorates would accept. There is no way in which Third World countries could combine to force the West into such a policy. Even mass desertion to the Soviet camp would be ineffective: it is difficult to imagine in itself, but if it occurred, it would be more ruinous to the Soviet economy than to those of the West. The only weapon of consequence which the poor countries possess is that of the Western conscience—which is apparent in only some of the Western countries, and in most of those is not obvious in government circles.

The desire for power is never the same as the possession of power, although it may be a factor in bringing about that possession. It is one thing to think that extra power would be beneficial, quite another to attain it by vague threats. The Third World campaign for a New International Economic Order certainly indicated a wish for greater economic strength, but only partly the desire for power over the Western economies. To the extent that it called for automatic and mandatory transfer of resources, it was a kind of call for universal world government, since only such a government could enforce the transfers; yet the Third World states would be the first to reject such a government, with the Soviet Union and its allies following closely behind. The claims, largely put forward on the advice of

economists in the UNCTAD secretariat and other similar
groups within the UN structure, were what are called, in
Australian wage arbitration procedures, 'ambit claims'—that is,
they were maximalist demands which were clearly unattainable
in themselves, but within the boundaries of which negotiation
could be carried forward.

Throughout, there has been a distinctly theatrical note to the
whole affair, with the UN and the specialized agencies as the
chosen venue. Governments of states with relatively little
connection with the international economy as a whole, and
whose concerns have been essentially practical, have lent their
voices and votes to large universalized demands which might or
might not affect their situations. Much of this has been activity
for activity's sake, not for results. Essentially, it has been a
coalition operation, with such disparate countries as those of
Latin America, Africa, the Arab states, and the Mediterranean
states involved. It has had some of the strengths but mainly the
weaknesses of such an operation. To regard it as a threat to the
economic, military and political power of the West is unrealistic.
The NIEO is in itself unattainable; the most that can be said for
it, from a general Third World standpoint, is that it provides the
parameters within which negotiation can proceed, sometimes
bilaterally between developed and underdeveloped states, sometimes on a regional basis.

VII

What, then, is the upshot of our consideration of the Third
World's impact on international society?

There is an international society, and it is both like and unlike
what Bull saw, especially if the international economy is taken
into account. The big fish in the pond have become bigger and
fewer, while the numbers have grown overall, and the 'big
fish'—the superpowers—treat it as if it were not single and
universal, but two separate societies, one led by the United
States, the other by the Soviet Union. As against this tendency,
the Third World and certain European states stoutly maintain
that there is an 'international community', and that its principal
venue is the United Nations, where the principles of individual
sovereignty and diplomatic equality are maintained. To put it
this way highlights one of the enduring facts about international
society: that it is ultimately subject to the will of the greatest

powers, but that in between their bitterest conflicts, it can be nourished and sustained by lesser powers to which it is a source of advantage.

There has been an apparent attempt at fundamental change in the rules by the Third World states, which has had some influence upon the institutions of the UN system; but this, while highly publicized, has been of little effect, since there is not sufficient of an international conscience to enable the Third World to overcome the attitudes, prejudices, and obvious interests of the Western powers—the Soviet Union and its associates having their own approach to the rules, but preferring to obey them where profitable and otherwise ignore them. The principal Third World effort has been in the economic sphere, exemplified by the demand for a New International Economic Order; but this has been a failure, largely because of the refusal of the Western states to commit themselves to mandatory transfers of resources, partly because of the inescapable dependence of many Third World countries on the West for markets and investment, and partly because the general lack of vigorous economic growth since the middle 1970s has made Western governments reluctant to provide much in the way of economic aid to the Third World. (It is also fair to say that the growth of Western military aid, and the willingness of Third World governments to accept it when offered, has been a factor in reducing economic aid and generalized attention to Third World problems: military aid is bilateral and much more effective in terms of the obligations which it incurs.)

In fact, the Third World is inextricably linked with the economies of the West: it cannot escape. This is whether 'it' means the Arab oil states, with their apparent riches and resources, since they have nowhere else to sell the oil; or the plantation economies, which are in the same position with their sugar and rubber and tea; or those which depend on mining exports; or even the Newly Industrialized Countries of East and South-East Asia, which could not continue their progress without the West and Japan as markets. Third World governments know that, in practice, they cannot do without the West, though they might get better terms if they prove politically troublesome. This ploy is difficult to manage, and can certainly not be achieved in global terms: bilateral activity is much more promising.

These are hardly the circumstances in which international

society can be disrupted by Third World countries. They are in fact junior partners in it: they cannot escape from the economy, they have enthusiastically embraced the diplomatic system and added to its intensity by their concentration upon its multilateral aspect, and their demands for recognition and concessions are not unlike those which minor states used to make in the days of a Eurocentric international system and society. Hedley Bull's writings in his last years suggest that he had come to much the same conclusion, allowing for differences of emphasis.

VIII

We come now to the question of international justice. Bull made this the subject of his 1983–4 Hagey Lectures at the University of Waterloo in Canada, entitled *Justice in International Relations* (from which the page references which follow are drawn). He was deeply interested in the philosophical question of justice: his ready acceptance of Aristotle's categories shows his concern for the range of meanings which he could see as applicable to a variety of circumstances (p. 2). It was justice in international relations, however, and especially the demands for justice of Third World countries, that occupied him particularly. He saw these demands as having involved equal rights of sovereignty or independence; national self-determination; racial justice or equality; justice in the economic domain (through NIEO and the other similar demands); and justice in matters of the spirit and mind (pp. 2–4).

Bull believed that these demands had been made upon the Western powers, often with the assistance of the Soviet Union—even though the Soviet Union, as the legatee of the Russian Empire, was itself potentially vulnerable to criticism as a colonial power. He was impressed by the extent to which the Third World states had been successful in their demands (pp. 25–7). He thought this success resulted from the psychological awakening of the Third World peoples from their sense of passive subjection; from the weakening of the Western will to maintain dominance; from the rise of the Soviet Union, which had been an inspiration to many anti-colonial leaders and had also given diplomatic support to the anti-colonial crusade; from 'a more general equilibrium of power', which had provided opportunities for penetration by Third World propaganda; and from a transformation of the legal and moral climate of international relations, which had been organized by the majority in the UN General Assembly (pp. 27–31). As a result of these influences, there had been a number of concessions by the West, though not in respect of all the demands made by the Third World.

He thought that in future the Western response should be one of recognition that the aim of the Third World struggle was to end European and North American domination. This would involve some adjustments which might be unwelcome because they meant a diminution of power. The West should, he thought, seek to accommodate the demands wherever possible, but should stand firm on some issues, such as human rights and freedom of information. In general, the West should remember that the Third World was 'striving towards political, economic and cultural freedom': these were basically aims which the West itself had fostered (pp. 32–3). At the same time, he was well aware that the interpretation of the rights which the Third World wanted was often different as between thc Western countries, their progenitors, and the Third World states in their official doctrines, as expressed at the UN (pp. 5–11). In particular, he recognized that those demands were normally couched in terms of the rights of peoples, which meant in practice the rights of states; the Western concern for individuals was often lacking.

Bull's own ideas on the concepts of justice in international relations which 'we should embrace' included the view that the rights of states and nations were subject to the rights of the international community, thus expressing a cosmopolitan and universalist concept which went beyond the directly state-centred demands of the Third World. His belief in the rights of individual persons was expressed in this context. It was necessary, he said, to take account of 'our emerging sense of a world common good'; this was to be accompanied by 'a new prominence in questions of distributive justice in international relations'. He did not believe, however, that these concepts were gaining much acceptance.

Bull obviously found it difficult to settle the question of the divergence between the Western view that justice was some-thing due to individuals, and the Third World's case for it, which assumed that it was due to communities, in particular to states. To some extent he agreed with concessions to states as instances of justice: the economic concessions, for example, could be made only to states, since most of them did not apply to individuals. He was still uneasy about the Third World's frequent disregard for human rights as applied to individual persons, and thought the West should not give in about these. Yet he recognized that, in the Third World, states were what mattered: demands for justice would be made in the name of the state, and essentially for its benefit. He wrote trenchantly on the role of the state in the *Daedalus* article:

Among the Third World countries the idea that we must all now bend our efforts to get 'beyond the state' is so alien to recent experience as to be almost unintelligible. Because they do not have states that were strong enough to withstand European or Western aggression, the African, Asian and Oceanic peoples, as they see it, were subject to domination, exploitation and humiliation. It is by gaining control of states that they have been able to take charge of their own destiny. It is by the use of state power, by claiming the rights due to them as states, that they have been able to resist foreign military interference, to protect their economic interests by excluding or controlling multilateral corporations, expropriating foreign assets, planning the development of their economies, and bargaining to improve the terms of trade.[13]

Given this situation, the concept of justice in international relations as justice to states has to be accepted, at least in part; otherwise, the notion of the Third World's demands as claims for justice falls to the ground.

IX

But is there much point in asking whether justice can be done to states? The problem is that, as Bull saw, there is no 'distributor' to determine or dispense justice. Justice between states must remain either an abstract ideal or a name given to the outcome of political struggle by those who approve of that outcome.

To elaborate this point, I suggest we look first at the domestic analogy, which is not justice as between man and man, which is decided by the courts or equivalent bodies, but the process known as 'social justice', whereby groups of people—farmers,

---

[13] Hedley Bull, 'The State's Positive Role in World Affairs', *Daedalus*, 108. 4 (Autumn 1979), 121.

pensioners, business associations, tenant associations, trade unions, and so on—obtain what they regard as their due. The process is formally carried out by a 'distributor', such as a parliament; but it is in fact one of pressures upon governments and political parties, of departmental bargains, and of consultation between governments and the groups which they consider important. It is a political process, not a legal one; and it is not governed by the ideals and beliefs of the formal distributor, which is largely an instrument for the forces brought to bear upon it. The ideas of fairness and equity prevalent in the community will have some effect on the result, and that effect may at times be great; but the upshot will be decided by political strength.

The same is true in the international sphere. There will be concessions if strong states think their interests will be served: the concessions may provide the strong with allies and associates, they may prevent hostile powers from gaining ground, they may forestall the inroads of other powers (hostile or not), they may protect trade and other economic interests, and they may expand the influence of the strong in directions which they consider advantageous. The interests of the strong state may chime with those of its citizens with consciences, who wish to help the weak. Is there any point in treating this process as a matter of justice, even if it is influenced by conscientious people who clothe it in that sort of language? It can be represented as a matter of justice for purposes of propaganda by both weak and strong; but that will not make it so. From the standpoint of the analyst the propaganda, while obviously an important element in the situation, should not be allowed to obscure the essentially political nature of the process. What we are faced with is a contest amongst states at a variety of levels, involving coalitions, trade-offs, and all the apparatus of international politics. Why worry about justice?

Bull could not help doing so. He had a sense of duty towards less fortunate people which he wished to transfer to the Western states. It arose not so much from a conviction about the cant Third World claim that the West was responsible for its problems—I doubt if he found this historically convincing—as from his hope that humankind would eventually recognize reciprocal and distributive rights which went well beyond the demands of states. Yet his inherent realism forced him to recognize the basic importance of the state; so, reluctantly perhaps, he found that he had to discuss the notion of justice for states, and to employ it as it was used in international discourse.

Nevertheless, we disguise the essentially political nature of the process when we use 'justice' to describe what goes on when particular states or groups of states make demands on others. It was in the name of justice to the German people that Hitler overwhelmed Czechoslovakia and Poland; Mussolini insisted that justice to the Italians required the conquest of Abyssinia. Justice—the righting of wrongs, the success of claims righteously made—is what every predator says he is seeking. It was a call for justice that sent the unfortunate Argentinians into the Falklands. This does not mean that all states are predators, or that every claim is unjustified; but all states are political in their procedures, and it is only by political means—pressure, negotiation, threats, alliances, even war—that states get what they want. No other distributor is in sight.

X

One can sum up Bull's views on the Third World as ultimately hopeful. He was interested in the problems it created for the international system, and for his favourite concept of international society. His sense of compassion made him sympathetic towards its calls for justice. Perhaps he did not analyse its components sufficiently. For example, his work does not show much awareness of how significant is the pursuit by the Arab and African groups of their specific aims through coalitions, how votes at the UN are arrived at, or how much the Third World depends upon the opportunities provided by multilateral diplomacy and the assumptions behind the UN General Assembly. He may not have given enough attention to the gap between the relatively sophisticated statements of Third World spokesmen (often prompted by lawyers and economists from within the UN system) and the actual problems encountered by their governments. He saw the Third World as raising big questions; that was to the good for the discussion of changing international relations.

His final attitude, which merged the notion of justice with that of order, can be quoted from an address given in Canberra in

1983. After indicating some of the shortcomings of Third World states, Bull went on:

Our policies towards Third World countries should not be merely supine or appeasing: we have legitimate interests and rights of our own in relation to them for which we have no need to apologize.

For all this the Western countries today, and especially the United States, display an appalling lack of vision in their policies towards the South. The Third World represents the great majority not only of the states but of the people of the world today. No international order can endure in the future unless these states and people believe themselves to have a stake in its continuance. The issue that this raises for the Western powers is not mainly or even chiefly a moral one. Nor is it chiefly, as the Brandt Reports are inclined to suggest, a matter of the economic interest we have in increasing their purchasing power. We must take the Third World seriously primarily because of the vital interest we have in constructing an international order in which we ourselves will have a prospect of living in peace and security into the next century and beyond.

This requires that we in the West should be ready to accommodate the demands of Third World countries for a redistribution of wealth and power in the international system. We should seek to find common ground with the political forces looking for a better life for the peoples of these countries, even though it requires us to make uncomfortable adjustments. We should have no truck with the ignorant view that sees nothing more behind these forces than Soviet machinations, or the crass and contemptible notion that the interests of the West in the Third World are to be described in terms simply of access to material resources.[14]

One can agree with this noble statement while doubting whether such sentiments are ever likely to commend themselves to the leaders of Western states. This doubt rests partly upon the ingrained conviction of leaders and peoples in the West that the Third World is essentially a set of countries which can be operated on rather than operate in their own right; partly upon the great difficulty of getting developed countries with such disparate backgrounds of experience in respect of colonialism as Britain, Japan, West Germany, and the United States to act together; and partly upon the enormous problems of organizing

---

[14] Hedley Bull, 'The International Anarchy in the 1980's', *Australian Outlook*, 37. 3 (Dec. 1983), 128–9.

massive transfers of resources without trespassing on the jealously preserved sovereignty of the Western powers. It also stems from the probability that the Western powers would never be inclined to act uniformly towards the Third World in any major venture: the temptation to reward friends and punish assailants, already obvious in the field of economic aid, is one which is likely to triumph.

5

Strategic Studies
and Arms Control

T. B. MILLAR

'STRATEGIC studies in its broadest sense', Hedley Bull wrote in a 1964 paper,[1] 'is the study of military force and its place in human affairs.'

A very high proportion of Bull's writings bore directly or indirectly on this subject: directly, because he was passionately interested in the world of nation states, in which there is so much overt conflict almost all the time; indirectly because, interested as he was in theories about relations between states, and in order and 'justice' in the world system, the use of force or the threat or capacity to use it is never far from the surface. The general sits at the ambassador's elbow. Political power, economic power, military power, are functions of one another.

Nevertheless, Bull has produced a whole corpus of literature that bears directly on strategic studies, and not least an assessment of the subject itself which emerged after he had become interested in arms control and indeed had written his lucid first book[2] on that topic which was so to exercise him for the rest of his life. His involvement with the Institute for Strategic Studies from its early days, with the Strategic and Defence Studies Centre at the Australian National University, and with university faculties and institutes in America occupied with strategic studies, gave him a series of vantage points from

---

This chapter does not attempt to record or assess every idea on strategic studies and arms control in Hedley Bull's written work. That would require a book in itself. Rather it seeks to pick out some of the main themes.

[1] 'Strategic Studies in a University,' unpublished paper, Jan. 1964
[2] Hedley Bull, *The Control of the Arms Race: Disarmament and Arms Control in the Nuclear Age* (London, 1961).

which to see whether this was a coherent subject, and one that could properly be studied in a university.

In the paper referred to above, written with respect to a proposed course at the London School of Economics and Political Science for an M.Sc. (Econ.) in 'International Relations with special reference to Strategic Studies', he had no problem in seeing it as a proper subject for academic enquiry, but he did have a problem in giving precision to what it was. Strategic studies is wider in scope than the study of war, because it includes aspects of the possession of force that may not lead to war. For the same reasons, it is wider than the study of strategy, either in Clausewitz's narrow sense of 'the art of employment of battles as a means to gain the object in war', or even in Liddell Hart's sense of 'the art of distributing and applying military means to fulfil the ends of policy'. On the other hand, strategic studies is narrower than the study of violence, or of conflict, which can include domestic violence or conflict at any level, from children fighting in the school playground to sizeable internecine combat not deploying military force. It is *military force* that distinguishes strategic studies from other related studies, and as most military force is deployed by sovereign states, the core of strategic studies lies in the study of international relations. Yet strategic studies transcends international relations, as a study of relations between states. It must include subnational or transnational groups who are international actors. The core area could shift to them (the PLO, Islam) or to an international organization which might, for example, breach the monopoly of nuclear weapons. The *study* of the core of strategic studies (the use of military force) has the same divisions, Bull argues, as the study of international relations: (1) studying the actors; (2) describing their conduct and the actual working of the international system, to illuminate choices available; and (3) studying the techniques pursued in these studies, whether historical, philosophical, or other methods adopted by the social sciences.

Strategic studies therefore

is concerned with military policies (the strategies and armaments policies) of particular States and other actors, and the bearing of these on their foreign policies; and it is concerned with the role or function of military force in the international political system as a whole. It is concerned to describe the actual development of the military policies of States and other actors, and to identify the actual roles played by military force in the States-system; but it is concerned also to illuminate the choices, ranging from all-out war to unilateral disarmament, with which modern states are confronted with respect to the utilisation of this military force, and to explore directions, ranging from a 'unit veto' system to a disarmed world, in which the international system might move or (conceivably) be moved.

Then, in an act of abnegation which was a sign of integrity as well as youth, he wrote:

It goes without saying that it is no part of the business of Strategic Studies actually to canvass lines of policy. The study of policy choices and the advocacy of policies are incompatible activities.

This seems to pave the way for strategic studies to be a proper subject of academic study, serving to advance academic purposes and to develop 'those habits and attitudes that are peculiarly in the custody of universities'. Yet the problem of ends and means immediately appears, a dilemma which seems more apparent to the reader than the writer. Just as economic study may lead to greater control of economic life (Bull writes), the study of government to a superior structure of government and administration, or sociology to better solutions of 'social problems', so (as a general principle) strategic studies may be expected to lead to better strategic policy. But, we may ask, are the political scientist and the sociologist not to study policy choices or advocate policies? Surely they do. And if they do, why not the strategic studies academic? Bull admits that the management of military force so as to promote the aims of social policy is a major, pressing, and permanent problem of modern society, equally as important as (and perhaps more immediate than) some of those problems on which economics, government, psychology, and other social sciences have focused. But perhaps it is not capable of rigorous intellectual analysis? Perhaps strategic 'policy scientists' (including some of the 'peace researchers') claim too much. A policy science can at best only relate means to ends, whereas 'in international politics the most important problems of policy are about the choice of ends; and there is no science of ends'. Again, strategic studies so far, perhaps because of its intrinsic nature, has failed to produce a cumulative body of knowledge affording a means of prediction and control. And finally, once more, 'there is an inherent antagonism between the activity of policymaking and that of study and inquiry'. If the university is to make a contribution, it must be to the public debate rather than in the private channels that connect that debate to government policy.

And after all there is a widespread interest in matters of war and peace; they are central to the political debate; the public is surprisingly credulous of the pronouncements of apparent authority, and needs to be better informed; and among official or unofficial institutes working in the field (some of which have produced good work) there is a lack of those virtues—independence of mind, breadth of perspective, high critical standards—which the university is intended to develop among its students. So let there be strategic studies at universities, preferably at graduate level. Outstanding ideas and writing in this field come out of American universities; why not also out of British ones? Yet much of the American teaching and writing about international politics, including strategic studies, is from the point of view of American policy. Bull deplores this: 'I do not think the proper alternative to a national policy is an "international" one, a "Western" one or a "world" one. The only proper perspective is an academic one.'

When that paper was written, the Vietnam war had not begun. Four and a half years later, after the 1968 Tet offensive and President Johnson's decision not to seek re-election and to wind down the war, and after Bull had done a stint as head of the Arms Control and Disarmament Research Unit at the British Foreign Office, he returned to the subject in an article in *World Politics*.[3] He had by now refined somewhat his definition of strategy: ' . . . in its most general sense it is the art or science of shaping means so as to promote ends in any field of conflict'. Strategy as 'military strategy' is 'the art or science of exploiting military force so as to attain given objects of policy'. But what of the civilian strategists who 'now constitute a distinct profession in the Western world', who have overwhelmed the military in the quality and quantity of their contribution to strategic studies, and have entered the citadels of power (especially in the US) and 'have prevailed over military advisers on most aspects of policy'? What are their distinguishing features? How valid are

[3] 'Strategic Studies and its Critics', *World Politics*, 20. 4 (July 1968). I appreciate that, given the usual time gap between submission and publication in a journal such as this, it was probably written before the Johnson decision, as internal evidence suggests.

their methods? How useful are they to society? Why is there such a barrage of criticism against them?

Bull felt that the civilian strategists have displaced the older generation of soldiers and civil servants, have obtained an influence unavailable to fellow intellectuals who have remained outsiders, and have thus become an object of resentment as well as a scapegoat for those who fear, or feel guilt about, modern war. And while society disagrees within itself (an offshoot of the Vietnam war) as to whether the state should use or even possess military force, there will be disagreement about the worth and utility of students of strategy.

I

Bull saw the specific complaints against the civilian strategists as follows:

1. They leave morality out of account: they are technicians indifferent to the moral standing of the causes for which war is undertaken or the means by which it is waged. (The most prominent target of this criticism was Herman Kahn, with his horrifying and apparently unfeeling calculations of the millions of deaths which nuclear war would cause.) There is a sense, Bull argues, in which strategic thinking does and should leave out questions of morality, in that 'pure' strategy relates given means to given ends. Strategic judgements should not be coloured by moral consider-ations, nor strategic enquiry restricted by moral taboos. Governments, on the other hand, should not take decisions only on the basis of strategic considerations, and strategist advisers must—and in fact do—realize that strategic imperatives are not categorical. It is just that these strategists assume a higher moral stature for American and Western political objectives, for which the risk of war must be undertaken, whereas many of their critics believe that virtue lies in avoiding the risk of war, in 'obeying the rules a world community might legislate if it existed and never in pursuing the different moral guides that are appropriate in a situation in which it does not'. A strategist adviser helps his government to advance its objectives at the expense of other governments. Is there an element of the immoral in that? It depends on the moral nature of the government

and its objectives, says Bull. Scientists who helped the
Allied cause in World War II did not act improperly.

2. Strategists take the existence of military force for granted
and consider how best to exploit it, thus ignoring a range
of alternatives such as disarmament or non-violent resistance. Fresh from his Foreign Office experience, Bull says
the strategists have no choice in the matter. The armed
forces exist, and may be reduced but are not going to be
eliminated. 'The capacity for armed violence between
states is inherent in the nature of man and his environment.' On the other hand (and here Bull begs the
question), if strategists are over-inclined to military
solutions to foreign policy problems—and they *are*—it is
up to the advocates of alternative methods to enter into
debate with them and correct their perspective.

3. Strategists are inclined to make unreal assumptions about
international politics. In comparing and costing alternative
strategies, they oversimplify, distort political reality, and
don't allow for change. True, says Bull. Some of the
classical analyses of America's problems in determining
military posture and choosing weapons have been based on
the assumption that international nuclear politics was a
game between identical twin states in a condition of
mutual hostility, a zero-sum game. General de Gaulle, by
withdrawing from NATO military planning and developing a French nuclear strike force, demonstrated what
ought to have been clear enough: that Paris and London
are not Washington and that nuclear forces have diplomatic as well as military functions. The strategists are
waking up to the follies of their 'strange logic'.

4. Civilian strategists are pseudo-scientific in their methods.
Their specialist techniques such as game theory, systems
analysis, simulation, and the writing of scenarios 'are
bogus when used to arrive at strategic decisions and serve
to give an air of expertise to positions arbitrarily and
subjectively arrived at'. This is basically an attack on game
theory, says Bull, but the majority of civilian strategists do
not use it. Some of the logic of game theory is implicit in
the way some strategists think, and their rigorous techniques should not provide a means of circumventing
political choices or be used as a political weapon to support

one arbitrarily chosen policy. But the techniques can still have value and validity within their limitations; and Western European governments have been at a disadvantage during the past decade compared with the US for not having access to a comparable body of strategic expertise. Problems can arise where the experts do not question the assumptions on which policy is based.

5. Alternatively, it can be said that the sin of the strategist is not his covert commitment to political purposes but his objectivity. He is detached and aloof, and has no right to be. The strategists are thus collaborators in the system and are 'speeding up its movement towards catastrophe', instead of using their influence to help America change the behaviour of Russia or China. This suggests a capacity for America to change Soviet policy, and a role for conciliation as against strength, which have yet to be demonstrated.

Bull concludes that the civilian strategists have at least charted a reasoned course where otherwise there might well have been drift; they have made a serious attempt to come to grips with the problem; they have developed considerable technical expertise as well as a necessary capacity to think in the abstract; compared with the situation in the Soviet Union, 'they have served us well'. They have elaborated the three central notions of deterrence, limited war, and arms control mainly in the context of the Soviet-American confrontation rather than in the polycentric diplomatic field that has come to exist, and even their fundamental assumptions are open to challenge. It is typical of Bull that in the spirit of independent enquiry rather than simple iconoclasm he should set out to challenge them, and he spent over a quarter of a century doing just that.

II

Hedley Bull's first published article in the area of arms control, which appeared in May 1959 in an Australian journal,[4] was a critique of Philip Noel-Baker's book, *The Arms Race*.[5] It demonstrated the ordered thinking and relentless logic that was

---

[4] 'Disarmament and the International System', *Australian Journal of Politics and History*, 5. 1 (May 1959).
[5] *The Arms Race: A Programme for World Disarmament* (London, 1958).

to determine his career. He began with a paragraph that could hardly have been written by anyone else, even if he was subsequently to publish a long and erudite book[6] whose title contradicted (in my view, incorrectly, but it was a piece of iconoclasm he found irresistible) the paragraph's central thesis:

The sovereign states of today have inherited from renaissance Europe an ordered system for the conduct of these relations which may be called an international society. For though sovereign states are without a common government, they are not in a condition of anarchy: like the individuals described by Locke in his account of the state of nature they are a society without a government. This society is an imperfect one: its justice is crude and uncertain, as each state is judge in its own cause; and it gives rise to recurrent tragedy in the form of war; but it produces order, regularity, predictability and long periods of peace, without involving the tyranny of a universal state... One of its institutions has been material armaments; and one of the preoccupations of Western thinking has been disarmament, the attempt to do away with or drastically curtail them. Yet if armaments are an integral part of the whole system of international relations, and stand or fall with it, there are serious objections to the notions both of the possibility and the desirability of disarmament.

Bull records that Noel-Baker's book is a restatement, adapted for the nuclear age, of the classic case for general and comprehensive disarmament, or at least for a reduction of armaments to a level and of a kind that would make oppressive war impossible, and miscreants dealt with by forces of a collective security system. Noel-Baker believed that the arms race is the major cause of international tension: Bull declared, with rather more history on his side, that it is both a cause and a consequence of international tension, but in any case it cannot be terminated unless the tension is ended. Disarmament does take place where there is an accommodation of interests between parties, but it is never comprehensive because a comprehensive accommodation of interests has never been found possible. Some states are, alas, predatory. States do have opponents, and see their security in balancing—preferably with an advantage—their opponents' power. Among many others, the history of nuclear Soviet-American negotiations bears this out, each side seeking and refusing to concede an advantage. As

---

[6] *The Anarchical Society: A Study of Order in World Politics* (London, 1977).

to 'collective security', whereby an erring state is brought to heel by the collective force of the others, this assumes that governments will be prepared to go to war when their own interests are not directly threatened—a regrettably unproven proposition. And in a bipolar world, if one of the superpowers is the miscreant there is no way it can be contained without resort to nuclear war, which because of its enormous destructivity is irrational and will always be so unless a satisfactory defence against nuclear missiles is discovered. 'In the international society states have a system which moderates their tendency to anarchy, and is not a blueprint or an aspiration but a going concern'. It rests not simply on armaments and a military equilibrium but on these *and* on a set of legal and moral rules. What about world government, to which Noel-Baker inclines? If it is designed to combat predatory powers, those powers will not subscribe to it. The United Nations lacks both power (with the guilt that goes with it) and responsibility. To call upon it to solve the problems the states themselves cannot solve is appealing but irrelevant. Thus it may plausibly be argued that 'in the present world states are not only unlikely to conclude a general and comprehensive disarmament agreement, but are behaving rationally in refusing to do so'.

For one who contributed so profusely to writings on strategic questions, including arms control, it is perhaps surprising that Bull wrote only one full-length book on the subject: *The Control of the Arms Race.*[7] This book was a logical development from the UN resolution on 'general and complete disarmament', the Campaign for Nuclear Disarmament in Britain, the 1960 ISS conference on the arms race, and a study group which the Institute set up with Bull as its central writer. Though other members of the group (including one general, two admirals, and an air chief marshal) contributed to the thinking, the book, the content, the style, were his. The book goes step by step over old ground and new, through the objectives, the implications for the balance of power, the conditions of arms control, the relationship

---

[7] I suspect that the reason for this was that his contributions at conferences—always lucid, sometimes abrasive, often provocative—brought him many invitations to write articles and chapters, which he accepted; but his real interests lay in wider and more profound issues, as is evident in *The Anarchical Society* and in the book he edited with Adam Watson and contributed to not long before he died: *The Expansion of International Society* (Oxford, 1984).

of arms control to disarmament, and the possibility of arms control *without* disarmament. He makes no excuses—indeed, he sees positive virtue—in not coming up with complete answers. The academic *should* not rush to judgement, should not be an advocate:

The object of this inquiry has not been to settle the controversy about war and disarmament, only to illuminate it by regarding with an innocent eye the difficulties that confront all policies. If the arguments that have been presented do not point unambiguously towards some set of policies that are the right road ahead, if they do not remove doubt and anxiety about what should be done to induce them, where before they did not exist, I make no apology for this. The strong advocacy of policies, the marshalling of arguments so as to suggest them, involves a certain wilful blindness and abdication of critical judgement.[8]

And on 'world government':

We cannot expect that the establishment of a universal government by contract among the nations rather than by conquest will be brought about by governments incapable of the most modest forms of co-operation; that the complete and voluntary elimination of national armaments will be put into effect by governments for all of whom there are issues over which they will resort to violence rather than admit defeat; or that the removal of the sources of political conflicts . . . will be undertaken by governments themselves absorbed in such conflicts.[9]

To stabilize the arms race requires stabilizing the whole field of political relations between antagonists, especially between the two superpowers. He acknowledges that there is value in reducing the damages of accidental war between these two; in attempting to get a balance of power in conventional arms that would release the Western powers from their reliance on the threat of initiating nuclear warfare; and in getting a balance in strategic nuclear weapons that would reduce the likelihood of premeditated war. The US-Soviet arms race is dangerous; so would be the expansion of the nuclear club. A successful anti-missile missile would be destabilizing, as are all measures aimed at making the powers invulnerable. Mutual vulnerability is essential. If wars occur, it is better that they be conventional. If strategic nuclear wars occur, it is better that they be conducted

---

[8] *The Control of the Arms Race*, p 202.
[9] Ibid., p. 203.

as military engagements in which strategic weapons are launched at strategic weapons, rather than that they become 'orgies of indiscriminate annihilation'. It is important to preserve conventional nuclear capacity, to try to ban all nuclear testing, to abstain from developing chemical and biological weapons. But finally, alas, 'The world is much more complicated than the arguments in this book, and the destinies of nations are not determined by simple choices of the soul'.[10]

III

Eight years later, at another ISS conference again in Oxford, Bull returned to take stock of the progress of arms control.[11] In the intervening period, the UN had established the Eighteen Nation Disarmament Committee (ENDC); the nuclear powers had signed the Hot Line Agreement (June 1963), the Partial Test Ban Treaty (August 1963), the tripartite declaration on outer space (October 1963), the Treaty on the Exploration and Use of Outer Space (January 1967), and the Nuclear Non-Proliferation Treaty, or NPT (1968). Both superpowers, with the US in the lead, had multiplied, dispersed, and hardened their nuclear missile sites; had improved submarine detection capability; and had begun the development of the Multiple Independently Targetable Re-entry Vehicle (MIRV). France and China had become nuclear weapons powers, and India was reaching towards membership of the nuclear club.

Bull noted how the trend of academic thinking had shifted from disarmament to arms control, which had become a reputable subject and included the possibility of shared interests and reciprocal action even between potential enemies. Arms control did not necessarily require disarmament. Stabilizing the balance of terror was itself an arms control measure. All this 'new thinking' had been infected with the optimism of the social sciences in America.

What was the result? In 1968 states were still sovereign; they retained their armaments. Political conflict continued. Nevertheless, the world was a safer place as regards the danger of

[10] Ibid., p. 212.
[11] 'Arms Control: A Stocktaking and Prospectus', in *Problems of Modern Strategy*, pt. 2, Adelphi Papers, 55 (Mar. 1969).

nuclear war (as the agreements listed above demonstrate), basically because each superpower could inflict unacceptable damage upon the other. While mutual deterrence was unstable *in principle*, and *potentially* through the anti-missile defence of some cities and the development of MIRVs, the balance of terror meant that deliberate resort to unlimited force by either side could not be a rational act. Yet, because of conflicts of interests, war always remained a possibility. The superpowers therefore should develop a doctrine of limited war and allow for it in their strategic planning and preparations. Fortunately each of the superpowers had developed confidence in the other's willingness to coexist with it—the process known as *détente*. Each felt the likelihood of war to be less.

But was this true? New political conflicts had arisen—between China and India, in Nigeria, in South-East Asia. But none of these was capable of giving rise to devastation comparable to that resulting from a Soviet–American conflict.

Not all hopes had been realized by *détente*. There was no actual reduction of armaments. There had been no progress in applying international inspection machinery to existing arms control agreements. And above all there had been no progress towards a formal arms control agreement that would stabilize the balance of terror at a minimum level. Instead the superpowers had stabilized the balance of terror, but at increasingly high levels.

The answer then, says Bull, is not to return to the notion of general and complete disarmament, which is irrelevant in practice, however desirable as an ultimate goal. Nor is it to pursue formal arms control agreements, which could be symbolic or hortatory; but rather to press for reciprocated unilateral action, reciprocated restraint, for which an informal agreement is more likely to be the outcome than a formal one. The politics of arms control discussion cannot be avoided, but nor should arms control be treated by the rest of us as the *only* great issue in a complex world.

Finally Bull returns to question the assumptions he has himself accepted. Is it true that the balance of terror is the chief foundation of international security? Is it true that the ballistic missile defence of cities is destabilizing? He poses the questions but does not attempt to answer them, although events were to overtake the second question.

Like most other civilian strategists, Bull saw great importance in the Strategic Arms Limitation Talks (SALT) that began in late 1969 and led to the agreement that came to be known as SALT I.[12] The two *agreements* of SALT I (as distinct from the Protocol on limiting SLBMs, and agreed or unilateral interpretation and statements) were (1) the Treaty on the Limitation of Anti-Ballistic Missile Systems (ABMs) and (2) the Interim Agreement on Certain Measures with respect to the Limitation of Strategic Offensive Arms. Under the first, the two superpowers agreed to deploy no more than two ABM systems—one of the national capital and one of an ICBM complex. Thus to the extent (completely undemonstrated and presumably undemonstrable) that an ABM system might be effective, it would only defend each nation's government apparatus and its capacity for a limited but damaging retaliation against attack, or second strike. The rest of each country would be wide open, thus ensuring mutual vulnerability. As a concession to Soviet sensitivities and a recognition of advances in technology, only 'national technical means' of verification for the ABM Treaty and the Interim Agreement would be used. Under the Interim Agreement,[13] the parties undertook to call a halt to ICBM launcher construction for five years, not to replace light launchers by heavy ones, and to contain the numbers of ballistic missile submarines. Bull asks: do the Agreements help to stabilize mutual nuclear deterrence, and is that in any case an acceptable goal?

Throughout much of his strategic analysis, Bull is blessed (or afflicted, acording to one's viewpoint) by the capacity to see both (or all) sides of a question—'on the one hand . . .' but 'on the other hand . . .'. On SALT I: on the one hand it 'makes a contribution to the stability of mutual deterrence by placing powerful inhibitions in the way of the development of an effective defence of cities and populations'. On the other hand, 'the Agreements taken together have not made any serious contribution to eliminating the possibility of development by one side of a disarming capacity'; although on the *other* hand mutual deterrence might still be assured by SLBM forces, bomber

---

[12] *The Moscow Agreements and Strategic Arms Limitation*, Canberra Papers on Strategy and Defence, 15 (Canberra, 1973).

[13] *The Moscow Agreements* gives comprehensive details of the two agreements, which there is no point in reproducing here.

forces, Forward Based Systems, and placing multiple re-entry vehicles on ICBMs to ensure that an expectable minimum surviving force has a disabling punch. The negotiations must have been educational for both sides, but there is no way of knowing how far they have committed themselves to 'the proposition that they have a common interest in preserving the stability of mutual nuclear deterrence'; the two Agreements 'signally fail to deal with threats to stability of the balance deriving from the development of disarming capacity'; and they indicate no commitment to reducing nuclear weaponry or to making the political accommodations required for a stable world. The Agreements, Bull concludes, provide for a rough overall parity, with each superpower having superiority in certain areas, but leaving the USSR with more room for expansion, which could be a diplomatic asset for it and a liability for the US.

America's allies have not indicated that the Agreements jeopardize their interests, but on the other hand he thinks perhaps they ought and will come so to feel. 'The demise of the American ABM screen [*what* American ABM screen?], the acceptance of parity or inferiority with Russia in offensive arms [a special interpretation of the figures], the steps taken towards sanctification of mutual nuclear deterrence, and the removal of obstacles in the path of secondary nuclear powers [again, debatable] all give ammunition to the critics of reliance on American power.' Giving, perhaps understandably, undue weight to restive elements of US opinion he concludes 'My view is that the American alliance system is in inexorable decline', and that both the US and its allies will attach less importance in the future to the preservation of American guarantees. What is needed is for the US and the USSR to seek to create a comity of nuclear powers (including especially China) which will generalize the restraints they have accepted for themselves.

In 1983, having returned to Oxford after ten years in Australia, Bull did a further reassessment of the arms control debate,[14] looking back nostalgically and with some satisfaction to his own earliest pronouncements which he identified with the 'classical approach'. This approach had five elements which still

[14] 'The Classical Approach to Arms Control: Twenty Years After', in Uwe Nerlich, ed., *Soviet Power and Western Negotiating Policies*, 2, *The Western Panacea* (Cambridge, Mass., 1983).

held true, despite the criticisms or assertions of 'arms control theorists', though these elements needed adaptation to the changed circumstances.

1. Arms control or disarmament is not an end in itself but only a means to an end—the enhancement of security, especially security against nuclear war. This has been lost sight of as the West, especially the US, has developed 'heavy bureaucratic machineries committed to the negotiation of arms control agreements so as to justify their own existence', and a host of other institutions similarly committed. Fortunately a reaction has now set in against the doctrine that agreements necessarily promote security.

2. Arms control is founded on the area of perceived common interests between antagonistic powers. This does not mean that agreements will always relax tension—they could occur in spite of the tension in an effort to avoid nuclear war,[15] but the agreements arrived at in the 1960s, in the event, contributed to a wider process of relaxation and to *détente*.

3. Adequate defence measures and arms control are not opposite or contradictory objects of policy but are, or should be, in harmony, both contributing in their different ways to security. This had become increasingly accepted. American strategic thinking was now (in Reagan's America) shifting back to a unilateral pursuit of military strength. One may sympathize with this in particular areas, while fearing that the arms-control dimensions of defence may be lost sight of. Like most people, Bull looked more closely at the rhetoric of Reagan's policies than the content, but there was not much content to go by.

4. Arms control goes much wider than concluding formal agreements, and includes informal agreements, and unilateral actions on a non-reciprocal basis directed towards interests held in common with the adversary. The superpowers' informal agreements (for which evidence is hard to find) include those not to use nuclear weapons, not to become engaged directly in military conflict with one another, not to violate spheres of influence, not to allow

---

[15] I find Bull's analysis in this point hard to follow. His criticism of 'the arms control theorists' seems to apply equally to the classical thinkers.

military expenditures to become ruinously high, not to engage in provocative behaviour. These have been more important than the formal agreements, although Western governments' arms control agencies have focused almost entirely on the latter.

5. The most important objective of arms control is to stabilize the relationship of mutual deterrence between the super-powers, as an expression of the balance of power. Despite the great advances in nuclear weapons technology, and despite the fact that at some times the balance has been less stable than at others, this objective has been achieved. But the level of strategic arms has not been reduced, nor the tempo of competition, and the belligerent rhetoric of the superpowers cannot be reconciled with the Third World's demand for redistributive justice. The American ambition to restore the military dominance, fuelled by the challenge posed by the Soviet build-up and also by US resentment at its loss of global political leadership, is incompatible with arms control as hitherto envisaged. Equally the Soviet Union is engaged in a military build-up because it has reason to believe that the distribution of power is shifting against it. It is now more difficult to define what a stable nuclear balance consists of, but we must still pursue it as the 'proximate goal': security against nuclear war remains cardinal, and there is no alternative to working for piecemeal co-operation between the super-powers.

IV

In a short summary like this it is impossible to do justice either to the breadth of Hedley Bull's thought on strategic questions or the complexities and logic of his argument. While sometimes reluctant to come to conclusions, he was relentless in pursuing and setting out the facts, the factors, the assumptions. The basic conditions of world politics tend to change slowly. Any frequent writing about them is bound to repeat themes and arguments, and Hedley Bull's could not be an exception because he wrote so much.

In addition to a continuing concern with arms control *per se*, he took up specific aspects, especially proliferation and non-proliferation, the role of the superpowers, the notion of the balance of power, chemical and biological weapons, civil violence. His ten years in Australia brought him to focus from time to time on strategic problems in Asia and the Pacific— Australia's own defence problems, relations with New Zealand, the Indian Ocean, the Third World. When he returned to Britain his perspective (never wholly removed to the southern hemisphere) became once again that of a European, a European *philosopher*, and despite his many connections with and friends in the United States he became increasingly critical of American policies and culture, tending at times to elide the fundamental distinctions between the superpowers.[16] But throughout the nearly thirty years that he thought and wrote about the world, it was the whole society that held his intellectual interest, the nature of *order*, the tendencies to anarchy, the question of means and ends; the role of force, of diplomacy, of law, of 'justice'. Strategic studies and arms control were not peripheral to these subjects, but functions (in the mathematical sense) of them. The world first had to be preserved. It had also to be understood. You could not have the one without the other.

[16] See e.g. his article 'The Great Irresponsibles? The United States, the Soviet Union and World Order', *International Journal*, 35. 3 (Summer 1980).

6

The Global Political System

ROBERT GILPIN

HEDLEY BULL was the most distinguished scholar of his generation to analyse and explore the uniqueness and genius of the modern European political order. In *The Anarchical Society* (1977), the subtitle of which is *A Study of Order in World Politics*, Bull carried forward a tradition of speculation and theorizing that extends from Hugo Grotius to Ludwig von Ranke to Bull's own mentor, Martin Wight. Bull, however, in his last major contribution to scholarship, went beyond the themes of these earlier writings and enquired whether the European experience of statecraft has any relevance for the emergent pluralistic international system composed of diverse civilizations with vastly different conceptions of international relations.

The seminal volume *The Expansion of International Society* (1984), edited by Bull and his colleague Adam Watson, was one of the first systematic attempts to explore this important issue. In the 1970s, when non-Western societies commenced their concerted effort for a new international economic and political order, Bull, Watson, and their collaborators addressed the question of the nature of the new international order: will it be based on the norms and precepts of the European 'society of states'; or will 'a new genuinely universal, and non-hegemonial structure of international relations' replace the once dominant European system of rules and institutions; or, as at least one contributor suggested, will the collapse of the European conception of an international order give rise to 'a new international disorder'? While the answer to these questions must await the test of time, the questions themselves are important for the scholar and for mankind in the closing decade of this century.

This chapter will consider the contemporary applicability of the European conception of international politics, with its emphasis on a society of states, as discussed in *The Expansion of International Society*. One must enquire into the nature of the European political system to evaluate its relevance to the emergent pluralistic and global international system composed of a number of fundamentally diverse and frequently conflicting civilizations. What were the intellectual and institutional innovations that led to the European system of statecraft? What were its norms and ordering principles? Why did it succeed over such a long and turbulent period of history? Why did it become increasingly anachronistic in the nineteenth century and eventually collapse in the twentieth to be succeeded by the bipolar era of the superpowers? In the postwar era characterized by the rise of other civilizations, what are the prospects for a global political order?

I

Throughout its history, the human race has known only three types of international order. Each has been based ultimately on the distribution of power among the dominant states in the international system. Efforts to achieve a different basis for international order, such as medieval Christendom, or collective security, or proletarian internationalism, have failed. Perhaps the efforts of scholars around the world to promote a world order based on what are perceived to be universal human values and aspirations may eventually prove fruitful. At present, however, the historical record provides only three models with which we can work.

The historical pattern has been civilizational conflict leading to universal empire. One state or civilization in an international system has tended to triumph eventually over the others and to create a unified empire. The unification of China by Ch'in, of India by the Mogul Empire, or of the Levant by successive Islamic empires are examples of this historic pattern. This type of political order, best exemplified by the *Pax Romana*, is one of complete domination and subordination of one civilization by another. In the age of nuclear weapons and of many vibrant civilizations, the age of such universal empires appears to be over.

A second and more ephemeral type of political order has been bipolarity. Athens/Sparta, Rome/Carthage, and United States/ Soviet Union exemplify bipolar structures. Although Kenneth Waltz has made an ingenious argument for the stability and superiority of this form of political order, it has seldom survived over long periods; it has invariably been transformed into either an imperial order or a multipolar system.[1] In the contemporary era, the American-Soviet bipolar system appears to be waning. Whether it will be replaced by a universal imperial order or a global multipolar system is a central concern of this article.

European civilization invented a third and novel basis of international order, the balance of power system. Its fundamental purpose was to prevent any state from unifying Europe and establishing a universal empire. In the words of Ranke, 'the concept of the European balance of power was developed in order that the union of many states might resist the pretensions of the "exorbitant" court, as it was called'.[2] The balance of power system and the institutions of European statecraft were not developed in order to prevent war, even though the deterrence of war was occasionally a consequence.

The European system of statecraft was the product of the Thirty Years War (1618–48). Although the motives and causes of this devastating conflict were many and complex, a central and crucial issue was the religious composition of domestic societies. Adherents of one faith warred against the adherents of another in order to change their religion. After three decades of Catholics and Protestants slaughtering one another, the statesmen who gathered at Westphalia to conclude the war agreed that henceforth religious and other domestic issues were not legitimate concerns for international relations. Thus the conception of national sovereignty and the principle of non-interference by one state in the internal affairs of another society were established.

The recognition of state sovereignty, the creation of the institutions of modern diplomacy, and the novel conception of warfare as an instrument of national policy were among the principal means developed to preserve the system. Although there were several notable attempts by the Habsburgs, Napoleon, and Hitler to unify the European continent, each was

---

[1] See Kenneth Waltz, *Theory of International Politics* (New York, 1979).
[2] Gordon A. Craig and Alexander L. George, *Force and Statecraft: Diplomatic Problems of our Time* (New York, 1983), 7.

defeated by the successful operation of the balance of power system. From the Treaty of Westphalia (1648) to the outbreak of the First World War in 1914, the European order was 'successful' at achieving its goal of resisting unification.

This so-called Westphalian system provided the basis for the conduct of international diplomacy for the next century and a half. Numerous wars were fought, but they were limited ones and were not concerned with the domestic values of society. Heterogeneity in political, social, and religious matters was respected. The object of foreign policy was to secure or advance the national interests of the state. Seldom during the classic age of the balance of power system in the latter half of the seventeenth century and the eighteenth century did governments fight over one another's internal affairs.

As Ranke and other students of European statecraft appreciated, Europe developed an international order based on the balance of power system rather than on a universal empire. Several conditions permitted this development. There was a level of cultural and political uniformity that facilitated the creation of strong states.[3] The geographical fragmentation of the continent differentiated Europe from Asia with its steppes, plateaux, and great river valleys that facilitated conquest and the creation of empires. First the Ottoman Empire and subsequently Great Britain had both the motivation and the power to intervene against any attempt to unify the Continent, but could not themselves conquer it. This situation, combined with the openness of the continental periphery, also thwarted its unification. States were unable to acquire decisive superiority over their neighbours because the available technology was insufficient for the task of imperial conquest and also diffused rapidly. In brief, as the Habsburgs were the first to learn, the costs of empire in Western Europe were too high to make it a feasible proposition for any state.

This 'diversity of elements harmoniously adjusted in freedom', to use the hyperbole of one German scholar, had preserved the 'liberties' of the Europeans;[4] parenthetically, the intense competition between the European powers caused them

---

[3] See Charles Tilly, ed., *The Formation of National States in Western Europe* (Princeton, 1975).

[4] Ludwig Dehio, *The Precarious Balance: Four Centuries of European Power Struggle* (New York, 1962), 7.

to grow strong and eventually enabled them to expand and suppress the liberties of other once great civilizations. While this success in maintaining the European balance of power and preventing ambitious powers from unifying the Continent was in part due to the favourable geographical, political, and technological conditions mentioned above, it was also a consequence of the human ingenuity expressed as the Europeans developed a set of novel political ideas and institutions. These innovations in the nature and conduct of statecraft have continued to influence international statecraft to the present time.

II

The European political order was based on three innovations in international affairs. The first was the emergence of the nation-state as the fundamental unit of political life. The second was the theory of political realism. And the third was the balance of power system. Although they can be distinguished from one another and analysed separately, in reality they were closely entwined parts of the same historical development.

For reasons that can be discussed only briefly here, the modern nation-state has increasingly displaced other forms of political organization. Traditionally empires, tribes, and city-states have been the foremost actors in what we today call international relations. The European concept of the nation-state supplanted these early forms primarily because it proved to be more efficient in the creation of wealth and the exercise of military power. This development has entailed state achievement of a monopoly of the legitimate use of force and command over the loyalty of its citizens. As shall be shown below, the supremacy of the state over other forms of association has been embodied in the doctrine of national sovereignty.

The triumph of the nation-state was due to its success in resolving the historic trade-off between loyalty and power. Both the tribe and the city-state were able to gain the intense loyalty of their members, yet these political forms found it difficult to amass great power; by their very nature they were inclusive, and extension of their territory diminished group cohesion. The empire was able to unify and draw upon a large territory and diverse peoples, but it was usually impossible for an empire to obtain the loyalty of its subjects; empires, therefore, have tended to be fragile structures that have easily fragmented internally or collapsed under external pressure.

The nation-state solved this fundamental problem in political organization. The loyalty of its people was achieved by the invention of what Niccolo Machiavelli called a 'civic religion'. The secular religion of nationalism and the symbols of patriotism made it possible for the nation-state to acquire the loyalty of a huge population. Moreover, the creation of new institutions and bureaucracies enabled the state to exploit the resources of a citizenry spread over a large territory. Other developments such as maps, tax systems, and 'political arithmetic' (statistics) gave rulers unprecedented control over their societies and increased their capacity to direct events in their favour.[5] The culmination of these innovations in political affairs and their significance have been summarized in the following words:

... the reorganization of political, economic, and military management that began to manifest itself as the eighteenth century neared its close was unique, not because other states in other ages had not also sought to increase their military power by internal reorganization, but because the scope and complexity of the techniques accessible to European administrators and soldiers had become enormously greater than in any earlier age. Rational calculation so enlarged the scope of deliberate action that, before the end of the century, managerial decisions began to change the lives of millions of persons.[6]

With these internal developments, the nation-state became the most efficient means to promote economic development and to wage war.

Although the nation-state brought domestic order to societies and ended the anarchy of the late Middle Ages, it did so at a very high price. As Jean-Jacques Rousseau observed, the internal cohesion of the state leads to an intensification of external conflict with other states; the more the members of the society are bound to one another through nationalism, the greater the antagonism towards their neighbours. In addition, again as Rousseau observed, the state, having no natural limits, has an insatiable propensity to expand and conquer other states;

---

[5] See George Clark, *War and Society in the Seventeenth Century* (Cambridge, 1958).
[6] William H. McNeill, *The Pursuits of Power: Technology, Armed Forces and Society since AD 1000* (Chicago, 1982), p. 158.

it expands lest the expansion of other states threaten its security. And third, the sovereignty of the state means that there is no authority superior to the state and no morality binding upon it; the state is the sole judge of right and wrong. Thus the nature of the modern nation-state itself runs counter to the concept of an international political order.[7]

III

A second West European innovation was the establishment of a tradition of reflection and speculation regarding the behaviour of states and the nature of international relations. Other civilizations have, of course, produced great political and social thinkers. The Chinese theorist of military strategy Sun Tzu, the Indian Kautilya with his deep insights into political behaviour, and, most impressive of all, the Arabic philosopher of history Ibn Khaldun rank as great students of international relations. They stand out, however, as individuals rather than (as in Europe) as part of a discourse spanning the centuries. Although Confucianism also ranks as an equivalent intellectual tradition, it is worth noting that it has been concerned with a hierarchical and authoritative ordering of human affairs. It is only in Western Europe with its international system composed of sovereign states that successive generations of scholars and thinkers over several centuries have addressed a common set of fundamental questions regarding modern statecraft.

This political tradition is that of political realism, which is at once a set of observations and reflections on the historic behaviour of states and, at its best, a set of rules prescribing appropriate and prudent behaviour. Its strength and its weakness as well have been due to its close association with the history of the European political order. Political realism has been accurate regarding the 'realities' of international affairs, at least among a particular group of states during a particular historical epoch. For this very reason, however, realism has been condemned by those who believe that it accepts, if not actually condones, the existing international system of war, domination, and injustice. Political realism, critics contend, cannot possibly

---

[7] See Stanley Hoffmann, *The State of War* (New York, 1965), for an excellent account of Rousseau's realism.

provide the intellectual basis for a more ideal international order.[8]

The intellectual roots of political realism are found in the writings of Niccolo Machiavelli as well as other political writers of the late sixteenth and early seventeenth centuries. Machiavelli's crucial contribution was the separation of politics and statecraft from morality and religion. In *The Prince* and other writings, he broke with the Christian tradition and enquired how states actually do behave rather than how they ought to behave. He spoke of the prudent or effective use of power and not of the just or unjust use of force and violence. His goal was to discover a set of precepts regarding the acquisition and management of state power.

In the seventeenth century, this evolving doctrine of political realism came under the influence of the new science of Newtonian physics that conceived the universe as a vast machine composed of discrete bodies and impersonal forces governed by objective and discoverable laws.[9] This mechanistic philosophy was transferred to the political world. International relations was conceived to be a mechanical system in which the discrete bodies were the Great Powers and where objective political laws governed interactions. In this rational political universe the power of these political bodies was believed to be objective and measurable. This concept of international relations as a 'system' provided the framework for political analysis and state action.

The third important innovation associated with the theory of political realism and the balance of power system was the concept of national interest.[10] As the state became the embodiment of the nation rather than merely the personal fiefdom of the ruler, the goal of foreign policy changed from pursuit of the dynastic interest of the prince to that of the interests of the society. In this new conception of statecraft, the objective of foreign policy was and, even more importantly, *ought* to be the advancement of the national interests of the society.[11]

Nothing illustrates this conceptualization of statecraft better

[8] See Richard A. Falk, *A Study of Future Worlds* (New York, 1975).
[9] See Alfred Vagts, 'The Balance of Power: Growth of an Idea', *World Politics*, 1 (1948).
[10] Craig and George, *Force and Statecraft*, p. 5.
[11] See Albert Hirschman, *Rival Views of Market Society and Other Essays* (New York, 1986).

than the decision taken at the Congress of Vienna to establish a Mathematics Committee to resolve the conflict over the disposition of Silesia.[12] In retrospect, the doctrine of political realism as it developed from the seventeenth century onwards was profoundly naïve. States are not black boxes whose power and interests can be objectively determined and whose interactions are governed by objective laws.

As generations of critics such as Friedrich Meinecke[13] and Woodrow Wilson have charged, innumerable evils have been committed in the name of political realism. Throughout modern history, the doctrine of *raison d'état* has been employed to rationalize ignoble policies. Thus E. H. Carr in *The Twenty Years' Crisis* invokes political realism to justify the sacrifice of Czech democracy at the Munich conference of 1938 in the higher interest of the peace of Western Europe.[14] The indictment of 'power politics', or what Meinecke called Machiavellism, cannot be swept away.

Another and more sympathetic interpretation of political realism, however, is possible. As Gordon Craig and Alexander George have argued, two variations of the theory can be distinguished.[15] One is what they refer to as 'vulgar' realism; in this version, power becomes an end in itself, the end justifies any means, and no moral or other restraints on state behaviour exist. The other view of realism is what Bull characterized as the Grotian tradition of statecraft; this normative version recognizes the role of power and the limits of moral restraints in international affairs, but it argues that a 'morality of states' does exist: states are believed to be bound by norms, institutions, and international law. Too frequently, this distinction between the two types of realism is neglected, or perhaps not even appreciated, by severe critics of realists, critics who condemn the realists as defenders of the crimes of modern statecraft.[16]

Hans Morgenthau, along with Bull, was one of the foremost proponents of realism in the contemporary era. He advocated this Grotian version of realism and the balance of power system.

---

[12] See E. V. Gulick, *Europe's Classical Balance of Power* (New York, 1955).

[13] See F. Meinecke, *Machiavellism*, trans. D. Scott (London, 1957).

[14] See E. H. Carr, *The Twenty Years' Crisis, 1919–1939* (2nd edn., London, 1946).

[15] Craig and George, *Force and Statecraft*, pp. 274–5.

[16] This is, essentially, the same distinction as that which Martin Wight makes between realism and rationalism. On this see James Richardson's and John Vincent's contributions to this book.

In the conclusion to his text *Politics among Nations*, Morgenthau continues a long tradition of 'advice to princes'. Drawing upon his vast and intimate knowledge of international affairs, he provides a set of precepts composed of 'four fundamental rules' of diplomacy and 'five prerequisites of compromise'. These precepts of prudent statecraft include: Thou shalt defend thine own vital interests; Thou shalt not violate thy neighbour's vital interests; Divest thyself of the crusading spirit; and Never be unwilling to compromise in matters that are not of vital interest.[17]

This tradition of political realism is one that attempts to ~Morgenthau~ balance national security and the necessity for compromise in an anarchic system of sovereign nation-states. It argues that foreign policy *ought* to be based solely on considerations of power and national interest. The 'crusading spirit', issues of universal justice, and ideological commitments should be divorced from the determination of foreign policy. If issues of morality and the redemption of one's opponents become objects of foreign policy, it becomes impossible for statesmen to reach compromises and solve the problems that lead to war. Realistically, then, the primary purpose of foreign policy is to safeguard the security and interests of the society.

This realist position is neither ignorant of nor unconcerned with what most people would consider to be matters of justice and morality. Many proponents of political realism are quite aware that the world is filled with injustice and that humankind has a moral responsibility to alleviate the injustices suffered by others. Nevertheless, as J. D. B. Miller has put it, realism acknowledges a world of diverse and frequently conflicting value systems wherein every group or state defines for itself what is right and wrong.[18] If the issues between states are defined in terms of right and wrong or just and unjust, compromises and the achievement of peaceful coexistence are impossible. While this concession of the realist to the evils of the world may dampen his moral sensitivities, it does limit conflict in a world where individual sovereign states are ultimately the only judges of moral issues.

---

[17] Hans J. Morgenthau, *Politics among Nations* (5th edn., New York, 1973), 540–50.

[18] J. D. B. Miller, 'Morality, Interests and Rationalization', in Ralph Pettman, ed., *Moral Claims in World Affairs* (New York, 1979), 36–51.

IV

The third component of the European political order has been the institutionalization of the European balance of power system. The concept of the balance of power is one of the most misunderstood and abused in the study and practice of modern statecraft. Usages and definitions abound. For some, it functions automatically as a universal principle of political behaviour.[19] For others, it is primarily a maxim of prudent behaviour in a competitive state system.[20] In this paper, however, it is identified as a specific international system that lasted from approximately the middle of the seventeenth century to the outbreak of the First World War.[21]

The balance of power system was the result of a series of intellectual and institutional innovations devised to prevent the unification of Europe by a universal empire and to manage the tremendous growth of power unleashed in the early modern era. It was based on a peculiar set of assumptions and conditions. As long as these conditions continued, the system functioned successfully, at least within its own terms. When the underlying reality changed, the system collapsed and was replaced by the bipolar reign of the superpowers. As the power of the United States and the Soviet Union dissipates in our own age, will conditions which earlier led to the operation of the European balance of power system provide the basis for a global political order?

In order to preserve the European political order and prevent the unification of the Continent, the European states developed a number of norms or institutions. Crucially important were European professionalization of diplomatic practice, the related doctrines of sovereignty and non-intervention in the internal affairs of other states, and the concept of war as an instrument of national policy. From the origins of the system at the Congress of Westphalia (1648) to its collapse in the First World War, these institutions, with several major lapses to be discussed below, characterized the European balance of power system.[22]

---

[19] See Kenneth W. Thompson, *Toynbee's Philosophy of World History and Politics* (Baton Rouge, 1985), for a discussion of what Toynbee held to be laws governing the automatic operation of the balance of power in all ages.

[20] For a good representative statement of the view that preserving the balance of power is an act of prudent statecraft, see David Hume, 'Of the Balance of Power', reprinted in Paul Seabury, ed., *The Balance of Power* (San Francisco, 1965).

[21] See Inis Claude, *Power and International Relations* (New York, 1962).

[22] For one of the most thorough analyses of the techniques of the balance of power system see Gulick, *Europe's Classical Balance of Power*.

The concepts and institutions of permanent diplomacy were transmitted to Western European statesmen from the Byzantine Empire via the Italian city state system.[23] States had to post ambassadors abroad and create expert corps of professional diplomats so as to maintain vigilance regarding the power and policies of other states, negotiate political alliances, and uncover threats to the system. The ambassador could no longer be the 'enemy amongst us', but became protected by international convention. The international congress was created to put the system back together again following the great wars of European history; the multilateral treaties produced by the Congresses of Westphalia, Utrecht, and Vienna became what one scholar has called the 'constitutions' of the system.[24] The principle of 'reciprocal compensation', that is, the exchange of population and territory between states, was instituted to maintain the balance between the Great Powers. One could extend the list of newly devised diplomatic practices and devices of statecraft. While injustices perpetuated by this professionalized diplomacy, such as the partitions of Poland, became legend, it helped preserve the 'liberties' of the Europeans.

A second important innovation of European statecraft was the product of mutual exhaustion. For three terrible decades in the Thirty Years' War, the major European powers fought with one another over the issue of Catholicism versus Protestantism. While the question of the religious affiliation of domestic society was only one of many issues, it intensified the conflict and made resolution of other conflicts more difficult. In response to this experience, the Europeans at the Congress of Westphalia adopted the principles of sovereignty and non-interference in the domestic affairs of societies. International relations was declared to be solely about the external interests of states: in order to moderate relations between states, the religion of a people, their political system, and the nature of the economy were judged illegitimate concerns. In effect, what we today refer to as ideological differences between states were no longer to be appropriate issues of international relations.[25]

---

[23] See G. Mattingly, *Renaissance Diplomacy* (Baltimore, 1964).
[24] R. B. Mowat, *The European States System: A Study of International Relations* (London, 1923).
[25] The standard work on the concept of non-intervention and its status in the post-war international order is R. J. Vincent, *Nonintervention and International Order* (Princeton, 1974).

The third and most important departure of European statecraft was a new concept of war. Throughout the history of the human race, war has tended to be a clash of societies. Most frequently the goal has been to vanquish or be vanquished: the defeated were put to the sword, reduced to slavery, or colonized. In the European context, war became an instrument of national policy rather than a means to destroy utterly one's opponents; after all, today's enemy might be tomorrow's friend. At the same time, however, the Europeans rejected the Christian concept of 'just war'. War was considered to be a natural aspect of international life; the purpose of international law was not to outlaw war, but to make it more humane with respect to such matters as the protection of non-combatants and the treatment of prisoners of war. Along with the new diplomacy, war became a legitimate means by which states defended and advanced their national interests.

V

The European balance of power system survived the upheavals of war and revolution for three centuries. The several attempts to unify the Continent were defeated as the human and material costs of these defeats continued to increase. By the middle of the nineteenth century, however, the functioning of the European mode of statecraft became more and more difficult to maintain. The social, political, and technological conditions on which it was based were undergoing a profound transformation and the assumptions underlying the European political order were decreasingly relevant. Eventually, it collapsed in the First World War, and following an interregnum was replaced by the bipolar system of the superpowers.

The political developments of the nineteenth century undercut the basis of traditional diplomacy. The democratization of political life transformed the world in which professional diplomacy, for all its cynicism and attendant evils, had moderated conflict and preserved the peace. No longer could statesmen operate diplomatic machinery free of the effects of emotionally charged public opinion. The rise of representative government, the increasing importance of public opinion, and the spread of nationalism, as Henry Kissinger complained in his book *A World Restored*,[26] made the task of the diplomat an impossible one. These developments made it unlikely that the statesman could employ solely rational criteria of national interest in the determination of foreign policy. The desire for justice, national honour, and simple revenge became a more important factor in international affairs. In a world where nationalist aspirations and the desire for national self-determination were important, the principle of 'compensation', which had been so important in keeping the balance, became difficult to maintain. This increasing emotionalism in international relations would reach its peak at the Congress of Versailles (1919) where the victors, in their desire to punish the vanquished, failed to put the world back together again and thereby laid the basis for the rise of totalitarianism and the Second World War.

The problem of ideology proved equally troublesome. From the very beginnings of the European political order, ideological differences, or what Martin Wight called 'international revolutions', have periodically broken through the restraints of political realism.[27] When this occurred the domestic order of states became the issue of international relations and threatened the system. Increasing interdependence and the 'modernization' of societies has made more difficult the containment of this ideological challenge to the European political order.

The European political order was based on the idea that the sole purpose of war and diplomacy was to safeguard the national interests of the state. The domestic affairs of other states were considered an illegitimate concern. Three times in modern history this commitment to non-interventionism has been violated and ideological conflicts have broken forth. The first was the religious struggles of the Thirty Years War, and the terrible devastation of this conflict led to the concept of state sovereignty. For the next century and a half, wars were limited and fought to secure the national interests of states. With the outbreak of the French Revolution and the triumph in France of the political ideology of republicanism, once again an unlimited ideological struggle engulfed Europe in the Wars of the French Revolution and of Napoleon. Following the defeat of France

[26] Henry Kissinger, *A World Restored* (New York, 1957).
[27] Martin Wight, *Power Politics*, ed. Hedley Bull and Carsten Holbraad (Harmondsworth, 1979).

and the rise to global pre-eminence of Great Britain, ideological concerns receded and limited wars again characterized European statecraft, but ideological conflict would reappear as a consequence of the First World War. By the 1930s, the world had become divided into three ideological camps—democracy, Communism, and Fascism—committed to vastly different conceptions of the socio-economic organization of domestic societies; the ideological clash between democracy and Communism continues to dominate contemporary international relations.

The third great change that destroyed the European political order was the democratization and industrialization of war. The French Revolution democratized war with the new concept of the nation-in-arms or *levée en masse*, and the French Revolution and the Napoleonic Wars became inter-societal conflicts. After the defeat of Napoleon the restoration of the European order rejected this idea of nationalistic warfare: it was too disruptive to European society. For the next hundred years European wars were limited affairs for professional soldiers. Underneath the surface of this stable order, however, nationalist stirrings were everywhere and the conservative domestic order was crumbling.

By the eve of the First World War, the industrial revolution had spread to the Continent and transformed the technology of warfare. As the prescient Polish banker Ivan Bloch appreciated, modern industrial civilization had made possible wars of attrition of unprecedented devastation. The combination of the emotionalism associated with the democratization of war, the spread of nationalism, and the new weapons of mass destruction ended war as a limited instrument of national policy. In the First World War and even more in the Second, war reverted to what it had been in the pre-modern era, that is, a clash of societies committed to one another's total destruction.

The European balance of power system broke down because of the unification of Germany in the middle of the nineteenth century, the devastation of the First World War, and the rise of non-European powers. Both internally and externally, the European order was increasingly an anachronism. The Second World War, delivering the final blow, would prepare the way for the new international order of the superpowers.

From the very beginnings of the European political order Germany has presented a problem of either excessive weakness or excessive strength.[28] When it was too weak, as in the Thirty Years and Napoleonic Wars, it was the object of its neighbours' ambitions and the cockpit of European conflict. When the Germans overcame their insecurity by unifying and achieving strength, they terrified their neighbours and became the aggressor. The unification of the German Reich in the middle of the nineteenth century destroyed the internal European balance. A unified Germany could not be contained by neighbours employing the traditional techniques of the balance of power. Instead Europe divided into the two great and inflexible alliances that made the First World War and its destruction of the European order inevitable.

The First World War itself delivered a blow to Europe from which it never recovered. With the application of modern science and the technologies of industrial civilization to warfare, the conduct of war reverted to what it had been in the earlier epoch of inter-civilizational conflict. For four terrible years the Europeans threw men and machines at one another. This internecine struggle was ended by the exhaustion of these societies and American intervention into European affairs. The European political order which had been based on a self-contained internal balance of power had destroyed itself.

The First World War was not only the beginning of the end of the European balance of power system, but it provided the transition to a new international political order. For nearly four centuries, European civilization had dominated world affairs. Both primitive peoples and great civilizations had come under the sway of the expanding and aggressive Europeans. Writing in 1904, when this European domination of other civilizations was at its zenith, the distinguished political geographer, Halford Mackinder, both caught its essence and also predicted its eventual demise:

When historians in the remote future come to look back on the group of centuries through which we are now passing, and see them foreshortened, as we to-day see the Egyptian dynasties, it may well be that they will describe the last 400 years as the Columbian epoch, and will say that it ended soon after the year 1900. Of late it has been a common-place to speak of geographical exploration as nearly over, and it is recognized that geography must be diverted to the purpose of

---

[28] Henry Kissinger, *The Necessity for Choice* (New York, 1961).

intensive survey and philosophic synthesis. In 400 years the outline of the map of the world has been completed with approximate accuracy, and even in the polar regions the voyages of Nansen and Scott have very narrowly reduced the last possibility of dramatic discoveries. But the opening of the twentieth century is appropriate as the end of a great historic epoch, not merely on account of this achievement, great though it be. . . . In Europe, North America, South America, Africa, and Australasia there is scarcely a region left for the pegging out of a claim of ownership, unless as the result of a war between civilized or half civilized powers. Even in Asia we are probably witnessing the last moves of the game first played by the horsemen of Yermak the Cossack and the shipmen of Vasco da Gama. Broadly speaking, we may contrast the Columbian epoch with the age which preceded it, by describing its essential characteristics as the expansion of Europe against almost negligible resistances, whereas mediaeval Christendom was pent into a narrow region and threatened by external barbarism. From the present time forth, in the post-Columbian age, we shall again have to deal with a closed political system, and none the less that it will be one of world-wide scope. Every explosion of social forces, instead of being dissipated in a surrounding circuit of unknown space and barbaric chaos, will be sharply re-echoed from the far side of the globe, and weak elements in the political and economic organism of the world will be shattered in consequence. There is a vast difference of effect in the fall of a shell into an earthwork and its fall amid the closed spaces and rigid structures of a great building or ship. Probably some half-consciousness of this fact is at last diverting much of the attention of statesmen in all parts of the world from territorial expansion to the struggle for relative efficiency.[29]

Within a decade of these prophetic words, the Europeans ripped apart their own civilization in the greatest war in history. The duration and destructiveness of this first world war greatly weakened European civilization, loosened Europe's grip on other civilizations, and began a process of decolonization that was to be completed following the second great world war. These wars led to the domination of world affairs by two European-derived civilizations, the United States and Soviet Russia. As the French thinker, Alexis de Tocqueville, predicted in the middle of the last century, these two expansionist and highly ideological civilizations were destined to confront one another and supplant the European domination of the globe.

---

[29] Halford Mackinder, 'The Geographical Pivot of History', reprinted in Mackinder, *Democratic Ideas and Reality* (New York, 1904), 241–2.

VI

Although the First World War had destroyed the European political order, the statesmen who gathered at Versailles in 1919 failed to create a replacement for the balance of power system, and what E. H. Carr so appropriately called 'the twenty years' crisis' occurred.[30] An unbridgeable chasm separated the new order based on the concept of collective security embodied in the League of Nations from the underlying realities of power.[31] Another and even more devastating world war would take place before a new and more stable order would be founded.

The First World War brought forth a new attitude towards war and international affairs. The scope and intensity of the war caused a rejection of the traditional European acceptance of war as a natural and legitimate aspect of international relations. Nations came to believe that other countries had been responsible for the terrible slaughter and must be punished. The obvious culprits were the vanquished; the onus for the war was placed on the Germans. They were made to pay morally (the guilt clause of the Treaty) and financially (the reparation clause) for the war, and thus was laid the basis for the rise of Hitler and for their revenge.

The Versailles Treaty and the League of Nations incorporated the new attitude towards war and international relations. President Woodrow Wilson, the author of what was intended to be a liberal world order of peace and justice, condemned the traditional European political order because it failed to preserve peace and was unjust. A 'community of nations' would be substituted for the balance of power. War was outlawed and the new doctrine of collective security was put in its place. Nations had an obligation to punish an aggressor without regard to the effect on their own national interests.

The failure of this liberal order rent the European and global order. By the eve of the Second World War, in place of Bull's Grotian order, three powerful ideologies and parochial conceptions of world order had clashed with one another. The Bolshevik Revolution (1917) in Russia brought to power V. I. Lenin and the Soviets, with their revolutionary conception of

---

[30] J. D. B. Miller provides a summary of the far-reaching effects of the First World War on world politics in *Norman Angell and the Futility of War* (London, 1986).

[31] See Michael Howard, *The Causes of War* (Cambridge, Mass., 1983).

international relations. This argued that since imperialistic capitalism was the cause of modern war and all other evils, its destruction would lead to world peace and a just order based on the international proletariat and the ideal of a Communist society. The liberal democracies also had their own ideological conception of a universal world and moral order based on the principles of self-determination, collective security, and the illegality of war; this was a pluralist order of liberal and humane societies. And with the rise of Italian Fascism, German Nazism, and Japanese militarism, ruthless imperialisms and aggressive ideologies attempted to establish domination over their neighbours.

The defeat of the Axis powers in the Second World War left the world with the struggle between the heirs of Lenin and those of Wilson. What began as a conflict of interests over the post-war disposition of Eastern Europe and Germany became a clash of opposed ideologies and a power struggle of unprecedented dimensions. Once again two powerful civilizations with vastly different views about the nature of the moral and political universe, with clashing value systems, and with intense conflicts of interest contended with one another for supremacy and domination over the entire international system. Under the threat of nuclear annihilation and in the atmosphere of the Cold War, they have attempted concurrently to triumph over one another and to negotiate a code of peaceful coexistence.

The concept of mutual deterrence has provided the main foundation for this international order. Each of the two giants has the military power to destroy utterly the civilization of the other. Despite the vain hope of President Reagan to remove this mutual threat by perfection of an impenetrable defence, the basis of the contemporary world order is and can only be the restraint imposed on states by the possibility of mutual annihilation. Replacing the universal empires of the pre-Columbian epoch and the succeeding European balance of power system, the superpower stand-off has given the world over four decades of relative peace.

The relationship of the United States and the Soviet Union has evolved during this time from that of wartime allies, to that of implacable enemies, to that of reluctant collaborators in an uneasy *détente* and what today is called 'a new relationship'. The process of working out their differences has been one of attempting to formulate a code of conduct, of disentangling specific conflicts of interests from the profound ideological clash between the two opposed civilizations, and of negotiating separate problems one at a time. Despite the serious differences that continue to divide these two powerful and hostile civilizations, the danger of nuclear warfare is forcing them to seek a way of living together in peace and of moving towards a more secure international order.

VII

The confrontation between the United States and the Soviet Union began as they attempted to resolve the differences between them that arose from the Second World War. What originated as a conflict of interest over the disposition of the German and Japanese empires in Eastern and Central Europe and in East Asia escalated into an ideological contest. In time, these conflicts of interest and of ideology were transformed into a power struggle accompanied by a historically unprecedented arms competition. The unwillingness of either side to resolve these fundamental differences through the use of military force led to the Cold War. Underlying this political, ideological, and strategic clash of the superpowers were fundamentally different conceptions of world order.

The United States fought the Second World War in the name of a universal liberal order based on the principles of an open world economy, the joint responsibility of the Allies for the management of the peace, and the guarantee to all peoples of the Four Freedoms. Following the war, this conception of world order was embodied in the Bretton Woods system of economic co-operation, in the Security Council of the United Nations, and in what Americans call 'the basic principles of human rights'. Thus the United States projected onto the rest of the world the liberal values of Western civilization.

The Soviet Union wanted to establish in Eastern Europe a sphere of influence which would provide a guarantee against the revival of a German or Western threat to its security. This interest was embodied in the creation along its western borders and in East Germany of subservient Communist regimes. The USSR also supported the efforts of Communist parties to take power even beyond the reach of the Red Army, and committed itself, at least verbally, to the promotion of world revolution. It intended to create and extend a world order based on the Marxist values of Soviet civilization.

Although the Cold War originated in the refusal of the United States to accept the incorporation of Poland and East Germany into the Soviet bloc, what began as a limited conflict of interest in central Europe rapidly escalated and became transformed into a global ideological struggle. The Russian effort to expand the Soviet system through the support of indigenous Communist parties and the American policies of containment converted the conflict into a universal contest between the two civilizations. The expansion and redefinition of this confrontation following the absorption of Czechoslovakia into the Communist system in 1948 was defined by the American political leadership (in the document NSC 68) in the following stark terms:

Thus unwillingly our free society finds itself mortally challenged by the Soviet system. No other value system is so wholly irreconcilable with ours, so implacable in its purpose to destroy ours, so capable of turning to its own uses the most dangerous and divisive trends in our own society, no other so skillfully and powerfully evokes the elements of irrationality in human nature everywhere, and no other has the support of a great and growing center of military power.[32]

Subsequently, this developing ideological conflict became manifest in the power struggle between two military blocs over many issues, including the American effort to consolidate West Germany, the Berlin blockade, the formation of the NATO alliance and the Warsaw Pact, the rearmament of West Germany, the Soviet explosion of an atomic bomb, the Korean War, and the American decision to develop a thermonuclear weapon. Through a process of action and reaction the superpowers became locked into a deadly and escalating arms race. This contest of wills threatened the survival of both civilizations.

In Asia as well, serious conflict began after the Second World War between two civilizations. Although the origins of the Korean War remain obscure, that war and subsequent American miscalculations caused hostility to intensify between Communist China and the United States. American leaders, incorrectly believing North Vietnam to be a puppet of the

---

[32] *Foreign Relations of the United States* (1950), p. 234.

Chinese, became increasingly antagonistic towards China; this situation led to the American involvement and eventual defeat in South-East Asia. As the distinguished French historian and political scientist Raymond Aron observed, America's defeat transformed American foreign policy and paved the way for the *détente* policies of Richard Nixon.[33]

The logic of the American policy of containment, as the prescient American journalist Walter Lippmann predicted soon after its original formulation, resulted in the open-ended expansion of American commitments throughout the world.[34] The Korean War was defensive (at least initially) and was fought by the United States to preserve the status quo resulting from the Second World War. However, the Vietnam War represented the extension of American power into an area which previously had had little historic or strategic interest for the United States, but which was of immediate concern to the Chinese. Defeat in the jungles of Vietnam brought this American expansionism to an end and provided the incentive for the *rapprochement* with Communist China. The confrontation between American and Chinese civilizations was over; that between Chinese and Soviet civilizations had begun.

The fragmentation of international Communism, the Soviet Union's achievement of nuclear parity, and the demands of America's European allies for a European political settlement laid the basis for the era of *détente* between the superpowers. In the same year that the United States suffered its ignoble defeat in Vietnam (1975), the United States and the Soviet Union at Helsinki ended the Cold War essentially on Soviet terms.[35] The United States granted to the Soviet Union what the United States had previously been unwilling to concede. It acknowledged *de jure* Soviet domination of Eastern Europe and recognized the legitimacy of the German Democratic Republic. In return, the Soviet Union agreed to respect the Western conception of human rights within its empire. In addition, the first significant arms control agreement was signed (SALT I) to prevent the deployment of anti-ballistic missile weapons systems.

[33] Raymond Aron, *The Imperial Republic: The United States and the World, 1945–1973*, trans. Frank Jellinek (Engelwood Cliffs, NJ, 1974).
[34] Walter Lippmann, *The Cold War: A Study in US Foreign Policy* (New York, 1947).
[35] Craig and George, *Force and Statecraft*, p. 169.

Détente, or what the Soviets prefer to call 'peaceful coexistence', permitted the process of the disentanglement and the settlement of specific issues dividing the United States and the Soviet Union to begin. The conflict of interest in Central Europe from which the Cold War had sprung was separated from other issues and 'settled'. The first important steps to manage the power struggle and bring the arms race under control were taken. But the more fundamental ideological clash between the two systems has remained; neither the Soviet Union nor the United States has been willing to concede its conception of world order. As the Soviet leader Leonid I. Brezhnev informed the Soviet party congress in March 1976, '*détente* does not in the slightest abolish and cannot abolish the class struggle.' The Soviet Union, he argued, could not be expected to give up its support of 'progressive' and 'liberation' movements throughout the world. And, as former American National Security Advisor Zbigniew Brzezinski was to put it, subsequent efforts of the Soviet Union to extend its influence in Asia, in Africa, and in the Middle East buried *détente* in the 'sands of the Ogaden'.

Under the banner of the Brezhnev Doctrine, the Soviet Union declared its historic obligation to defend the 'achievements of socialism'. In Afghanistan, using the pretext of defending an externally threatened Marxist regime, Soviet armed forces for the first time crossed those boundaries between East and West which had been agreed upon at the Yalta Conference in the closing days of the Second World War. As happened with the United States in Vietnam, the Soviet Union began attempting to expand its political control and sphere of influence again, and this brought the Soviet Union into deeper conflict with China. What began as a limited exercise to save the Kabul regime escalated into a Soviet confrontation with Chinese and Islamic civilizations. It finished, as in Vietnam, with the superpower cutting its losses.

The ideological confrontation between the United States and the Soviet Union has become a stalemate. Neither power can successfully impose its value system upon the other without risking a nuclear war destructive to both societies. Although the ideological and military competition between the two superpowers and political clashes in peripheral areas continue, the two antagonists are not contesting one another's vital interests, at least not at the present. In this situation President Reagan (and now President Bush) and Chairman Gorbachev have been seeking what President Reagan described to the American people as a 'fresh start'. Although in both societies powerful forces oppose efforts to renegotiate the terms of 'peaceful coexistence', both leaders have the overwhelming support of their societies.

On a still larger canvas, however, what is taking place is a transformation of the international political system. Although the United States and the Soviet Union possess unprecedented military power, neither has been successful in employing its massive arsenals to achieve important political gains. Both are squandering their wealth on machines of war and thus weakening themselves in the economic contests unfolding around them and in what Mackinder called the struggle for 'relative efficiency'. The diffusion of Western techniques of military power, industrial production, and economic organization is giving rise to new centres of power willing and able to resist the ambitions of the superpowers.

Japan's long-term economic challenge is increasingly viewed as a major concern for the United States, while the Soviet Union may have more to fear from an industrialized and nuclear-armed Communist China than it does from the capitalist United States. As has occurred so frequently in history, the contest between two dominant civilizations has opened the way for the rise of their potential rivals. Perhaps some faint glimmer of this historical tendency and of the significance of the diffusion of power to the periphery of the system and towards long-submerged civilizations is encouraging American and Soviet leaders in their attempts to moderate their ideological and military confrontation.

It is important to note that since the end of the Vietnam War, the agenda of world politics has been filled primarily by the conflicts within and among these re-emergent civilizations: Persian versus Arab; Chinese versus Vietnamese; Vietnamese versus Cambodian; Ethiopian versus Somali. One could easily extend the list of intra-Third World conflicts. It is true that there have been a few notable exceptions to this pattern, such as the Soviet invasion of Afghanistan and the British–Argentine war, but as a rule the Europeans, the Americans, and the Russians have not been major parties in the disputes that have arisen. While the United States and the Soviet Union have not been disinterested in many of these clashes, it is significant that the conflicts have been largely beyond their control. And the subconscious fear of both superpowers that they might become inadvertently drawn deeply into these conflicts in Asia, Africa, and the Middle East is surely a factor in their renewed efforts to work out the terms of their coexistence.

As the world moves from the bipolar era of the superpowers to a more pluralistic international system, what are the prospects for a global political order? Will, as Hedley Bull hoped, the European concept of an international 'society' provide the basis for a relatively stable international order? Will there be a return to the inter-civilizational conflicts of the pre-modern era, or will it be possible to work out some basic rules of global coexistence? The only model available to us of an alternative to inter-civilizational conflict or the triumph of one civilization over another is the European balance of power system. Can this system and its ordering principles provide the foundations for a global system composed of diverse civilizations?

VIII

The purpose of the European balance of power system was to preserve the independence of the major states in the system, and the fundamental ordering principles of European statecraft promoted this objective. The three most important principles were (1) the basic and only task of foreign policy was to promote the security and national interests of the state; (2) the domestic values and structures of other societies were not legitimate concerns of foreign policy; and (3) war was a limited instrument of foreign policy rather than a means of destroying other societies. Upon these ordering principles were constructed the institutions and practices of modern diplomacy, such as the cardinal concept of diplomatic immunity and the Grotian morality of states. Recent events in Iran, Lebanon, and elsewhere where wars have manifested a clash of societies threaten a return to the previous conception of civilizational conflict.

It is obvious that these principles of European statecraft were frequently violated, and terrible injustices were committed. They did not operate at all times to the benefit of every state in the system. Furthermore, the preservation of their own 'liberties' did not inhibit the Europeans from subjugating and colonizing other civilizations. Yet the idea that the business of international relations was the interests and security of states rather than the imposition by one society on another of its values or way of life tended to moderate conflict. An international politics based on interests may not be perfect, but it has the advantage that conflicts can be kept limited, differences can be negotiated, and compromises may be found. In contrast, an international politics based on conflicts over social, economic, or religious matters means that conflicts become unlimited and non-negotiable as one society and its values must eventually triumph over the other.

In a world composed of diverse civilizations based on vastly different value systems and armed with nuclear weapons, political realism and a politics of national interests are the only conceivable basis of a stable global order. In contrast to liberalism and Marxism, realism is a universal political theory which every society can understand and which can provide a basis for coexistence. Every society can accept its three fundamental principles: (1) the state as the basic unit of international relations; (2) security as the primary goal of the state; and (3) the fundamental role of power in securing and defending the national interests of the society. Only the Grotian doctrine of the 'morality of states' can provide the basis for compromise and the negotiated solution of international disputes.

Three times in modern history the basic principles of the European political order have been challenged. The first occasion was the French Revolution and the Napoleonic Wars, which were fought over the political organization of domestic societies: that is, aristocracy versus republicanism. The second great struggle arose in the 1930s with the challenge of Axis totalitarianism. The third is the contemporary contest between East and West. In these latter two conflicts, the fundamental issue involved has been the entire social and economic organization of domestic society.

In contrast to the earlier contests between conflicting value systems and ways of life, East and West have yet to resort to the use of force as a means of resolving their fundamental differences. The mutual threat of nuclear weapons has restrained both the Soviet Union and the United States. Although the dangers of a breakdown of this system of mutual deterrence are ever present, time has been gained in which to formulate rules of peaceful coexistence. The Soviet Union, which once denounced traditional diplomacy as a corrupt bourgeois institution, has become its most staunch supporter. For the moment at least, the Soviet Union is not talking about 'burying American capitalism', and the United States is not referring to the Soviet Union as the 'evil empire'. Nevertheless, one would be foolish to be too sanguine that this 'new start' to improved relations between these two hostile and rival civilizations will long endure.

In the contemporary world the revival of older and subordinated civilizations is overtaking the conflict between the superpowers. As noted earlier, some awareness of the significance of this historic development may underlie the efforts of the United States and the Soviet Union to reach agreement on arms control and to prevent their ideological differences from escalating into a dangerous confrontation. They have yet to learn, however, that neither liberalism nor Marxism can provide a basis for order in a truly global system composed of societies with conflicting values. Both of these ideologies need to accept the goal of fashioning an international political order based on the Grotian morality of states doctrine.

The proven tradition of European statecraft, the ordering principle of mutual deterrence, and the increasing importance of the struggle for 'relative efficiency' have moderated the conflict between the United States and the Soviet Union by providing foundations upon which these two hostile offshoots of Western civilization can attempt to work out the terms of their coexistence. Do these same factors provide a basis for a global political order for the emergent and pluralistic world of diverse civilizations? The rivalries between many of these civilizations have existed for centuries; the hostility between Islamic and Hindu civilizations, for instance, has only been suppressed in recent times by British domination of the subcontinent. Whether these ancient feuds will be renewed or whether a foundation for true peaceful coexistence will be established is crucial. Will inter-civilizational conflict return, or will a world order of interdependent civilizations finally be achieved?

The closing decades of the twentieth century may one day be acknowledged as a watershed or critical turning-point in world history. Overshadowing the Cold War and the American–Soviet confrontation, the re-entry or entry into world history of ancient and new civilizations, not as objects of other civilizations but as moulders of international affairs in their own right, will be considered the crucial feature of our age. Today the revival of Islamic, Chinese, and Hindu civilizations, as well as the emergence of potentially powerful new or previously isolated civilizations, in particular Japan, Brazil, and Mexico, suggests that a new era is opening.

The central question raised by Bull in his major writings has yet to be resolved: can the European 'society of states' become the model for the emerging global system? The transformation in international relations taking place now makes immediate the question of what type of world order will succeed American and Soviet domination. The history of the world has largely been one of inter-civilizational conflict: Greek versus Persian, Roman versus Carthaginian, Mogul versus Hindu, Han versus Mongol, Islam versus Christianity. Lacking common values, unifying conceptions of the universe, and common interests, rival civilizations have found it difficult to achieve a peaceful coexistence. One civilization has eventually triumphed over the other, or coexistence has been the product of mutual exhaustion after decades, if not centuries, of deadly confrontation. Will the era into which we are entering be a return to inter-civilizational conflict, or is it possible to devise a basis for the creation of a global society and peaceful coexistence?

7
The Academic Study of International Relations

JAMES L. RICHARDSON

HEDLEY BULL's approach to the study of international relations is usually identified with his influential critique of behavioural-ism, published in *World Politics* in 1966, 'International Theory: The Case for a Classical Approach'.[1] From one perspective this stands as the classic refutation of the pretensions of the behaviouralist school, from another as the classic illustration of the wrong-headedness and obscurantism of the traditionalists. While the issues raised by this debate must form part of any discussion of Bull's views on the study of international relations, they should not be allowed to dominate it. His comments on the subject as a whole and on the role of the scholar in international relations range far beyond the issues canvassed in the behavi-ouralist controversy, as well as offering a more positive appraisal of the work of the leading behaviouralist scholars than is evident in the 1966 paper. His view of the subject was unusually broad, questioning, and critical: it is to this, rather than to his particular view of methodology, that his influence as scholar, teacher, and colleague may be attributed.

The first section of this chapter will discuss his views on the nature of the subject and its academic study, drawing on his writings as a whole, and in this context will re-examine some aspects of the 1966 paper and its influence. It is noteworthy that, despite its title, that paper offers little more than a tantalizing sketch of what is involved in the classical approach itself. The

The author would like to acknowledge the assistance of Robin Ward in identifying source materials for this chapter, and helpful comments by the two editors and by Ursula Vollerthun.

[1] Reprinted in Klaus Knorr and James N. Rosenau, eds., *Contending Approaches to International Politics* (Princeton, 1969), 20–38.

second section attempts to fill out this sketch, to counter some frequent misunderstandings, and to identify some of the more substantial critical questions that have been raised in relation to the classical approach.

This approach is not to be identified with Bull's own approach, which falls within it but, like the work of other leading scholars who may be included within this general school, has its own distinctive features reflecting his particular intellectual background and interests. The third and final section discusses what is distinctive and especially valuable in Bull's approach, and illustrates this with reference to his main theoretical study, *The Anarchical Society*. The chapter concludes by drawing attention to some major issues which are raised in his later work, but which he was unable to consider further.

I

As Adam Roberts has stated, Bull 'saw the house of International Relations as having many mansions, and many different views of the world, each coherent, plausible and intellectually defensible'.[2] Even while forthrightly upholding his own position, he acknowledged the strength in others. While never limiting himself to a synthesis of other views, he reinforced his own approach by incorporating insights from other perspectives. Thus, despite his predilection for the uncompromising extreme, his conclusions tended towards a judicious balance between competing considerations.

His principal statement on the subject as a whole, 'International Relations as an Academic Pursuit', presents the subject as one with a well-defined focus, but one which cannot be studied in isolation from ancillary subjects; one which is not a single discipline but 'the scene of contending approaches and techniques', in which history and theory, country studies, and the international system all have an essential place.[3] Writing in the early 1970s, he saw the generally accepted focus of the subject as the contemporary political relations among states. Of the various suggestions for changing or broadening the focus, he expressed some sympathy for broadening it in the direction of

---

[2] 'Hedley Norman Bull (1932–1985)', *Balliol College Annual Record* (1985), 26.
[3] Hedley Bull, 'International Relations as an Academic Pursuit', *Australian Outlook*, 26. 3 (Dec. 1972), 251–62.

'world politics', that is to say, the 'global political system of which . . . the states-system is only part, even if it is the most important part'.[4] While rejecting several familiar arguments in favour of this, he acknowledged the need to study transnational organizations and groups, and suggested that normative issues relating to justice could not be adequately addressed in terms of the sovereign state, but required discussion of the individual, on the one hand, and the potential global community, on the other.

Why are history and theory, country studies and the global system, the four essentials? History, he argues, is the only vehicle through which we can grasp the individual ('singular') characteristics of states: the United States is not just a great power, but one with unique traditions, values, and institutions. History is the essential starting-point for the study of international relations, and the essential companion to theoretical study, providing the cases against which theory must be tested, and creating an awareness of the way in which theories themselves are conditioned by historical circumstances. Theorctical enquiry is essential in order to identify and evaluate the general assumptions which underlie all discussion of international relations. It may be critical or constructive, normative or empirical, comprehensive or partial, policy-oriented or not, 'classical' or scientific.[5] Country or area studies, like history, bring out the unique features of each actor, emphasize the domestic dimension of all foreign policy, and correct the otherwise inevitable tendency to project one's own frame of reference on to states with quite different cultures, traditions, and perspectives. But this needs to be complemented by an understanding of the international system and the country's place in it, and of the forces shaping the development of world politics as a whole.[6]

Knowledge of international law and international economics is 'desirable as part of the intellectual equipment' of the student of international relations, as part of the context of international politics, but not as part of the subject itself.[7] In his own work Bull showed a great deal of interest in the inter-relationship of international law to international politics, but not in the

---

[4] 'International Relations as an Academic Pursuit', p. 255.
[5] Ibid., pp. 255–9.
[6] Ibid., pp. 259–62.
[7] Ibid., p. 252.

international economy. He did not deny its importance, but rather left it to others; however, while avoiding economic issues in the technical sense, he was keenly aware of the power struggles which underlie economic conflicts and became increasingly interested in the ethical issues raised by North–South economic relations. In contrast to many contemporaries, Bull does not seek to locate international relations among the social sciences, but nor does he simply project his own intellectual background in defining the essential components of the subject: there is no mention of philosophy in this general overview, but it may be assumed that he saw it as essential for the scholar who seeks to contribute to the development of theory.

Bull's book reviews illustrate the breadth of his conception of the subject in another way, that is, in the range of different contributions which he was ready to acknowledge, and the breadth of his scholarly criteria. In every instance but one, a review of a Soviet publication in 1972 which he found to be 'self-righteous and polemical', containing 'no breath of self-criticism or of questioning of Soviet policy', instead relying on 'name-calling, ranting and smearing, in place of argument',[8] his criticism was balanced by a recognition of the scholarly qualities of the work under review. One such quality was to address (rather than resolve) large issues. 'This is an admirable study which raises some large questions and, in a modest and scholarly way, breaks some new ground.'[9] Another work shows 'a willingness to identify the big questions and make judgments about them'.[10] Even John Burton's *World Society*, a work which he characterizes as consisting mainly of 'mere assertions of a loose and general nature, not accompanied by any careful argument', raises 'large and important questions, and there is much to be said for the answers Dr Burton gives to some of them'.[11]

F. H. Hinsley and Richard Falk are credited with 'penetrating analyses', of nationalism and the Treaty of Westphalia,

[8] Bull, review of *Problems of War and Peace: A Critical Analysis of Bourgeois Theories*, in *American Political Science Review*, 68 (1974), 1850–1.

[9] Bull, review of Astri Suhrke and Lela Garner Nobel, eds., *Ethnic Conflict in International Relations*, in *Ethnic and Racial Studies*, 3 (1980), 366.

[10] Bull, review of F. S. Northedge and M. Grieve, *A Hundred Years of International Relations*, in *American Political Science Review*, 67 (1973), 724.

[11] Bull, review of J. Burton, *World Society*, in *American Political Science Review*, 68 (1974), 857.

respectively; the work of the latter author, despite Bull's many criticisms, represents 'one of the most significant points of departure in the study of world politics today'.[12] He singles out Peter King's contribution to an edited volume on strategy, 'Critique of Strategic Studies', for its challenge to accepted views, 'striking a rare note of irreverence and intellectual honesty'.[13] T. B. Millar's *Australia in Peace and War* may not address theoretical issues nor offer a novel interpretation, but offers the first comprehensive history of Australia's external relations, characterized by 'an underlying structure of sound common sense and . . . many penetrating observations' reflecting 'a deep and more than merely bookish knowledge' of the subject.[14] Though he rejects the 'false precision' of some of the quantitative findings of Gary Hufbauer and Jeffrey Schott's study of economic sanctions, they are right to seek a more comprehensive and systematic treatment of the subject in place of the usual narrative accounts.[15]

His greatest accolade, profundity, is reserved for a paper on international justice by Julius Stone, Henry Kissinger's *White House Years*, and Raymond Aron's *magnum opus, Peace and War*. Kissinger offers 'brilliant sketches', 'penetrating observations', and 'magisterial surveys of the issues with which he had to grapple'.[16] In Aron's 'great contribution',

> there is not an issue that is dodged, a passage that smacks of faltering comprehension, an item that is redundant or irrelevant, or a judgment that is glib or pedantic. More remarkable even than the intellectual depth of this book is the example it provides of fidelity to the principle of scholarly integrity. . . . Mr Aron's conclusions are the most modest and austere that the copiousness of his argument will permit.[17]

Bull's writing on the history of the study of international

---

[12] Bull, *The Anarchical Society* (London, 1977), p. ix. The reviews are in *American Political Science Review*, 69 (1975), 374 (Hinsley) and *International Organization*, 26 (1972), 583–8 (Falk).

[13] Bull, review of D. Ball, ed., *Strategy and Defence: Australian Essays*, in *International Affairs*, 60 (1984), 454.

[14] Bull, review of Millar, *Australia in Peace and War*, in *International Affairs*, 55 (1979), 503.

[15] Bull, 'Economic Sanctions and Foreign Policy', *World Economy*, 7 (1984), 218–22.

[16] Bull, 'Kissinger: The Primacy of Geopolitics', *International Affairs*, 56. 3 (Summer 1980), 484–7. For his comment on Stone, see Bull, 'International Law and International Order', *International Organization*, 26. 3 (Summer 1972), 584.

[17] Bull, review of R. Aron, *Peace and War*, in *Survival*, 9 (1967), 371.

relations is on theory, not on the subject as a whole, but if theory is understood as he defines it—'By theory of international relations I mean simply the body of general propositions that may be put forward about relations among states, or more generally about world politics'[18]—a history of theory is essentially an intellectual history of the subject. By concentrating on the central ideas in each phase, this approach provides a sharp focus.

International relations theory in this sense began long before its academic study.

The theory of international relations is at least as old as the debates about it recorded in Thucydides' *History of the Peloponnesian War*, and it is arguable that the most important body of systematic theoretical writing on the subject is still that of the classical international lawyers.[19]

Classical works are those whose 'relevance and topicality are experienced afresh by each succeeding generation'; they provide the 'standard or most excellent expressions' of particular views.[20] He refers to the Catholic tradition of just war doctrine and the works of Callières and Clausewitz, but does not offer a historical account of international relations thought. He sees the fifty years from the beginning of the academic discipline in 1919 as divided into three distinct phases: the 'idealist or progressivist', the 'realist', and the 'behaviouralist'. At the time of his latest writing on the topic, 1975, his view of the next phase was still tentative.

Bull finds little of lasting value in the writings of the first phase. The forerunners, publicists such as Lowes Dickinson and Brailsford, are credited with raising significant questions, even if their answers no longer impress us. Their academic successors such as Zimmern amplified the same answers, but never questioned the assumptions that the growth of democracy, the spread of international enlightenment, and the working of the League of Nations were transforming the international system, and that 'their responsibility as students of international

---

[18] Bull, 'New Directions in the Theory of International Relations', *International Studies*, 14. 2 (Apr.–June 1975), 277.

[19] Bull, 'The Theory of International Politics, 1919–1969', in Brian Porter, ed., *The Aberystwyth Papers: International Politics 1919–1969* (London, 1972), 49.

[20] Hedley Bull and Carsten Holbraad, eds., 'Introduction' to Martin Wight, *Power Politics* (Harmondsworth, 1979), 10, 20.

relations was to assist this march of progress'.[21] They did indeed offer a general view of the nature and recent history of international relations, but this 'now strikes us as superficial. The "idealists" were not remarkable for their intellectual depth or powers of explanation, only for their intense commitment to a particular view of what should happen'.[22] In their 'narrow and uncritical rectitude' they showed no awareness of the moral dilemmas of international politics. 'The quality that shines through all their work is innocence', the tendency to accept externals at face value.[23] Thus Bull goes beyond the realist critique of particular doctrines, identifying more fundamental intellectual weaknesses in the thought of the 'idealists'.

His assessment of the 'realists' is not so positive as might be expected of an author frequently identified as one, at a time when the realist 'paradigm' once again dominates discussions of international theory. While endorsing their critique of their predecessors, and characterizing their work as 'an important starting point of theoretical understanding of international relations', superior to much recent work, he maintains that 'the stream of thinking and writing that began with Niebuhr and Carr has long run its course.'[24]

Again, while endorsing some of the contemporary criticisms of the realists, he goes beyond them. Their polemical starting-point, the critique of Anglo-Saxon legalism and moralism, provides too narrow a foundation for the theoretical analysis of fundamental continuities in international relations, or of the major changes which transformed the international agenda between the 1940s and the 1970s. In debunking a narrow moralism, the realists neglected the role of values in international relations, and provided no foundation for the reasoned moral judgements which should have a central place in the scholarly study of politics. Moreover, each of the major realist authors draws on quite different theoretical traditions: it is only in the polemical sense that they form a school. Their invoking of the national interest diverts attention from the larger question of the conditions of international order.[25] These criticisms arise

---

[21] 'The Theory of International Politics, 1919–1969', p. 34.
[22] Ibid., p. 35.   [23] Ibid., p. 36   [24] Ibid., p. 39.
[25] Ibid., pp. 38–9; Bull, *'The Twenty Years' Crisis* Thirty Years On', *International Journal*, 24. 4 (Autumn 1969), 625–38.

from two of his own central interests, international order and the place of ethics in international relations.

If the assessment of the realists is unexpectedly harsh, Bull's assessment of the overall contribution of the 'behaviouralist' or 'scientific' school, as distinct from their methodological aspirations, is unexpectedly positive. There is high praise for Kaplan's 'arresting demonstration of what is involved in the attempt to formulate a fully rigorous theory of the international system', not least for exposing the inadequacies of previous attempts at such theory.[26] Deutsch's work on political communities is important for raising a new set of questions and, along with that of Haas and others, for providing a foundation for any future work on integration. Likewise the major strategic analysts, whatever specific criticisms one might raise, have provided a thorough examination of the momentous issues raised by nuclear weapons, and the ideas of one of these theorists, Thomas Schelling, have become 'part of the general intellectual culture of the age'.[27]

Reviewing the development of international relations theory since 1919, Bull discerns only limited and fitful progress. Too often there is regression, through neglect of the discussion of fundamentals in the classics, old or new; too much pursuit of novelty for its own sake, too great a concern for methodological niceties rather than major issues. On the other hand, there is a greater level of sophistication, less 'innocence', explanations are 'deeper and more many-sided' than fifty years earlier. This he attributes to the general advance of the social sciences rather than progress within international relations itself.[28] The new concern for methodology has exposed much 'intellectually shoddy' reasoning and has enhanced the rigour and precision of the subject. Certain lines of enquiry have been shown to be unfruitful, but these have been 'instructive failures'; meanwhile, other lines have provided a well-reasoned and researched foundation for future enquiry. In addition to the work of Karl Deutsch, noted above, he instances Kenneth Waltz on the causes of war and Inis Claude on collective security.[29]

Writing in 1975, he identified three potential developments

---

[26] 'The Theory of International Politics, 1919–1969', p. 42.
[27] 'International Relations as an Academic Pursuit', p. 258.
[28] 'The Theory of International Politics, 1919–1969', pp. 48–51.
[29] Ibid., pp. 51–4.

which held out promise for the future. The first of these, the study of values—both the role which values actually play in international relations, and normative enquiry in its own right—has been among the notable developments since then. The second, prominent in the 1970s, has receded in the 1980s: concern with transnational and global issues, the role of non-state actors and his own special interest in the prospects for a cosmopolitan global culture. Finally he identified an area of such difficulty that, with a few notable exceptions, there has been little advance: the 'liberation' of international relations theory from its 'parochial' Western perspective by relating it to the Marxist tradition and to ideas from the Third World.[30]

The startling omission here is a dimension of the subject which has moved into the mainstream of theorizing in the ensuing years, international political economy. This no doubt reflected his relative lack of interest, and indeed background, in economics, but it may also be related to his ambivalence about the social sciences in general. On the one hand, as we have seen, he acknowledged the positive influence of the general advance of the social sciences; on the other hand, the sole reference in his historical overview to the British 'traditionalist' school of theory was to individuals who stood out against the dominant trend, scholars who 'sought to warm the coals of an older tradition of historical and philosophical reflection during the long, dark winter of the "social scientific" ascendancy.'[31]

Bull does not offer a systematic exposition of his view of the role of the scholar in international relations, but it is outlined in a paper, cited above, which was first read to colleagues and graduate students, in which he notes that his answers to the large questions which he raises are necessarily brief, assertions rather than arguments, his purpose on that occasion being 'to provide a general point of view, in relation to which others can take their bearings'.[32] The paper concludes on a challenging note: 'The most important task is to maintain the intellectual integrity of the subject . . . this task is also the most difficult'.[33]

---

[30] 'New Directions in the Theory of International Relations', pp. 283–7. For a discussion of the Marxist tradition, see V. Kubalkova and A. Cruickshank, *Marxism and International Relations* (London, 1985).

[31] 'The Theory of International Politics, 1919–1969', p. 48.

[32] 'International Relations as an Academic Pursuit', p. 251.

[33] Ibid., p. 265.

The strength of his own commitment to scholarly integrity impressed all who knew him, and was widely acknowledged in the tributes at the time of his death. It was even such as to enhance the standing of the subject of international relations as a whole: Adam Roberts notes in his tribute that the standard comments that the subject is no more than high-class journalism, a poor relation of history, or a subject without a discipline, were little heard in Oxford after his appointment there.[34] Such comments, however, point towards one of the reasons for the difficulty in achieving scholarly integrity in the subject: its novelty as an academic subject dealing with issues so much at the focus of public attention. Bull commented on this, 'the lack of agreed standards and demands on all sides for instant wisdom',[35] and expressed concern that punditry or public advocacy would not only divert academics in the subject from their central task, but would also tend to dilute intellectual standards.

Among the qualities which he most prized were the Socratic questioning of received opinion and determination to penetrate to a more fundamental level of understanding, and the courage to take an unorthodox or extreme position, provided always that it was seriously argued, not merely idiosyncratic. There is also his widely noted plea 'for the recognition of complexity in the moral, military and political issues raised by modern war: for confronting this complexity, rather than turning away from it: for rigorous study and anxious questioning, in place of the pursuit of panaceas'.[36] Later he was to draw attention to the intellectual honesty of authors such as Aron and Walzer who, in the face of complexity, acknowledged their inability to resolve all the problems or eliminate all the loose ends in their arguments.[37] He proclaimed the need for a 'rigorous and undiscriminating scepticism', yet even so, while 'trying not to regard any question as closed which could possibly be regarded as open,' he observed that 'the most important open questions always pass us by.'[38] His irreverence, also much commented on and a quality

---

[34] 'Hedley Norman Bull (1932–1985)', p. 27.

[35] 'International Relations as an Academic Pursuit', p. 265.

[36] Bull, *The Control of the Arms Race: Disarmament and Arms Control in the Nuclear Age* (London, 1961), p. ix.

[37] Review of *Peace and War*, pp. 371–3; Bull, 'Recapturing the Just War for Political Theory', *World Politics*, 31 (1979), 591.

[38] 'International Relations as an Academic Pursuit', p. 265; *The Control of the Arms Race*, p. xiii.

which he admired in others, served as a means of identifying especially cherished assumptions and breaching their outer defences.

The influence of John Anderson's thought, discussed below, is evident in Bull's summing up of the problems created by the political character of the subject:

> The tradition of detached and disinterested study of politics is, I believe, a very delicate plant. It exists at all in relatively few countries, and even in these it has a precarious existence. Its survival depends on a form of commitment that is not political, but intellectual and academic: a commitment to inquiry as a distinct human activity, with its own morality and its own hierarchy of priorities, that is necessarily brought into conflict with the prevailing political values in any society—whether these values derive from the established order or from movements of protest against it. Political movements of all kinds—radical and conservative, good and bad—are interested in ideas not for their own sake but as a means of acquiring power and influence, and are always interested in imposing limitations on political inquiry.[39]

Within Western societies the direct subordination of scholarly values to political ends is the lesser danger: even so, he notes the early 1970s fashion for committed scholarship as 'potentially a menacing development', and on the other hand, excessive closeness of academics to government, as in the case of the Kennedy Administration, as substituting the preoccupations of decision-makers for the concerns of scholarship.[40] The more insidious danger, however, is the unquestioning acceptance of a moral and political framework, the extreme example of which is provided by the first generation of international relations academics, the 'idealists'. But even when research is rigorous, scholarly, and professional, as in the contemporary American discipline, it is impaired by a climate of 'stifling intellectual and political conformism, as evident in the new radical orthodoxies as in the old conservative ones'.[41] In a review of a number of American studies of Soviet naval power, for example, he draws attention to the common failure to pose any question not suggested by the immediate US strategic perspective.[42]

---

[39] 'New Directions in the Theory of International Relations', p. 284.
[40] 'International Relations as an Academic Pursuit', pp. 262, 264.
[41] Ibid., pp. 263–4.
[42] Bull, 'The Rise of Soviet Naval Power', *Problems of Communism*, 30. 2 (Mar.–Apr. 1981), 60–1.

The 'detached' or 'disinterested' approach is emphatically not to be identified with 'value freedom'. 'There is, of course, no such thing as a "value-free" inquiry into international relations or any other social subject.' By political objectivity or detachment, he means awareness of, and a critical attitude towards, one's moral and political premisses: that one should 'treat the investigation of moral and political premisses as part of the subject'.[43] This involves *inter alia* an awareness that the views, and the silences, of academics have practical consequences, and an awareness of the conflicts between intellectual and political values sometimes simplified in the notion of 'the treason of the clerks'. The role of normative questions in the study of international relations, one of the central features of his view of the subject, is explored more fully below.

This perception of the conflict between intellectual and political values lies behind the apparent ambivalence in Bull's comments on the academic's relationship to policy. On the one hand, he rejects the idea that there are 'solutions' to the larger dilemmas and uncertainties posed by international politics. On the other hand, he sees the discussion of policy issues as a normal part of the academic subject, yet, insisting that it is an intellectual subject, not a practical one, he deplores the tendency for academics to seek to become policy-makers, the example of Kissinger notwithstanding.

It is only the first of these points, the rejection of 'solutions', which is developed at all fully. It is not stated as an absolute principle, but emerges in the conclusions of his own principal works and in his critiques of others. He finds that the arguments in *The Control of the Arms Race* 'do not point unambiguously towards some set of policies that are the right road ahead', and that in these circumstances, 'the strong advocacy of policies, the marshalling of arguments so as to suggest them, involves a certain wilful blindness and abdication of critical judgment'.[44] *The Anarchical Society*'s 'implicit defence of the states system' is 'a conclusion ... in need of continual reassessment', and reflects an 'incomplete' examination of the conflicting claims of order and justice. It provides no 'solid basis' for practical advice: '... while there is a great desire to know what the future of

---

[43] 'International Relations as an Academic Pursuit', p. 262.
[44] *The Control of the Arms Race*, p. 202.

world politics will bring, and also to know how we should behave in it, we have to grope about in the dark with respect to the one as much as with respect to the other'.[45] His main criticism of *Peace and War* is that Aron has made concessions to the readers' expectation for an 'apparent solution', but that Aron's rules of prudence do not offer an escape from the moral dilemmas which he has so convincingly enunciated.[46] And Richard Falk in *This Endangered Planet* has succumbed to the attractions of advocacy, setting aside uncertainty and engaging in 'rhetoric, exaggeration, denunciation and the slurring of issues' in pursuit of 'world order activism'.[47]

However, the discussion of policy issues forms 'a large part of the academic discussion of politics'.[48] We may assume from the example of his own writing that he saw this as the critical examination of the general direction of policy—its goals and means, its appropriateness in relation to changing circumstances—leaving the fine tuning to the practitioners. Why, then, should the academic not from time to time seek to translate thought into practice? Why is Kissinger's example, 'acting out the secret dreams of countless academic experts on international relations', so 'unfortunate'?[49] Does this apply to academics in all the social sciences, or is international relations a special case?

Unfortunately Bull does not address these questions systematically. Should his comment, then, be regarded as an example of his thinking aloud, stating a point in characteristically uncompromising form? If the statement is read in the context of his concern for the dangers to the intellectual integrity of the subject, the dangers of political commitment and of too close a relationship to government, and his principle that 'it is only if they remain themselves that academic students of international relations are likely to have anything distinctive to contribute to the discussion of foreign policy problems',[50] we may conclude that there was serious consideration behind his comment on the Kissinger precedent. If the attraction of policy-making, with all the intellectual constraints that it entails, exerts greater sway

---

[45] *The Anarchical Society*, pp. 318–19, 320.
[46] Review of *Peace and War*, p. 373.
[47] 'International Law and International Order', p. 588.
[48] 'International Relations as an Academic Pursuit', p. 262.
[49] 'Kissinger: The Primacy of Geopolitics', p. 487.
[50] 'International Relations as an Academic Pursuit', p. 264.

within the discipline than the desire to make contributions to scholarly understanding, its *raison d'être*, these contributions are likely to be meagre and, in so far as dubious policy assumptions are left unchallenged, the practical as well as the intellectual consequences are likely to be for the worse.[51]

In later years Bull gave two different accounts of the purpose of his 1966 critique of what he termed the scientific approach to the subject. At a Canberra seminar in 1972 he stated that:

The article is devoted partly to convincing opponents of the 'scientific' movement in International Relations Theory that they should take it more seriously, and that they needed to meet it with 'rational criticism' rather than 'facile abuse'.[52]

He also reaffirmed that theory should be 'scientific' in the sense that it should be coherent and precise, and 'consistent with the philosophical foundations of modern science', and drew attention to his high praise for the contributions of Kaplan, Deutsch, and Schelling. In his Martin Wight Memorial Lecture in London in 1976, however, the imagery is very different:

Wight's attitude towards the behaviourists was the source of one of my own disagreements with him. I felt that they represented a significant challenge and that it was important to understand them and engage in debate with them. The correct strategy, it appeared to me, was to sit at their feet, to study their position until one could state their arguments better than they could and then—when they were least suspecting—to turn on them and slaughter them in an academic Massacre of Glencoe. Wight entertained none of these bloody thoughts.[53]

Whichever of these intentions may have been uppermost at

---

[51] He would surely have agreed with Hoffmann's comment on this issue: 'Once one starts rolling down the slope from research-with-practical-effects to practical-advocacy-derived-from-research, the tendency to slight the research and to slant the advocacy . . . will become insidious. Which means that the author may still be highly useful as an intelligent and skilled decision-maker—but not as a scholar. Either his science will be of little use, or else, in his attempt to apply a particular pet theory or dogma, he may well become a public danger. This does not mean that the experience of policy-making is fateful to the scholar . . . A scholar-turned-statesman can, if his science is wise and his tactics flexible, find ways of applying it soundly; and he can later draw on his experience for improving his scholarly analytical work. But it is a delicate exercise which few have performed well.' Stanley Hoffmann, 'An American Social Science: International Relations', *Daedalus*, 106 (1977), 56.

[52] 'International Relations as an Academic Pursuit', p. 258.

[53] Bull, 'Martin Wight and the Theory of International Relations', the second Martin Wight Memorial Lecture, in *British Journal of International Studies*, 2. 2 (July, 1976), 104.

the time, a review of the controversy provoked by the article leaves the overwhelming impression that there was in fact little rational debate, little taking up of claim and counter-claim, but rather a reaffirmation and refinement of existing standpoints. Even the attempts by various 'bridge-builders' and 'research pluralists' to promote a methodological synthesis—albeit in the idiom of the behavioural sciences—are more indicative of the direction of their own work than of intellectual interchange with the warring protagonists.[54] The authors of the methodological essays of the time were not seeking to persuade one another, but appealing to a wider audience, or at least to the next generation of graduate students. Bull himself, who had less taste for methodological refinements than most of his adversaries, did not re-enter the 'debate' but, as noted below, reaffirmed the most important of his claims, while omitting to press others.

The impact of the 'Massacre of Glencoe', however, was much more decisive, at least among those already predisposed to traditionalist approaches. As Martin Indyk commented in the Australian context:

In this short piece Bull managed to encapsulate all the reservations and suspicions of the British school and its Australian offshoot to behavioural approaches. It was therefore easy for Australian academics to breathe a sigh of relief and get back, with clear consciences, to what they had been doing. Bull saved everybody else the trouble of taking the behaviouralists seriously.[55]

The vehemence of Bull's polemic was at odds with his interest in promoting rational criticism. To the extent that the work of the behaviouralist school was disregarded, rather than examined critically, the subject in Britain and Australia was impoverished, issues which might have been regarded as open were treated as closed, innovations which might have been welcomed for their potential were all too readily derided, and the extent and the limitations of the behaviouralists' contribution to research were not assessed. The suggestion is not that this should be attributed entirely to Bull, but that his arguments provided the rationalization.

[54] See e.g. Michael Haas, 'A Plea for Bridge Building in International Relations', and Robert C. North, 'Research Pluralism and the International Elephant', in Knorr and Rosenau, eds., *Contending Approaches*.

[55] Martin Indyk, 'The Australian Study of International Relations', in Don Aitken, ed., *Surveys of Australian Political Science* (Sydney, 1985), 276.

Is the debate, such as it was, of continuing relevance, or is it now only of historical interest? Bull's specific claims have a certain air of the 1960s, as do the critiques of the behaviouralist approach in other branches of political science at the time.[56] The subject has moved on. Some of the developments, such as the revival of interest in normative questions, fall squarely within the traditionalist approach, while others, such as the new emphasis on international political economy, cannot be clearly assigned to either camp. Recent theoretical debates, in particular those focusing on realism and on positivism, are analogous to those of the 1960s only to a limited extent. They raise, explicitly at least, more fundamental philosophical issues: 'positivism' is a broader concept than the scientific approach condemned by Bull, who does not go far enough to satisfy its contemporary critics.[57]

On the other hand, the behaviouralist school is far from vanquished, but lives on vigorously, retaining a prominent place in the leading American journals. A major publication of the early 1980s, the *Handbook of Political Conflict*, edited by Ted Robert Gurr, is devoted entirely to reviewing the progress of quantitative 'empirical' studies.[58] While there is now a good deal of support in general terms for combining traditional and behavioural science methods, and there are important examples of such research, much work tends towards one or other end of the spectrum. To the extent that Bull raised important questions, then, they remain relevant, and can now be addressed in the light of a much greater corpus of completed research than in the mid-1960s.

Moreover, the debate between Bull and the behaviouralists— which is what it was, since he received applause but little reinforcement from the traditionalists—can be seen as one round in a perennial dispute between two schools of thought concerning the study of man and society, the one arguing for the essential unity of all the sciences, the other for the uniqueness of

---

[56] See e.g. Christian Bay, 'Politics and Pseudo-politics: A Critical Evaluation of Some Behavioral Literature', *American Political Science Review*, 59 (1965), 39–51; Leo Strauss, 'An Epilogue', in Herbert J. Storing, ed., *Essays on the Scientific Study of Politics* (New York, 1962), 305–27.

[57] See e.g. Richard K. Ashley, 'The Poverty of Neorealism', *International Organization*, 38 (1984), 225–86.

[58] Ted Robert Gurr, ed., *Handbook of Political Conflict: Theory and Research* (New York, 1980); see, in particular, Gurr's Introduction, pp. 1–6.

the social sciences. The opposition has been expressed in different ways at different times—between (scientific) explanation and (interpretative) understanding, between rationalism and historicism, between positivism and hermeneutics, and so forth.[59] To suppose that such a philosophical cleavage could be brushed aside by a little light banter, as did some contributors to the 'great debate', testified to a degree of arrogance which unfortunately is proving to be of long duration.[60]

In returning to Bull's critique, then, the question is not whether he was correct, but whether he was raising important issues, and whether these might need to be reformulated a generation later. Not all of the seven propositions which he advanced against the scientific approach were of equal importance, and some can be seen to raise questions for the traditionalists as well.

His first proposition was that in confining themselves to deductive reasoning and strict ('operational') procedures of verification, scientific researchers were unable to come to grips with the substance of the subject.[61] The subsequent accumulation of quantitative studies on issues of great substance—for example, the causes of war, crisis decision-making, the determinants of dependency—has been accompanied by persistent questioning of the 'validity' of such studies. That is to say, do the operational indices actually measure what they are supposed to measure, and are the quantifiers really addressing the questions of causation, especially structural or systemic causation, which have been at the heart of the subject? Are they testing the theories which they purport to test? Are they providing explanations, or merely correlations, more complete and precise descriptions? Authors such as Kenneth Waltz, Robert Jervis, and Raymond Duvall argue that certain major

---

[59] See e.g. Georg von Wright, *Explanation and Understanding* (London, 1971).

[60] David Singer, for example, the only contributor to the Knorr and Rosenau symposium who responds directly to Bull's arguments, opens his attack by referring to 'the all-too-familiar propositions by which it will once again be proven that the bee will never fly, the weather will never be predicted, the atom will never be smashed . . .', and so on. Singer, 'The Incompleat Theorist: Insight Without Evidence', in Knorr and Rosenau, eds., *Contending Approaches*, p. 64. For contemporary attitudes, see Gurr, ed., *Handbook of Political Conflict*.

[61] For Bull's seven propositions, see 'International Theory: The Case for a Classical Approach', in Knorr and Rosenau, eds., *Contending Approaches*, pp. 26–37. He gave a number of examples of questions of substance, relating to the international system, a common culture, war, intervention, and the causes of major international events.

quantitative studies lack validity in this sense, and fail to address the theoretical issues which prompted them in the first place.[62] To the extent that these criticisms have force, Bull's first proposition, updated, still identifies a basic and unresolved issue.

This is even more evident in the case of his second proposition, that behaviouralist scholars necessarily employ 'classical', interpretative methods to supplement their pro-claimed methods, and that the value of their work depends mainly on the former. The need to supplement rigorous, 'parsimonious' analyses with 'thick descriptions' and with judgements concerning the extent to which the particular case is an instance of the concept in question is widely acknowledged.[63] Not all will be persuaded by Bull's dual claim, but the issue which it addresses remains one requiring more searching analysis than it has yet received.

The third proposition, that the prospects for major progress through the cumulation of scientific studies are 'bleak', can now be examined in the light of a considerable cumulation of such studies, as a stocktaking exercise such as the *Handbook of Political Conflict* makes clear. Once again, the conclusion reached depends on the presuppositions of the enquirer, but the claims of the optimists are now strikingly modest.[64] After a generation of behavioural research, the issue remains.

These three propositions, the heart of Bull's critique, are strongly reaffirmed in his later references to the debate.[65] He did not reaffirm his fourth proposition, his general condem-nation of the use of models, and this indeed is the least convincing of the seven, ruling out, as it appears to, any role for

---

[62] Kenneth Waltz, *Theory of International Politics* (Reading, Mass., 1979), 13–16; Robert Jervis, 'The Costs of the Quantitative Study of International Relations', in Knorr and Rosenau, eds., *Contending Approaches*, pp. 177–217; Raymond D. Duvall, 'Depend-ence and Dependencia Theory: Notes toward Precision of Concept and Argument', *International Organization*, 32 (1978), 51–78.

[63] See e.g. Robert O. Keohane, 'Theory of World Politics: Structural Realism and Beyond', in Ada W. Finifter, ed., *Political Science: The State of the Discipline* (Washington, 1983), esp. pp. 506, 531; J. Donald Moon, 'The Logic of Political Inquiry: A Synthesis of Opposed Perspectives', in Nelson W. Polsby and Fred C. Greenstein, eds., *Handbook of Political Science*, 1 (Reading, Mass., 1975), 131–228.

[64] See e.g. Dina A. Zinnes, 'Why War? Evidence on the Outbreak of International Conflict', in Gurr, ed., *Handbook of Political Conflict*, pp. 331–60.

[65] 'International Relations as an Academic Pursuit', pp. 257–9; 'New Directions in the Theory of International Relations', pp. 278–80.

models or ideal types in clarifying concepts and assumptions. His critics were on strong ground in arguing that the misuse of models is one thing, but to deny them any role in the social sciences is quite another.

The fifth proposition, that work may be 'distorted and impoverished by a fetish for measurement', adds little to the issues raised by the first three. The sixth, that rigour and precision are essential but can be accommodated within the classical approach, raises major issues for the understanding of that approach and is therefore postponed for discussion below. The seventh and final proposition, that the 'scientists' had cut themselves off from history and philosophy, thus depriving themselves of self-awareness and self-criticism, raises interesting issues for both approaches. It is arguable that the members of the discipline in all methodological schools have become more aware of the issues raised by the history and philosophy of science, not least through the repercussions of the work of Thomas Kuhn. But in many cases this remains a rather peripheral interest, and it is not at all clear that, in general, traditionalists have a greater awareness of historical and philosophical issues than behavioural scientists. Thus certain of Bull's later propositions raise questions for the classical approach—questions which he did not pursue. It is now time to turn our attention to that approach.

II

It is frequently supposed that the 'classical approach' is to be identified with the characteristic British approach to the study of international relations, and the latter is taken to mean the historical approach in its 'idiographic' sense, that is, the view which denies the possibility of general theoretical propositions, which insists that 'international relations are understandable only through a detailed study of the history, values and institutions of each state.'[66] Bull, however, explicitly rejects this view. While, as we have seen, he regards the study of international history and of individual states as essential, and indeed sees historical understanding as 'more central' in the

---

[66] Roger Tooze, 'International Political Economy', in Steve Smith, ed., *International Relations: British and American Perspectives* (Oxford, 1985), 111.

study of international relations than in other branches of politics, he insists on the equal—or even greater—importance of theoretical enquiries.[67] It is true that there is a strong tradition in British political science of scepticism towards theory and commitment to the idiographic approach; Bull is at odds with this tradition.

A second, usually unstated, misconception is that the classical approach refers to the subject as a whole. But Bull's discussion in 'International Relations as an Academic Pursuit' shows that it refers to theory—as the title of the relevant article also indicates—not to the whole of the subject. He expresses a great deal of respect for in-depth country studies and the 'intellectual structure of hypothesis and argument' which is characteristic of historical narrative: these have their intellectual autonomy within international relations. Indeed, along with classical theory, these might be regarded as essential components of the subject as a whole, as seen by practitioners of a 'traditional' approach. But he does not discuss the methodology of historical or institutional research. His methodological discussion is limited to theory, the 'body of general propositions' about international and world politics.

Even more than his comments on the subject as a whole, Bull's account of the classical approach to theory is a sketch, not a full portrait—an outline, not a detailed discussion. Stanley Hoffmann rightly comments on the unity of method and substance in Bull's work, but it is evident that his primary concern is with questions of substance. For Bull, it is important to think through the problems of methodology, to arrive at a coherent position and to address the main challenges to it. He does not, however, pursue the detailed issues of methodological controversy very far: there is not the fascination with methodological principles of a Weber, a Myrdal, or some of the behaviouralists. He is more interested in putting his methodology to work on large questions such as the bases of international order and the relevance of the experience of the European states system to the contemporary world.

Moreover, the concept of the classical approach to theory is coloured to some extent by the polemical context in which it is put forward. Some of his comments on E. H. Carr's great

---

[67] 'International Relations as an Academic Pursuit', pp. 256–7.

polemic—its 'artificial dichotomies' and 'breathtaking equations'—might be turned against his own discussion, but it might also be added that these 'characteristic defects of a polemical work . . . do not detract from the main points that he has to make'.[68] The 'classical approach', like the 'scientific approach', is essentially an ideal type, a construct which groups together many variants of theory. Particular theorists are always reluctant to accept that their work can be characterized in terms of such constructs, yet they serve to mark broad distinctions in theoretical styles. For some purposes, as David Singer comments in a different context, one is interested in fruit, not the special characteristics of oranges, apples, and so on—in the *genus*, not the *species*.[69] For example, there are many, partially conflicting definitions of 'behaviouralism', accenting different characteristics and inadvertently excluding some theorists, yet for some purposes it is convenient to proceed on the basis of one or other definition. The test of such a construct is not that every individual case can be made to fit, but that it identifies major intellectual continuities and cleavages in an illuminating way.

At the beginning of his discussion of the classical approach, Bull indicates that what he means by this is something much wider than the study and criticism of the classics of the subject: this is just one of the methods included under the classical approach, one that is particularly fruitful.[70] The classical approach to theorizing is derived from philosophy, history, and law—from three long-established disciplines, each with its well-defined methods of reasoning and evaluating evidence. Any of these methods are thus available to students of international relations, according to the nature of their enquiry. This does not mean that these are the only appropriate disciplines: for example, he expresses admiration for Aron's capacity to draw on a wide range of social science disciplines as well, working them into his own 'integrated argument'.[71] There is no disciplinary exclusiveness about the classical approach, no attempt to erect artificial boundaries around the subject.

The central feature of the classical approach is its 'explicit reliance on the exercise of judgment': general propositions

[68] '*The Twenty Years' Crisis* Thirty Years On', pp. 627–8.
[69] Singer, 'The Incompleat Theorist', p. 77.
[70] 'International Theory: The Case for a Classical Approach', p. 20.
[71] Review of *Peace and War*, p. 371.

about international relations 'must derive from a scientifically imperfect process of perception or intuition' and can have only a 'tentative and inconclusive status'.[72] A problem may be discerned in this formulation. One of Bull's critics, Roderick Ogley, has no difficulty in finding frequent, and by no means atypical, examples of dogmatic utterances by leading classical authors, far removed from tentativeness or inconclusiveness.[73] Furthermore, the aim of some of the classical political philosophers was to establish secure foundations for their views. Bull's account of the classical approach is plausible only if we take him to be referring to *our* view of earlier philosophical speculation, not the view of the philosophers themselves. As a statement of the contemporary view of the methodology of the classical tradition, contrasted with the methodological claims of behavioural science, his definition may stand.

His principal argument in favour of the classical approach takes the form of rejecting the alternatives, pure deduction and strict verification. Deductive reasoning from axioms or from formal models tells us nothing until their correspondence with the real world can be established, but this requires a process of interpretation or judgement which is necessarily open to question and is not itself verifiable by strict operational procedures. The kinds of generalization which can be established by these procedures—answers to questionnaires, trade statistics, or data on communication flows, for example—cannot in themselves establish propositions about public opinion, dependency, integration, and the like.[74] An intermediate process of reasoning, involving judgement, is again required.

The exercise of judgement is not arbitrary, and does not depend on appeals to intuition or authority, but is 'verified or falsified by examination of the world'.[75] This is not, however, to be understood as the observation of simple, unambiguous items of evidence, or 'data'. The best guides to understanding 'the workings of the human mind in international politics' are 'historical imagination, the insights of philosophy or introspective

---

[72] 'International Theory: The Case for a Classical Approach', p. 20. A contemporary reader might question his assumptions concerning natural science, but this issue need not be pursued in the present context.

[73] Roderick C. Ogley, 'International Relations: Poetry, Prescription or Science?', *Millennium*, 10 (1981), 177.

[74] 'International Relations as an Academic Pursuit', p. 259.

[75] 'New Directions in the Theory of International Relations', p. 279.

psychology, or even some works of fiction'.[76] The concept of judgement, then, is taken to include the interpretation of the particular case in terms of the kind of theory deemed appropriate to it. This might suggest that Bull is close to Weber's concept of *Verstehen* and, more generally, the hermeneutic tradition of social thought. However, while there are obvious affinities, in so far as this tradition emphasizes the unique case—the individual person, society, or culture—this is at odds with Bull's primary concern, the procedures by which general propositions about international relations may be established.

Bull's 'classical approach' faces in two directions. The first of these, in accordance with the hermeneutic tradition, insists that judgements are grounded in the observation of complex situations, not on homogenous 'data' abstracted from them. These observations, our understanding of complex situations, derive from historical narratives, and 'putting together the conclusions' from different narratives is again no simple matter, but requires 'uncovering the intellectual structure of each and marrying it with that of the other'.[77]

Whereas the hermeneutic tradition is oriented essentially towards linguistics, history, and the interpretation of texts, the classical approach is oriented equally, or even more, towards philosophy. This is true not only of Bull's own theoretical contribution, but of his assumptions concerning the approach more generally—the need for the criticism of premises, the need to search for fundamental principles or foundations, however tentative their ultimate status. This is articulated most clearly in relation to ethical theory, discussed below, but is of general import. The making of judgements is, first and foremost, the framing of general propositions, and the starting-point for these is to be found in everyday assumptions as well as in the hypotheses in the existing theoretical literature.

Among contemporary scholars it was Arnold Wolfers who came closest to Bull in his characterization of theory. He, too, was especially interested in the theoretical assumptions which underlie the views of statesmen and citizens.

The choice is not between theory and no theory, but between relatively

---

[76] 'New Directions in the Theory of International Relations', p. 279.
[77] 'International Relations as an Academic Pursuit', p. 257.

informed, sophisticated and objective theoretical propositions carefully formulated in the course of disciplined and dispassionate professional analysis, and crude hit-and-miss 'theories' against which the statesman . . . may not be able to immunise himself.[78]

He was equally convinced of the continuity between the methods of classical political thought and contemporary social science, and of the dangers of too purist a view of the latter:

Yet before turning away contemptuously from the inadequate work of his predecessors, the social scientist of today . . . should ask himself how much better he is able to validate the hunches on which he is forced to base himself. He would have to remain within a narrow circle of rather marginal problems if he excluded all but scientifically unimpeachable investigations, particularly of the controlled experiment or quantitative kind . . . Like the political philosophers before him, then, he would find himself mustering all the evidence that history, personal experience, introspection, common sense, and the gift of logical reasoning, put at his disposal.[79]

Wolfers goes on to consider in what ways the contemporary political scientist might be expected to improve on the work of his predecessors, and his reply singles out not technical advances, the greater precision and reliability of his findings, but broader intellectual values expressing the ideals of the liberal scholarly tradition: 'a keener recognition of the controversial nature of his reply, a greater effort to consider alternative answers, and a more conscious attempt to remain dispassionate and objective'.[80]

This could serve as a summation of certain of the values which permeate Bull's writing, and which underlie his criteria for the evaluation of scholarly work. It is reasonable to regard his conception of the classical approach to theory as consisting not only of methodological principles but also of broader scholarly values and criteria, as does the scientific approach, with its criteria such as precision, reliability, parsimony, explanatory power, and the like.

One important criterion of the classical approach is critical self-awareness. As we have seen, for Bull the 'attempt to remain

[78] Arnold Wolfers, *Discord and Collaboration: Essays on International Politics* (Baltimore, 1962), p. xiv.
[79] Ibid., pp. 236–7.
[80] Ibid., p. 237.

dispassionate and objective', to maintain scholarly integrity, requires sustained conscious effort. In his view, as his seventh proposition on the weaknesses of behaviouralism shows, contemporary social science may be undergoing regression in this respect. There is, he claims: 'an uncritical attitude towards their own assumptions . . . an insensitivity to the conditions of recent history that have produced them, provided them with the presuppositions and perspectives they have, and coloured these in ways of which they might not be aware.'[81] Theorists in this frame of mind take their own objectivity for granted, rather than recognizing the need for continuous questioning and self-criticism in order to come closer to it. All this is reminiscent of the 'innocence' which Bull detected in the first generation of international relations academics. While he is suggesting that such innocence and intellectual conformism are characteristic of the behaviouralists, the same question may be raised concerning scholars attracted to the classical approach—perhaps not the major theorists, but the many who follow in their footsteps without engaging in theoretical enquiry of their own.

The classical theorist, then, should assimilate the perspective of the sociology of knowledge. Awareness of the way in which social and historical forces condition our thinking is the beginning of theoretical sophistication, but the end of innocence does not in itself create any theory: it is merely a precondition for a self-critical approach to theorizing. The weakness which he discerns in *The Twenty Years' Crisis*, for example, was that, in important respects, Carr stopped short at exposing the ideological character of the ruling ideas of the time. His moral relativism prevented him from taking the next crucial step, actually formulating a theory (in this case an ethical theory) in its own right.[82]

A second general criterion for classical theory is the need for rigour and precision, which he concedes has often been lacking: there has been a failure 'to define terms, to observe logical canons of procedure, or to make assumptions explicit'. In all these and related ways—he refers to a 'residual providentialism' in some classical authors—theory should be 'consistent with the philosophical foundations of modern science'.[83] He acknow-

---

[81] 'International Theory: The Case for a Classical Approach', p. 37.
[82] '*The Twenty Years' Crisis* Thirty Years On', pp. 628–30.
[83] 'International Theory: The Case for a Classical Approach', p. 36.

ledges that the behaviouralist movement has introduced new standards of conceptual clarity into the subject. It may be added, however, that it is not the only source of the demand for greater conceptual clarity. Linguistic philosophy influenced the intellectual climate in the same direction, especially in Britain, and the study of the history of ideas also enhanced the awareness of conceptual nuances. It is noteworthy that major analyses of the ambiguities and multiple meanings of 'balance of power' appeared quite independently from an American social scientist, Ernst Haas, and an English historian of ideas (if such a disciplinary tag may be attached to Martin Wight).[84] The need for more rigorous and systematic theoretical discussion is a recurring theme in Bull's reviews of works which make some claim to be presenting theory in the classical style.

In the light of his view that theoretical assumptions underlie all study, indeed all discourse on international relations, it is not surprising that many of his criteria are common to studies of all kinds, whether explicitly theoretical or not. This is true of the criteria discussed earlier—the importance of addressing large issues, of penetrating beneath surface appearances, above all, perhaps, the need to relate new work to the foundations laid by earlier scholars. In relation to F. H. Hinsley's *Nationalism and the International System*, for example, he complains of an 'oracular' tendency and an apparent lack of awareness of other work on the same issues.[85] It is suggested below that theory in the classical tradition, free from the 'scientific' aspiration to build knowledge cumulatively, may be especially prone to this particular weakness.

There are also certain criteria peculiar to works of theory, or at least especially relevant to them. One of these is expressed in a comment on Schelling's 'philosophical skill in thinking out problems in terms of their basic elements',[86] an idea which is amplified in Wolfers's comments on the prospect of moving beyond the 'fire and water' stage of the discipline by becoming more aware of the 'simple elements and forms' that abound in

[84] Ernst Haas, 'The Balance of Power: Prescription, Concept or Propaganda?', *World Politics*, 5 (1953), 442–77; Martin Wight, 'The Balance of Power', in Herbert Butterfield and Martin Wight, eds., *Diplomatic Investigations: Essays in the Theory of International Politics* (London, 1966), 149–75.
[85] Review of Hinsley, *Nationalism and the International System*, in *American Political Science Review*, 69 (1975), 374.
[86] 'International Theory: The Case for a Classical Approach', p. 29.

human relationships.[87] Bull's recurring references to 'penetrating analyses' and to intellectual depth also point to a criterion especially relevant to theory, which is less easily spelled out but is related to his insistence that enquiries be pressed on beyond conventionally agreed premises, and beyond familiar ideological stopping-points, in search of more 'illuminating' perspectives or more adequately reasoned foundations.

Bull's view, noted earlier, that critical examination of moral issues is essential to the study of international relations, as part of any substantial enquiry, may be regarded as a central assumption of the classical approach. There appears none the less to be some distinction between the way in which he sees ethical discussion entering into international studies in general, and the way he envisages ethical enquiries in their own right. Each of these throws light on his view of how classical theorizing should be undertaken.

While rejecting the notion of value-free social science, he endorses the view that there is a fundamental logical distinction between value judgements and statements of fact[88]—a view which is shared by the linguistic philosophers as well as the behavioural scientists. His position on the role of value judgements in the social sciences may usefully be compared with the well-known position of Gunnar Myrdal, who also endorses the fact/value dichotomy and holds that value judgements have an essential place in all social science. In the interests of objectivity, Myrdal's principal recommendation is that the value premises which underlie any social science enquiry should be made explicit—a task which is more demanding than it sounds, in that it may be the unspoken and unrecognized assumptions which play the greatest part in shaping an enquiry.[89]

Bull goes beyond Myrdal in calling, in addition, for the critical examination of such premises, as a means of achieving as close an approximation to objectivity as the nature of social enquiry permits.[90] This represents a considerable advance. It is

---

[87] Wolfers, *Discord and Collaboration*, pp. xv–xvi.

[88] See e.g. his discussion of the Yale school of international law, 'International Law and International Order', pp. 585–6.

[89] Gunnar Myrdal, *Objectivity in Social Research* (New York, 1969).

[90] 'International Relations as an Academic Pursuit', p. 262.

true that the explicit statement of value premisses exposes them to criticism, whereas silence or the claim to value-neutrality seek to protect them from criticism. An examination of competing ethical claims, however, can offer far more clarification than a mere formulation of premisses. The problem with Myrdal's principle is that, if there is to be more than a mere statement of certain premisses, there is likely to be advocacy: the justification of a certain ethical position, with little or no consideration of alternatives. In *Asian Drama*, for example, Myrdal spells out the 'modernization ideals' which underlie his study, but does not treat other values as offering any serious challenge to them.[91] Bull's principle requires that competing value positions be stated strongly: thus a study's value premisses are clarified by subjecting them to critical comparison, not merely presenting them in a persuasive form.

Bull's principle may be illustrated by reference to *The Control of the Arms Race*. Prior to the detailed strategic analysis which constitutes the greater part of the book, he undertakes a succinct but wide-ranging examination of the ethical premisses of pacifists, nuclear disarmers, and supporters of deterrence.[92] His principal theme is the complexity of the moral choices posed by nuclear weapons: the need to understand the complexity of the strategic situation in order to fully grasp the ethical issues, the partial validity of competing ethical positions, the need to recognize that there is no simple choice of good over evil, and the need to acknowledge uncertainty. Serious ethical disputants are those who have thought through the implications of their position, squarely facing its costs and uncertainties. He has little respect for those, of whatever persuasion, who express dogmatic certainties or believe that the burden of exercising moral judgement can be evaded through a simple assertion of principle or necessity.

In the case of studies whose primary purpose is moral enquiry—'political theory' rather than 'social science'—while Bull never provided a full account of his ethical position, it is possible to discern three consistent themes in his later writings. The central theme is his assertion of ethical pluralism, his perception of antinomies which cannot be resolved through

[91] Myrdal, *Asian Drama: An Inquiry into the Poverty of Nations* (New York, 1968), 49–69, for the 'modernization ideals'; other values are treated as outmoded, pp. 71–125.
[92] *The Control of the Arms Race*, pp. 20–9, 77–91.

rational argument, on the one hand, combined with his rejection of a cynical relativism, his insistence that moral issues are 'susceptible of rational investigation', on the other.[93] There is no generally agreed, compelling foundation for morality in the world as a whole: there may be 'conflict about the most basic moral ends, and when that occurs there is sometimes no rational way of choosing between them'.[94] But this only becomes clear after a process of rational enquiry.

For example, if one takes seriously the competing claims of order and justice at the present time, he finds no good reason to side with those conservatives who would assign a general priority to order, nor with those revolutionaries who would do the reverse. While supporting the 'liberal' preference for seeking to reconcile the competing claims, he is clear that this is not always possible. 'There is a deeper wisdom in the recognition, common to the conservatives and the revolutionaries, that terrible choices have sometimes to be made.'[95] Which choice one who is committed to both values should make, however, will depend not only on weighing the competing values but on one's assessment of the particular situation: to what extent is justice embodied in the existing world order, and is that order robust enough to stand the shock of violence in the interests of greater justice? Even if one holds that in some sense order is prior, since it is the prerequisite for realizing all other values, 'it does not follow that order is to be preferred to justice in any given case'.[96] Moral reasoning cannot resolve the choice, but it can clarify it.

A second theme, expressed in his discussion of Walzer's *Just and Unjust Wars*, is the need to seek to establish the foundations of one's ethical position. Despite a highly positive evaluation of Walzer's argument within its chosen limits, he sees these limits—the absence of any attempt to formulate the philosophical and ethical foundation of his position—as seriously diminishing the value of the argument, in that it addresses only those who share the author's liberal individualism.[97] Walzer does not, at the level of philosophical analysis, address the range

---

[93] Bull, 'Natural Law and International Relations', *British Journal of International Studies*, 5 (1979), 180–1.
[94] Ibid., p. 181.
[95] Bull, *Justice in International Relations*, the 1983–4 Hagey Lectures (University of Waterloo, 1984), 18.
[96] *The Anarchical Society*, p. 97.
[97] 'Recapturing the Just War for Political Theory', pp. 596–9.

of different positions which Bull himself, at the level of policy analysis, attempts in *The Control of the Arms Race*. The search for foundations will not, of course, resolve all differences, but it will take the argument to a deeper level. Only by seeking out principles more basic than those incorporated in familiar ideologies is there a possibility of establishing common ground with adherents of other doctrines or, alternatively, clarifying the essential differences.

A third theme is Bull's interest in the natural law tradition, which for many centuries provided a widely accepted foundation for political thought. Even though, consistent with his pluralism, he sees no possibility of the achievement of such a universal foundation at the present time, he is attracted by the idea of something analogous to natural law, that ethical discussion might identify *some* universally shared values (such as moral rules protecting life, property, and the sanctity of agreements), and this is related to his interest in the prospects for a global international society.[98]

The most telling critiques are not the polemical responses from within a different 'paradigm', but those which share some common ground with the position under attack. Thus there is little further to be gleaned from the immediate responses to Bull's 1966 article, but more searching questions are raised in two articles published in the UK in 1981, by Roy Jones and by Roderick Ogley.[99] Although the 'English school' discussed by Jones is only one sub-group within the classical genre, it includes the most prominent contemporary British theorists, and the article raises issues relevant to the classical approach as a whole. These issues may be grouped under four headings: (1) neglect of the social sciences; (2) holism versus precision; (3) the influence of personalities; and most importantly, (4) a barrier to intellectual progress.

1. *Neglect of the social sciences.* Jones comments that the style of the English school is easily recognizable 'for what it leaves out:

---

[98] 'Natural Law and International Relations', pp. 171–2, 180.
[99] Roy E. Jones, 'The English School of International Relations: A Case for Closure', *Review of International Studies*, 7 (1981), 1–13; Ogley, 'International Relations', pp. 170–85. The latter article was written shortly after Bull's 1966 article, but not published until 1981.

few statistics, no geometry and less algebra',[100] and Ogley translates Bull's methodological suggestions into a 'Mosaic code':

Thou shalt not make unto thee a graphical image; thou shalt not commit arithmetic . . . thou shalt do no experiment . . . thou shalt not steal the ideas of thy colleague in other social sciences, nor his research techniques, nor apply to international relations anything that is thy colleague's.[101]

It is too easy to respond that this is skilful parody of one particular article, but misrepresents Bull's overall view of the subject, as indeed it does. Bull does not exclude the social sciences from the subject, and indeed he sees its development as pervasively influenced by the overall state of the social sciences. However, even while paying the highest tribute to some of the 'scientific' researchers, such as Kaplan and Schelling, he insists that they succeed despite rather than because of their novel methods, and that what is of greatest value in their work depends on their tacit use of the classical approach.[102] There is no encouragement here to experiment with new methods, and indeed there is little room for doubt that, where the general intellectual culture is antipathetic to the introduction of new techniques into political studies, as in the UK and Australia, the impact of Bull's methodological writing was to discourage the use of the typical methods of social science research—surveys, statistical analysis, the use of simple graphs and models—and, more importantly, the kinds of enquiry which require such methods. Explicitly, Bull's critique was directed only against the behaviouralist methodological creed, not against the everyday methods of the social sciences: in practice, its repercussions extended to these as well.

2. *Holism versus precision.* Jones sees 'holism' as a fundamental tenet of the English school, that is, the study of the international system, society, community, or cosmos as a whole, at the expense of more specific topics.[103] He overstates his case in claiming that his authors confine themselves to this level: this is manifestly not true of two of the authors in question, Bull

---

[100] Jones, 'The English School', p. 1.
[101] Ogley, 'International Relations', p. 176.
[102] 'International Theory: The Case for a Classical Approach', pp. 28–9.
[103] Jones, 'The English School', pp. 2–4, 6–8.

himself and F. S. Northedge. But it is true that the main English theorists have written extensively on the society of states, and Jones's contention is that this leads to metaphysics, in the case of an author such as Charles Manning, or else to vagueness, whereas precise analysis requires the methods of the sciences:

[Science] splits things up. It does not flounder about in the cosmos. It makes a careful study of minute things as well as of immense things, and it relates the two ... In contrast, the English school ... deals exclusively in big things ... The essence of scientific method is the formulation of precise questions to which exact and falsifiable answers are possible. The question 'what is the nature of the society of sovereign states?' is not scientific. It is essentially a rhetorical metaphysical declaration.[104]

Thus, contrary to Bull, Jones contends that rigour and precision cannot be achieved within the classical approach. This is an issue which is best examined in relation to particular cases, and discussion is therefore postponed until the next section, which seeks to show in what ways Bull achieved rigour and precision in his own work. But to argue that this is possible within the classical approach does not establish that it is characteristic of it. The standards of precision in the sciences are well understood and are normally observed; there is no such agreement on standards of precision relating to classical theory, and Bull's book reviews show that, in his judgement, they are frequently not observed. At this stage in the discussion it has to be conceded that Jones has placed a question mark against Bull's claim concerning the rigour and precision of the classical approach.

3. *The influence of personalities.* His attention focused on Manning and Wight, Jones is concerned over the lack of specific methods of research which might be applied independently by others. The holistic view of the subject is, as it were, complemented by a holistic method.

On the basis of his writing I am at loss to see how a student of international relations could practise Manning's method without sacrificing his personality to Manning's. ... How could an undergraduate student of international relations deploy Wight's historical learning?[105]

[104] Ibid., p. 8.
[105] Ibid., p. 9.

Once again, the case is overstated: of the many scholars who have been stimulated by Manning or Wight, none has taken over their methods *in toto*. Once again, however, an important issue has been raised. Whereas in the case of social scientists there is usually no difficulty in distinguishing the scholar's view of the subject as a whole, and its methods, from his own specific contribution, this distinction is not so evident in the case of some classical theorists. This chapter attempts to portray the distinction in the case of Bull, but it is not clear that the work of Manning or Wight would so readily yield to such an analysis. To the extent that leading scholars in the classical tradition each develop a unique approach to the subject, integrally bound up with their own work, the discipline will indeed be highly influenced by personalities, and communication between different schools within it will be limited.

4. *A barrier to intellectual progress?* To the extent that these criticisms have force, to the extent that the classical approach leads to imprecision, the neglect of the social sciences, and the fragmentation of the subject into separate intellectual worlds, it will indeed represent an obstacle to intellectual progress. In Jones's view, 'repetition has set in and is likely to get worse as the years pass . . . pupils caught up in this sterile regime move inevitably from scholarship to scholasticism', their isolation from external stimulus becoming progressively more complete.[106] Or, to adopt a different terminology, the classical research programme is degenerating.

It is argued in the next section that Bull's work is not open to such strictures: he seeks to build on the foundations laid by others, he addresses a wide range of opposing views, and his work opens up new issues of substance. Does this imply that Bull is as much social scientist as classicist? His work *could* be viewed as part of a potential 'progressive research programme'. However, it has to be acknowledged that for the most part it has not been viewed in this light. The reason may be that, when the general intellectual culture is dominated by the classical approach, the tendencies which Ogley and Jones have identified have a strong hold. Certain of Bull's methodological principles may be observed more in the social science culture of the United States than in the classical culture of Britain. This is

---

[106] Jones, 'The English School', pp. 1, 12.

especially true of the principle of taking one's starting-point from the classics (or their contemporary equivalent), the standard works which can provide a widely understood foundation for the study of particular topics, rather than embarking on each topic afresh, with no recognition of what has gone before.

Two examples of the contrasting *modus operandi* of the American and British schools may serve to illustrate the point. The first concerns the critical discussion of Bull's *The Anarchical Society* and Waltz's *Theory of International Relations*, works of comparable scope and level of abstraction. Each has been subject to polemical critique, Bull's work as part of Jones's target, 'the English school', Waltz as the principal target of Richard Ashley's critique of 'neo-realism'.[107] The striking contrast, however, is the way in which Waltz's work has become the focal point of theoretical debates on 'neo-realism' (or 'structural realism'). It has provided the frame of reference for other theories, or has been widely construed as such—theories which take greater account of change than his, or theories at a lower level of generality and abstraction, such as theories of international regimes or of decision-making.[108] In the British context either *The Anarchical Society* or Wight's *Systems of States* would lend themselves to such theoretical development, yet nothing of the kind has taken place. A work such as *The Community of States*, whose title suggests that it might contribute to this kind of development, includes discussions from a variety of perspectives, addressed to a common issue, but with no common theoretical focus or point of reference.[109]

A recent work by Robert McKinlay and Richard Little, *Global Problems and World Order*, constitutes only a partial exception.[110] Its central thesis is that the main approaches to international order—liberal, socialist, and realist—are an expression of incompatible ideologies which define incompatible sets of

---

[107] Ashley, 'The Poverty of Neorealism'.

[108] Keohane, 'Theory of World Politics', pp. 503–49; Robert Gilpin, *War and Change in World Politics* (Cambridge, 1981); Stephen D. Krasner, ed., *International Regimes*, special issue, *International Organization*, 36 (1982). Some of the main contributions to this debate, including a response by Waltz, have been brought together in Robert O. Keohane, ed., *Neorealism and its Critics* (New York, 1986).

[109] James Mayall, ed., *The Community of States: A Study in International Political Theory* (London, 1982). For a highly critical review by Bull, see *Millennium*, 12 (1983), 276–8.

[110] R. D. McKinlay and R. Little, *Global Problems and World Order* (London, 1986).

problems and solutions. Although this is a substantial work, it is essentially at the level of the sociology of knowledge, not a theoretical analysis in its own right.

A second example is provided by normative writing on North-South relations. In the United States since the late 1970s the debate has been structured either by reference to different ideologies or to major statements of extreme positions by Charles Beitz and by Robert Tucker.[111] British scholars have contributed essays offering a wide range of philosophical, historical, and practical insights, but with virtually no reference to the American theoretical debates and with no alternative theoretical focus.[112]

The critique serves to emphasize that the classical approach is not only an ideal type in the descriptive sense, but also a scholarly ideal in the normative sense, its values widely acknowledged but only partially observed, the negative features of the wider intellectual culture of which it is part being insufficiently recognized. It remains to examine Bull's work as an example of this ideal, to establish how far he was able to avoid the pitfalls and, more importantly, how his work can illustrate the potential of the classical approach.

III

The classical approach offers many options. Bull does not, for example, engage in historical research or the kind of in-depth study of political culture and national style which Stanley Hoffmann has undertaken in his interpretation of American foreign policy. His approach may be described as philosophical, but in order to understand in what sense it is so, it is necessary to take account of Bull's conception of philosophy. After examining this, and outlining his method of analysis in general terms, this section will illustrate it in more detail by considering

[111] Charles R. Beitz, *Political Theory and International Relations* (Princeton, 1979); Robert W. Tucker, *The Inequality of Nations* (New York, 1977). For an intermediate position, see Stanley Hoffmann, *Duties beyond Borders: On the Limits and Possibilities of Ethical International Politics* (Syracuse, NY, 1981), 141–87. For the ideological approach, see Richard W. Cox, 'Ideologies and the New International Economic Order: Reflections on Some Recent Literature', *International Organization*, 33 (1979), 257–302.

[112] See e.g. James Mayall, 'The Liberal Economy', in Mayall, ed., *The Community of States*, pp. 96–111; Moorhead Wright, ed., *Rights and Obligations in North–South Relations: Ethical Dimensions of Global Problems* (London, 1986).

his approach and methods in *The Anarchical Society*. The chapter will conclude by noting some of the major questions which Bull's work leaves open: some of these he raises himself, others arise from an examination of issues which he did not pursue.

As was noted in Chapter 1, Bull acknowledged that his 'greatest intellectual debt' was to John Anderson, Professor of Philosophy in the University of Sydney from 1927 to 1958. It is impossible to characterize this debt at all precisely, but other accounts of Anderson and his influence provide some indications.

In a passage which captures the essential Andersonian values, Eugene Kamenka writes of the 'recurrent weekly drama' in the Philosophy Room:

It was one in which Socrates faced his accusers and died for his beliefs; one in which superstition, self-interest and sentimentalism were exposed; one in which thought triumphed over all; one in which even the young and partly educated could find—in criticism, in logic and argument—the intellectual force and confidence to rout philistinism, obscurantism, censorship and taboos, and to expose the shallow, the fashionable and the unreflective. In that room, Anderson's students became heirs to, and participants in, a universal culture that knew no boundaries of nation, race or creed . . .[113]

In his commitment to the Socratic pursuit of the argument irrespective of where it might lead, his sharp eye for illusion and rationalization, his suspicion of orthodoxies, and his scorn for superficiality, Bull remained quintessentially Andersonian. From Anderson he also derived a sense of philosophy as a living tradition, and a presumption that the best statement on any question of enduring interest is more likely to be found in one of the classics than in contemporary theory. It is tempting to compare his high evaluation of the classical international lawyers, writing before international relations became an established subject, with Anderson's admiration for the pre-Socratic philosophers.

Bull had the strength of personality and quickness of mind to set aside some of the characteristic Andersonian doctrines and stances. He did not, for example, share the alienation from society of the 1950s Libertarians, yet the intense experience of

---

[113] Eugene Kamenka, 'John Anderson', in Leonie Kramer *et al.*, *The Greats: The 50 Men and Women who Most Helped to Shape Modern Australia* (Sydney, 1986), 226.

philosophical discussion within that milieu must have strength-ened his capacity to stand back from the immediate preoccu-pations of those around him, and thus to achieve a certain detachment from prevailing values.[114] His intellectual style shows the influence of Anderson's philosophical realism and formal logic. Anderson has been credited with the most thoroughgoing, uncompromising statement of the 'New Realism' of the early decades of the century, which may be described as a commonsense theory of reality and knowledge (there *is* a real world of familiar objects; propositions state—or mis-state—what *is* the case), but one which is buttressed by a formidable array of arguments against competing philosophical views.[115] Bull also appears to have derived from—or shared with—Anderson 'an unusually powerful combination of two normally separate abilities—on the one hand the capacity for precision, the ability to analyse and to make distinctions and on the other hand imagination, creativity and a strong sense of connection, of systematic interrelation'.[116]

Finally, Bull was undoubtedly influenced by Anderson's conception of philosophy, as by no means a separate, technical subject but as the critical examination of foundations—the foundations of cultural values and of academic subjects, *any* subject. To quote Kamenka once more:

Philosophy, as John Passmore has stressed, elevates and concentrates upon argument in the same way science elevates and concentrates upon experiment as the only court of appeal. Philosophy is *not* the teaching of conclusions. It is the consideration and testing of the process by which conclusions are arrived at and the working out of their implications with a view to testing them further. Everything that is done in intellectual life and in practical life has a philosophical dimension and is subject to philosophical criticism.[117]

This is not the philosophy of the traditional metaphysical

---

[114] For the social views of Anderson and the 'Andersonians', see A. J. Baker, *Anderson's Social Philosophy* (Sydney, 1979); John Docker, *Australian Cultural Elites: Intellectual Traditions in Sydney and Melbourne* (Sydney, 1974), 131–55.

[115] For a recent analysis, see A. J. Baker, *Australian Realism: The Systematic Philosophy of John Anderson* (Cambridge, 1986). Anderson's main papers are included in John Anderson, *Studies in Empirical Philosophy* (Sydney, 1962); J. A. Passmore's Introductory Essay provides an overview.

[116] Kamenka, 'John Anderson', p. 224.

[117] Kamenka, 'John Anderson, Philosophy and Criticism in Australia', (seminar paper, History of Ideas Unit, Austalian National University, 1986), 1.

system, though Anderson is closer to this than to Oxford linguistic philosophy. In some respects it is closer to the twentieth-century understanding of the philosophy of science, though within a wider frame of reference: for Anderson there was no dichotomy between science and the humanities. The emphasis on criticism and the exposure of illusion suggests points of contact with 'critical theory', but there is nothing of its emancipatory utopianism in Anderson or in Bull, whose rejection of illusory 'solutions' is squarely in the Andersonian tradition. On the other hand, Bull's conception of ethics, in particular his views on moral judgements and moral reasoning, is quite different from Anderson's, even though it is quite consistent with Anderson's social pluralism. Bull was no disciple, but the strength and originality of his contribution to international relations owed much to Anderson.

Within international relations itself the most evident influence was that of Martin Wight, as Bull also warmly acknowledged. Wight showed him that it was possible to discern a long history of enquiry and speculation about international relations, to some extent reflecting the better-known history of political thought. Despite his well-known disparagement of these writings in 'Why is there No International Theory?', he postulated that three continuing traditions of thought could be identified, the Hobbesian, Grotian, and Kantian, and this provided the framework for Bull's view of the subject. Bull makes clear that it was no more than a framework, that there were many important questions which could not be 'related significantly' to the three traditions,[118] and his approach to the framework itself is essentially philosophical, in contrast to Wight's historical approach; that is to say, he is concerned to examine the logical implications and general plausibility of the central propositions advanced within each tradition rather than to carry further the task of their historical reconstruction, or indeed to enquire into the historical validity of Wight's basic hypothesis that the three approaches capture the essentials of earlier thought.

Bull's extensive publications may be grouped under five headings, three of which represent the 'large questions' which

---

[118] 'Martin Wight and the Theory of International Relations', p. 111. The above is Bull's terminology for the three traditions.

provided the focus for most of his work, and which are treated in separate chapters of this volume.

1. Questions relating to arms control and the dilemmas of security in the nuclear age predominate in his work in the 1960s and continue throughout.
2. His major theoretical writings on international society and international order begin with his sketch for *The Anarchical Society* included in *Diplomatic Investigations* in 1966, and culminate in the publication of that work itself in 1977.
3. During this same period he published the four papers on international relations theory and on the subject as a whole, which have been discussed extensively above.
4. From the mid-1970s three issues, closely interrelated in his thought, provide the focus of his later work: justice, the relations between the West and the Third World, and (his particular perspective on this) the expansion of international society.
5. In addition, from the time of his return to Australia in the late 1960s there are discussions of current policy issues, initially in Australian foreign policy, later for the West as a whole or (occasionally) the United States in particular. These, characteristically, place the current issues within a wide frame of reference and draw on his thinking within the three core areas.

In examining these questions Bull developed an approach, derived mainly from philosophy, which was appropriate to his chosen subject-matter—there is no suggestion that it be followed in all classical theorizing and analysis. He describes *The Anarchical Society* as an attempt to 'think through' a large and complex topic, and this could be said of each of his central themes.[119] The first step in preserving the outcome of this thought process is the formulation of a number of central questions, intended to clarify the issues and to open them up for discussion. The second step is the definition of concepts and drawing of distinctions, to the extent required by the degree of imprecision in existing discussions of the topic. The third is the systematic examination of the principal considerations bearing on the topic, thus defined and clarified. The choice of these considerations takes into account the contentions of others with

---

[119] *The Anarchical Society*, p. x.

a 'serious' view of the topic, but is not limited to these: he may introduce other, neglected considerations which he deems more weighty than those prominent in the existing discussion.

The rigour and precision which he seeks to strengthen in the classical approach is most evident in the second of these stages, definitions and distinctions, but also needs to be followed through in the third stage. It is here that the criterion of systematic analysis is uppermost, and it is also noteworthy that in this stage, in contrast to his mentors Anderson and Wight, Bull seeks to address the full range of views held by others. His work is located squarely within the existing scholarly debate, not developed in splendid isolation. Needless to say, the method as summarized here is something of an ideal type: in the case of some of his writings, especially his later work on arms control, there is greater emphasis on specialist detail, and less of the grand overview. For this, one must return to his early work.

In what sense can this method be described as philosophical? In its emphasis on the general premises underlying particular views, the critical examination of these premises, and the systematic discussion of the more general aspects of a topic, placing it in a broad intellectual context, the method is in accordance with the conception of philosophy which Bull derived from Anderson. It is true that for at least one of his critics, E. B. F. Midgley, Bull is not philosophical enough. Midgley refers to his 'semi-philosophical' thinking, conditioned by an 'Anglo-Saxon ideology', and urges him to go more deeply into the foundations of philosophy and natural law.[120] He is, in a sense, turning Bull's critique of Walzer against himself. However, even though it is true that Bull does not offer a general account of his philosophical and ethical foundations, his method may none the less be regarded as philosophical in the sense that it is derived from this discipline, and may be contrasted with the historical approach of a Wight, on the one hand, and the social-scientific approach of most American international relations scholars, on the other.

The same methods are to be found, interwoven in a more complex pattern, in Bull's major theoretical study, *The Anarchical*

---

[120] E. B. F. Midgley, 'Natural Law and the "Anglo-Saxons": Some Reflections in response to Hedley Bull', *British Journal of International Studies*, 5 (1979), 260–72.

Society. This addresses what he had earlier defined as 'the pre-eminent problem of international relations', namely, 'that of identifying and strengthening the foundations of international order'.[121] He pursues the enquiry at the level of the international system as a whole, in terms of its continuing, enduring features, not the global issues of the immediate present. The work offers essentially a critical evaluation and systematization of existing theoretical ideas; not a completely new perspective, but the kind of systematization which is itself original and advances theoretical understanding.

The problem is broken down into three central questions, each of which in turn opens up a wide range of issues. The first is simply, 'what is order in world politics?'[122] Under this heading he introduces his concept of order (discussed in chapter 3), and explains his concept of international society: an international system in which there is a consciousness of common interests and values, and an acceptance of certain rules and institutions. He argues that in the modern states-system the element of society has always been present in some degree, and goes on to discuss order and justice as basic values in international society, values which can sometimes be combined but, as we have seen, sometimes pose 'terrible choices'.

In answering his second question, 'how is order maintained within the present system of sovereign states?', he does not consider contemporary organizations such as the United Nations, but 'institutions of international society that arose before these international organizations were established, and that would continue to operate ... even if these organisations did not exist'.[123] He identifies five such institutions of the modern (post-seventeenth-century) states system: the balance of power, international law, diplomacy, war, and the role played by the great powers. In each case he discusses the institution itself, how it contributed to international order in the past, changes affecting it in the contemporary world, and whether (and how) it still contributes to international order.

The third question, 'does the system of sovereign states still provide a viable path to world order?', leads him to canvass the major contemporary criticisms of the system and the alternatives

---

[121] *'The Twenty Years' Crisis* Thirty Years On', p. 637.
[122] For the three questions, see *The Anarchical Society*, p. xi.
[123] Ibid., p. xiv.

which have been projected by a number of schools of thought. Some of the critics argue that the system is disastrously incapable of coping with urgent global problems, others that it is being superseded by new transnational actors or the networks or 'cobwebs' of transnational relations. The alternatives range from radical changes of system—to world government or a 'new medievalism'—to changes within the states system, such as general disarmament, reorganization into regional blocs, a new Concert, or the strengthening of the United Nations. In some cases he questions the values implicit in the projected alternatives, in others their feasibility, or he questions whether they would be likely to achieve their stated goals, but even though his scepticism comes through very strongly, to the point of alienating some readers, he regards his endorsement of the existing states-system, as we have seen, as 'a conclusion in need of continual re-assessment'.[124] This is not a second 'Massacre of Glencoe.'

To investigate these questions requires a variety of methods. In the first part of the book the emphasis is on conceptual and normative analyses: philosophical reasoning predominates, but there are also excursions into the history of ideas (a sketch of the 'Grotian' tradition of thought on international society), and the discusssion of the maintenance of rules in international society draws on anthropology and political sociology. Broad historical judgements are prominent in the discussion of the five basic institutions in the second part, but there is also conceptual clarification, and the discussion of the contemporary role of the institutions necessarily rests on general judgements whose 'tentative and inconclusive status' Bull had acknowledged in his critique of behaviouralism, but which, he had also insisted, are not arbitrary but rest on a scholarly interpretation of evidence. The third part relies on a combination of philosophical critique, the examination of the generalizations and normative premises underlying the various alternatives to the states-system, and judgements concerning cause-and-effect relationships, seeking to ground speculation as firmly as possible on plausible general propositions about international politics.

Bull draws on social-scientific theories at certain points, and it is arguable that there might be further scope for this, but there

---

[124] Ibid., p. 319.

are no specialized techniques in the social sciences which he could have drawn on in lieu of his primary historical and philosophical methods. Among reviewers of *The Anarchical Society*, only one, Richard Rosecrance, maintains the contrary view, claiming that the analysis is vitiated by Bull's failure to distinguish between independent and dependent variables.[125] This remains little more than assertion, however, in that Rosecrance does not attempt to show how complex historical judgements about institutions, still less arguments about alternatives to the states-system, can be reformulated in the way that he advocates. It is in the nature of a work of this kind that its judgements are open to challenge, but this would have to be through more cogent philosophical reasoning or through better-supported historical judgements.

It is not the task of this chapter to examine the validity of Bull's arguments: whether he has indeed succeeded in 'identifying and strengthening the foundations of international order'. But it is necessary to take account of one line of criticism which recurs in a number of reviews of *The Anarchical Society*, which questions the appropriateness of Bull's general approach. Drawing attention to the high level of abstraction of much of the analysis, the concern with centuries-old institutions but not with burning contemporary issues, the disparagement of 'solutions' and the claim that the study of world politics is an intellectual activity, not a practical one, the critics question whether such a work can indeed contribute anything to strengthening the foundations of international order.[126] What these critics overlook, however, is that while Bull disclaims any definitive solutions, he does indeed offer some suggestions for 'preserving and strengthening' the element of international society within the present states-system in the face of what he perceives as adverse trends: these relate mainly to maintaining and extending the precarious consensus about common values, interests, and rules.[127] Moreover, while he does not discuss immediate issues in *The Anarchical Society*, his analysis of the foundations provides

[125] Richard Rosecrance, 'International Theory Revisited', *International Organization*, 35 (1981), 698.

[126] Reviews of *The Anarchical Society* which raise these questions include those by Joe P. Dunn, *Annals of the American Academy of Political and Social Science*, 434 (1977), 199–200; *The Economist*, 262 (19 Mar. 1977), 131–2; and Frederick S. Tipson, *Virginia Journal of International Law*, 17 (1977), 805–11.

[127] *The Anarchical Society*, pp. 315–17, 319.

him with a unique vantage point for doing so in other contexts, where he relates its general views to the particular circumstances of the present.[128]

It has to be acknowledged, however, that Bull's suggestions for strengthening international order are not very substantial in relation to the weight of the analysis which has preceded them. This may be related to other lacunae in *The Anarchical Society*, not only the striking omission of the economic dimension of international society but also the relative lack of attention to questions of causation. In contrast to a work such as F. H. Hinsley's *Power and the Pursuit of Peace*, for example, Bull does not seek to identify the underlying forces which make for order or disorder in different periods of history, and the scope which these leave for the conscious pursuit of order.[129] While from some points of view *The Anarchical Society* may be as definitive as any work on the topic can be, it raises as many questions as it resolves. It is, as Michael Mandelbaum has commented, 'that rarest of books: it is not the last, but the first word on its subject'.[130] It represents a foundation on which others may be encouraged to build or, if not convinced that the foundation itself is sufficiently secure, a demonstration of how foundations may be laid and a challenge to do better.

Bull himself chose to build one kind of structure, which became *The Expansion of International Society*, but he also envisaged the possibility of extending the foundations—a study of justice in world politics might be 'envisaged as a companion volume' to *The Anarchical Society*—or even the need to do so—'a study of order in world politics . . . needs to be complemented by a study of justice.'[131] The Hagey lectures, *Justice in International Relations*, may be regarded as a sketch for such a work. A full-scale work might be expected to examine earlier thought on justice, develop the conceptual distinctions outlined in *The Anarchical Society*, and thus place present concerns more squarely in the context of philosophical discussion. Conceivably

---

[128] See, in particular, 'The Great Irresponsibles? The United States, the Soviet Union and World Order', *International Journal*, 35. 3 (Summer, 1980), 437–47; 'The International Anarchy in the 1980's', *Australian Outlook*, 37. 3 (Dec. 1983), 127–31.

[129] F. H. Hinsley, *Power and the Pursuit of Peace* (Cambridge, 1963).

[130] Michael Mandelbaum, review of *The Anarchical Society*, in *Political Science Quarterly*, 92 (1977), 575.

[131] *The Anarchical Society*, pp. xiii, 319.

such a study might call in question Bull's endorsement of the states-system, which is based on his study of order alone.

A second potential line of development, not suggested by Bull himself but arising from some of the preceding comments, is the discussion of world order at the present time at a level which could bridge the gap between Bull's discussion of fundamentals and the study of immediate policy issues. Such a development would need to take more account of economic issues than Bull does. It is the essential political character of order, so much neglected in contemporary economic studies, which it is most important, and difficult, to study, but none the less the task of 'bridging' studies would be to bring out the interrelationships between the political and the economic.

Might the concept of 'regime' provide the bridge? Regimes have recently been defined by Stephen Krasner, the editor of a substantial volume on the subject, as 'sets of implicit or explicit principles, norms, rules, and decision-making procedures around which actors' expectations converge in a given area of international relations'.[132] However, the concept has been developed in ways very different from Bull's concept of international society, even by those whom Krasner refers to as 'Grotians', and the concept itself has been questioned in ways which have not been sufficiently addressed by its supporters.[133] Theories about regimes have been linked to 'structural realism' but not to international society. The possibility of doing so is worth further examination: the general approach of the regime theorists is closer to behavioural science than to classical theory, but the questions which they study are close to those which Bull investigates in *The Anarchical Society*.

A further topic, suggested more indirectly in Bull's work, is the history of thought on international relations. Wight, not Bull, was the pioneer in this terrain, but through sharpening Wight's hypotheses and through some of his asides Bull draws attention to the paucity of scholarly research on the history of ideas in the subject. Pacifist thought has been studied more than

---

[132] Stephen D. Krasner, 'Structural Causes and Regime Consequences: Regimes as Intervening Variables', in Krasner, ed., *International Regimes*, p. 186.

[133] Susan Strange, '*Cave! hic dragones*: A Critique of Regime Analysis', in Krasner, ed., *International Regimes*, pp. 479–96. Krasner responds to Strange's critique as that of a 'conventional structural realist', thus declining discussion of most of the issues which she raises. The ethical premises of regime theories, in particular, are in need of critical examination.

thought about international relations; there is no full-length study apart from Friedrich Meinecke's history of the doctrine of *raison d'État*, published more than sixty years ago.[134] Histories of international law, beyond the introductory level, are equally lacking. The deepening of the subject which Bull sought will require that its history be recovered and interpreted from more than one perspective, a task which the discipline has scarcely begun to recognize.

Bull is one of the handful of scholars outside the United States who has made a major contribution to the contemporary study of international relations. His work could assist the discipline in its American heartland to achieve that 'triple distance' of which Hoffmann has written—away from its contemporary preoccupations, from the perspective of a super-power, and from the glide into policy science—'back to the steep ascent towards the peaks which the questions raised by traditional political philosophy represent'.[135] To those predisposed to the classical approach, it sets a challenge to identify the next significant questions and a formidable standard to emulate in pursuing them. The best service to his memory is not to endorse his conclusions but to approach his work in the critical, but ultimately constructive, spirit which he brought to the subject.

[134] Friedrich Meinecke, *Machiavellism: The Doctrine of Raison d'État and its Place in Modern History*, trans. Douglas Scott (New York, 1965). For a history of a different strand of international thought see Heinz Gollwitzer, *Geschichte des Weltpolitischen Denkens*, 1, *Vom Zeitalter der Entdeckungen bis zum Beginn des Imperialismus* [*History of World-political Thought*, 1, *From the Age of the Discoveries to the Beginning of Imperialism*] (Göttingen, 1972). A Ph.D. thesis in progress at the Australian National University, Ursula Vollerthun, 'The Idea of International Society', examines the thought of Grotius and his predecessors in the context of the Wight-Bull concept of a 'Grotian tradition'.

[135] Hoffmann, *Duties beyond Borders*, p. 59.

8

Conclusion: Hedley Bull and International Relations

CARSTEN HOLBRAAD

MOST of the authors of this volume have tried to decide where Hedley Bull stood within the study of international relations. Robert Gilpin finds that he was closely identified with political realism, not of the 'vulgar' kind, in which power is seen as an end to be pursued by any means, but of the 'normative' version, according to which the international conduct of states is somewhat restrained by moral, institutional, and legal bonds. All of his writings, Gilpin notes, present a blend of realism and morality. Stanley Hoffmann admits that Bull at first glance seems close to realism, but lists three important differences between Bull's approach and that of the realists. Ultimately his work, Hoffmann finds, is a blend of intelligent social science and humanism. The apparent difference between this assessment and Gilpin's is one of terminology rather than substance. J. D. B. Miller, by analysing and criticizing his ideas from a realist point of view, also brings out the difference between Bull's position and the realist tradition, at the same time, however, acknowledging his inherent realism. R. J. Vincent, using Martin Wight's distinctions and terminology, finds that Bull, despite frequent alignment with the realists and much rarer excursions with the revolutionists, stood four-square in the rationalist tradition. Realism and rationalism, Vincent concludes, were yoked together in his nature. None of the authors is able to classify Bull as a rationalist without acknowledging the presence of at least a streak of realism.

A further common feature of the characterizations of Hedley Bull's ideas about international relations is an emphasis on development and change. Apart from the tendency which some authors note to oscillate between rationalist and realist positions in the treatment of particular topics, all of them see a shift of emphasis over time in Bull's concerns and views. It was a shift from a philosophy strongly influenced by realist doctrines to one increasingly sympathetic to revolutionist concerns. Though the development was an evolution without marked turning-points, it is possible to distinguish three phases. The first, in which the focus was often on the realist element in his thinking, may be seen as covering much of Bull's earlier career in England. The second, in which the essentially rationalist quality of his philosophy became more clear-cut, seems broadly to have coincided with his subsequent period in Australia. The third phase, in which revolutionist tendencies came to complement the more dominant elements of his philosophy, became linked particularly with the later period in England.

To some extent, the realist element in Bull's world view no doubt reflected intellectual influences to which he was exposed in his formative years. According to Bull himself, the strongest influence was that of John Anderson. Just how powerful it was is difficult to say. But the impact of Anderson's mind and example must have been a very considerable factor in developing the sceptical temperament, enquiring spirit, and critical mind which came to characterize Bull's own intellect. Both of the authors who knew the Faculty of Arts at the University of Sydney in the early 1950s, J. L. Richardson and J. D. B. Miller, recognize the effect of Anderson's teaching on Bull's later intellectual style. Whether that teaching, with its strong emphasis on social conflict, also affected the contents of Bull's later views is more doubtful. At any rate, since Anderson himself had no special interest in international politics, any influence he may have had on Bull's thinking must have been more philosophical and general than related specifically to the field of study to which Bull devoted his career.

Within the academic field of international relations, the strongest formative influence apparently came from Martin Wight. In an acknowledgment of his debt, Bull pointed to Wight's lectures on International Theory as having made a particularly strong impression. The distinction between three traditions of thought about international politics presented in those lectures provided a framework for the thinking of Bull— as it did for many other scholars interested in the field. The realist, also called the Machiavellian, tradition focused on conflict between states. The rationalist, or Grotian, tradition centred upon co-operation or intercourse between states. The revolutionist, or Kantian, tradition emphasized the unity or solidarity of mankind. Though Bull noticed a certain ambivalence in Wight's own approach, he saw him as being, in a loose sense, a realist. What Wight had in common with other realist thinkers was above all his pessimism, which was expressed primarily in a lack of faith in progress towards a more peaceful and just international order and in a view of international history in terms of recurrent patterns. The sources of this pessimism, Bull recognized, lay in Wight's religious faith, which was of a particularly orthodox kind. This Christian pessimism was not shared by Bull. Yet elements of the realist position, as presented in Wight's account of earlier thinkers in this tradition and communicated through some of his own convictions, undoubtedly struck a sympathetic cord with Bull.

Students, of course, choose their teachers, in the sense that the intellectual relationship which develops between the parties depends on a degree of correspondence between their minds. The effect of the influence of Anderson and Wight, and of other teachers or senior colleagues of the realist mould whom Bull encountered in his earlier years, must have been to draw out and develop what was already there. The pronounced realist streak in Bull's thought stemmed from an inherent realism, which coloured particularly his earlier contributions to the study of international relations, and which throughout his life checked different inclinations which also found expression in his work. Characteristically, some of the most outstanding manifestations of his realist bent took the negative forms of devastating attacks on the superficiality and innocence of various idealist thinkers, such as the Anglo-Saxon school of the inter-war years, and of scathing rejections of utopian schemes and facile solutions. Prominent among the more positive manifestations of the realist strand were his penetrating analysis of the system of states and his ready acceptance of the element of power and the inevitability of conflict in international politics. His willingness to consider all aspects of an issue and to take account of every obstacle to a proposed course of action may also be seen as a realist characteristic.

The rationalist part, the dominant element in Bull's philosophy of international politics, may also be linked to certain influences in his earlier years. Among his teachers at Oxford in the mid-1950s, H. L. A. Hart may have left the strongest impression, especially through his work on the bases of political order in society. Subsequently, at the London School of Economics, C. A. W. Manning and Martin Wight, both in their different ways preoccupied with the nature and foundations of international society, were the major influences. Wight's work on the common interests, values, and obligations of the society of states, which later led to his paper on 'Western Values in International Relations', was particularly important. But the basic sources of Bull's rationalist philosophy must be found in his own character. Behind the sceptical temperament and critical disposition were a deep moral concern and a cautiously constructive spirit. Though rarely inclined to be optimistic about the motivations and abilities of men, Bull was not without hope for the future of the world.

Again characteristically, the rationalist foundation in Bull's thought is revealed most explicitly in his critique of the realist position. The realist writers, though they demonstrated some of the intellectual weaknesses in their predecessors, the idealists of the inter-war years, presented shortcomings of their own, he pointed out. In rejecting the legalism and narrow moralism of the idealists, they tended to overlook the role of values in international relations. They failed to provide a foundation for rational investigation of moral issues. Bull himself, as Stanley Hoffmann and others point out above, never fully laid out the foundations of his moral position. Nor did he disclose how aware he was of the conditioning influence exercised by his Anglo-Saxon background on his own moral and political thought. What he did make clear was that he considered rational investigation of moral issues an essential part of the study of international politics.

Rationalism, in the sense used here, was implicit in Bull's whole thinking about international relations. Its central core was the idea of a society of states. In the tradition of Wight and others, he defined this as a system of states in which the members are conscious of having a number of common interests and values and are aware of the existence of a variety of rules and institutions. One of the fundamental goals of international society was order. The middle period of his professional life was devoted mainly to exploring the foundations of international order, the identifying and strengthening of which he once described as the pre-eminent problem of international relations. Though at other times he concentrated on different goals of international society, his general concern was always with the societal elements of international relations. Never confining himself within the narrow lanes of the states system or entering fully into the open spaces of the global society of mankind, he belonged essentially to the *via media* in the study of international relations.

The burgeoning revolutionist ideas that distinguished the later phase of Bull's thinking may also be partly ascribed to the influence of a small number of individuals. The subtle and perceptive interpretation of current regional and global affairs from a Third World perspective presented by Sisir Gupta, a colleague at the Australian National University in the late 1960s and early 1970s, left an impression, as did the subsequent contact with Ali Mazrui. The period at the Jawarhalal Nehru University in Delhi in the mid-1970s seems to have been a particularly stimulating experience, helping to give Bull a new perspective on the world.

Among the inner sources of Bull's new ideas was again a keen sense of morality. Indeed, his later writings show an increasing emphasis on ethics. In earlier enquiries into the moral basis of international society he had started by recognizing the absence of a generally accepted foundation for morality in the states system at large and by accepting the existence of conflict about basic moral ends. Now, when he was becoming increasingly concerned with the problems of the Third World and, in particular, the difficulties associated with the geographical expansion of international society, this ethical pluralism became more marked. But he still hoped that through rational enquiry and ethical discussion it might be possible to identify some values which were broadly shared by states, including the new ones. However, in his pursuit of a limited ethical consensus he increasingly went beyond the state-centric framework which in the past had generally provided the context of his moral thought. In discussions of international justice, he broadened the focus in the direction of world politics by sometimes shifting attention from the proclaimed rights of states to the rights of individuals. In a parallel, though less elaborate, pursuit of a degree of cultural consensus, he paid tribute to the emerging conception of the common good of humanity when he stressed the need to develop the more widely shared parts of world culture.

Thus an admixture of revolutionist ideas made Bull's philosophy of international politics richer, and his world view more complex. But the new element did not annihilate his basically state-centric outlook. Ultimately his realist appreciation of the enduring importance of the state checked his cosmopolitan and universalist inclinations.

Bull's philosophy of international relations, marked as it was by continuous development and increasing complexity, informed the entire range of his publications. These have been divided into five groups. The first to be considered here consists of his papers on the theory of international relations and on the subject as a whole. The others, which deal with a wide range of subject-matters, have been grouped under four headings: strategic studies, arms control, and other issues relating to international security; the society of states and international order; the Third World and international justice; and current issues of international politics. Each of the groups that deal with a particular set of subject-matters presents some tension or other between different strands of thought. Yet the author's overriding concern with international society, its foundations and goals, gives unity to all of his work, which is reflected in this book.

Hedley Bull's writings on international relations theory and the subject as a whole, as J. L. Richardson shows in his analysis of this section of his work, display considerable philosophical consistency. If there is a tension here, it is between the author's temperament and style and his intellectual concerns. Particularly his earlier contributions to the methodology of the subject may be open to such criticism. The vehemently polemical form of his famous critique of the behaviouralists, Richardson explains in his discussion of the article of 1966, to a certain extent defeated some of its purposes. If these, as the author once claimed, included convincing the opponents of the scientific movement in international relations theory of the need to engage in rational argument with the behaviouralists, he was less than successful. Little rational debate in fact ensued. Bull's forceful critique in effect encouraged many in Britain and elsewhere to ignore the contributions of the behaviouralists, an outcome which no doubt was detrimental to the study of the subject. In the United States, on the other hand, the behaviouralist school lived on vigorously. Thus the victims of Bull's 'Massacre of Glencoe' may not all have been in the enemy's camp. That some of the issues raised by his article, particularly by those first three of the seven propositions which constitute the heart of the critique, are of lasting relevance makes it all the more regrettable, Richardson thinks, that the onslaught did not lead to a mutually fruitful debate.

Bull's account in this article of the classical, or traditionalist, approach to theory, Richardson goes on to note, is somewhat marred by the polemical context of its appearance. Since the principal argument advanced in its defence consists in a rejection of the alternatives, the case for the approach becomes rather sketchy. Yet its main characteristics, as presented by Bull, stand out clearly. It is derived from three well-established disciplines, namely philosophy, history, and law; and its central feature is an explicit reliance on the exercise of judgement. Given the nature of the process by which they are reached, general propositions about international relations can be only tentative and inconclusive. In principle, the methodology of this approach is thus in contrast with that of behavioural science.

It is when the analysis moves on to Bull's own approach to the subject that one becomes most aware of the unity of method and substance to which Stanley Hoffmann drew attention in his chapter. The approach is essentially philosophical. In the Andersonian tradition, Bull emphasized the need for a critical examination of moral and intellectual foundations. Quick to reject the tendentious or the sanctimonious, he gave equally short shrift to simplistic structures and unrealistic schemes. Scholars engaged in the study of moral issues, he thought, should try to overcome subjectivity and lay out the foundations of their positions. While ultimately leaving to others the task of revealing the foundations and analysing the structure of his own position, he became in his later years, when he grew more interested in ethics, a little more explicit about his commitment in such matters.

Bull's way of starting even a major piece of writing was not usually to engage in the finer points of methodology, but to move directly to matters of substance. Characteristic of his study of international relations is that he asked big questions and tackled central issues. Instead of undertaking massive library research, he typically set out to think through the complex topic that he had chosen. 'Thinking is also research' was a saying adopted by him. The principal stages in this process were listing the central questions, defining the relevant concepts and drawing distinctions, and examining the principal consider-ations. Most of the authors of this volume pay tribute to Bull's ability to make distinctions, a good many of which long since have become standard implements in the study of international relations. Richardson, however, draws attention particularly to Bull's systematic analysis of major considerations bearing on the topic, a process which was distinguished by an attempt to address the full range of the contentions of other scholars—that is, those deemed worthy of serious attention.

The three largest issues tackled by Bull were those of international security, international order, and international justice. Each of them he dealt with in the context of international society, which remained the basic concept. As we shall see, his work on international security, order, and justice reveals a gradual development, and eventually a tentative change, in his notion of international society.

Hedley Bull's work on the theme of international security in an age of nuclear powers deals largely with the field of strategic studies in general and the issues of arms control in particular. Tom Millar's chronological account of the two sets of writings reveals just how pronounced the realist strand is in this part of Bull's work, but also how closely entwined it is with the rationalist main strand. In the papers on strategic studies, the realist, or conflictual, element shows up both in the conception of the subject and in the discussion of the role of civilian strategists. In an article written after his period as head of the Arms Control and Disarmament Research Unit of the British Foreign Office, Bull defined strategic studies as 'the art or science of shaping means so as to promote ends in any field of conflict', and argued that strategic studies should not be coloured by moral considerations, nor strategic enquiry restric-ted by moral taboos. In the writings on arms control, the realist element is equally apparent. In the first article Bull published in this area he presented armaments as an integral part of the whole system of international relations and voiced serious objections to the notions of both the possibility and the desirability of disarmament. His principal work in the field, *The Control of the Arms Race*, is suffused with realist notions. And in a later article, in which he discussed the balance of terror as the chief foundation of international security in the nuclear age, he advocated acceptance of the doctrine of limited war.

However, though approaches and doctrines usually associated with the realist position are a prominent feature, Bull's work on the theme of international security also carries the unmistakable mark of the author's rationalist convictions. The very term 'international security', the security of the society of states as a whole, implies a rationalist commitment, as Stanley Hoffmann suggests when he hints at the difference between his own more Hobbesian and Bull's more Grotian view of international relations. Bull's whole contribution to strategic studies may be seen as an integral part of a wider enquiry into the nature and foundations of international society. His very first article dealing with arms control, as shown by the long passage quoted by Tom Millar, contains in outline the idea of an anarchical society of states, a system without a government but with a set of rules and a number of institutions, which he was to develop in his principal work on international relations. *The Control of the Arms Race*, to the extent that it can be seen as an attempt to apply the classical European doctrine of the balance of power to a world dominated by nuclear powers, deals with what he, like Martin Wight, considered to be one of the principal institutions of international society. In a chapter written twenty years later,[1] he reiterated that the most important objective of arms control was to stabilize the relationship of mutual deterrence between the superpowers. In the same chapter, as well as in certain other writings from his later period, he pointed to those tacit and informal rules which the superpowers seemed to have developed for regulating their rivalry, and presented them as one of the more promising developments of international society. That realist ideas of conflict and force appeared in the setting of the rationalist notion of a society of states gave both tension and subtlety to Bull's analysis of international security.

Hedley Bull's writings on international order, which was the

---

[1] See 'The Classical Approach to Arms Control: Twenty Years After', in Uwe Nerlich (ed.), *Soviet Power and Western Negotiating Policies*, 2, *The Western Panacea: Constraining Soviet Power through Negotiation* (Cambridge, Mass., 1983).

central concern of his theoretical efforts and the main theme of his principal work *The Anarchical Society*, was clearly in the rationalist tradition. Yet his analysis also presented strong traits of realist thought as well as some early hints of revolutionist tendencies. R. J. Vincent's analytical survey of Bull's writings on order in international politics, while placing them squarely in the rationalist category, brings out also the two lesser strands of his philosophy. The rationalist, or societal, constituent comes out most clearly in Bull's discussion of the existence and maintenance of order. The evidence for its existence he saw in the common interests of all states in achieving the elementary goals of social life—the security of life against violence, the sanctity of promises, and the stability of possessions—and in the rules that they had established and the institutions they had developed to that end. Here he took a special interest in international law. He did not, in the way of some writers with more faith in international law as a factor in international politics, see such law as actually producing order among nations. Rather its functions lay in identifying the constitutive principle of the society of states, stating the basic rules of their coexistence, and providing a language for their formal relations. For this reason, he attached importance to signs that countries of the Third World basically accepted international law and expressed their claims in legal terms, which he saw as evidence of the expansion of international society. For the maintenance of international order, he looked in the first place to the consensus that sustained the society of states. In a global society of states, he pointed out, order would have to depend on a development of this consensus. This might well require not only a widening and strengthening of the awareness of common interests but also a deepening and enrichment of the basis of common culture, from which shared values, rules, and institutions usually stemmed. Though there are strong undertones of scepticism, occasionally even of pessimism, in his speculations about future order in a global society, the prevailing note does seem to be one of progressivism, which was among Bull's own criteria for distinguishing rationalists from realists. But it was the whole complex of societal ideas which linked him with this tradition.

The realist streak in Bull's thinking asserted itself particularly in his discussion of the various institutions that helped to sustain international order. Prominent among them was the balance of power. Its functions in relation to order were performed within the system of states. They were three: preventing a transformation of the system into a universal empire, protecting the sovereign independence of its units, and providing conditions in which other institutions of international society might play a role in maintaining order. An essential part of the machinery of the balance of power was war and, not least in the central balance of the contemporary world, the threat of war. War and the threat of war had always played a major role in determining the shape that the international system would assume at any one time, and ultimately also in deciding whether the balance of power would endure or would give way to the preponderance of one dominating power. Thus war itself could be seen as, traditionally, an institution of international society. In the management of the balance of power, including the occasional resort to war or threat of war, the great powers had the most important part. Their role, in relation to each other as well as towards lesser members of the system, rested basically on their superior military strength. In focusing on the system of states, analysing the functions of the balance of power, accepting the part of war, and recognizing the role of great powers, Bull drew heavily on the realist tradition of international thought. But as in his strategic writings, the context of the analysis was the rationalist conception of international society. His repeated warnings that order in international relations must always be precarious, and at times will be only very minimal, may rightly be seen as a product of opposed theoretical influences—as indeed may the paradoxical title *The Anarchical Society*. But, as this title also indicates, it is a case of a rationalist position qualified by realist considerations, not the reverse.

It was when Bull contemplated the contemporary world and speculated about future international order that early signs of revolutionist tendencies appeared. Though order so far had rested largely on the society of states, this might not always be the case. Noting various current developments that could be seen as pointing towards a global polity, he allowed for the possibility that order one day might come to rest on a more integrated world society. Such a world order, he argued, would be more fundamental than, and morally prior to, the existing international order, because it would be composed directly of the individuals that make up mankind, and not largely of the states into which they were now organized. However, it was not till he tackled the issue of international justice that the apparent inclination towards a more solidarist point of view became more pronounced.

The third of the major issues that occupied Hedley Bull became the principal theme of the last phase of his writing career. Like the chief concerns of the two earlier phases, his interest in international justice was part of an enduring preoccupation with the society of states. It was in the context of a broad enquiry into the impact on international society of the emergence and policies of the new states of the Third World that he developed his novel ideas on justice. They appeared in their most advanced form in the paper of 1983, 'Justice in International Relations'.

At this stage of his life, as J. D. B. Miller points out in his critical analysis of Bull's ideas on the Third World, he was considerably more sympathetic than in the earlier years to at least some of the Third World claims and demands for justice. Historically the demands had taken the form of assertions of rights to sovereignty or independence, to national self-determination, to racial equality, to economic justice, and finally to cultural recognition. For a number of reasons, they had on the whole had a remarkably successful response. In the future too, Bull thought, the Western powers should accept that the Third World was struggling essentially to end the European and North American domination of its regions, and should seek to accommodate its claims for political, economic, and cultural freedom. But they ought to stand firm on issues that involved basic Western values, such as human rights and freedom of information. Here he came up against the difficulty that the demands of the Third World, which usually were couched in terms of the rights of peoples, in effect of states, took little account of the rights of individuals.

According to Bull's concepts of justice in international relations, the rights of states were subject to the rights of the global community, of individual persons throughout the world as a whole. In upholding the rights and defending the benefits of individuals on a global scale, he transcended the state-centric view that he had adopted in most of his writings on international security and international order and introduced a more cosmopolitan angle. When he, in a concurrent search for a global cultural consensus, brought in the modern notion of the common good of the human species, he introduced also a universalist angle. Thus his basically international perspective was complemented by, on the one hand, a cosmopolitan dimension pertaining to the rights of individuals in the social cosmos, and on the other hand, a universalist dimension pertaining to the interests of the human species in the physical cosmos. But Bull stopped short of establishing a revolutionist position. The direction he was moving, in the words of Stanley Hoffmann, was not so much 'beyond and after the states system' as towards a 'states system plus'. Developed in the context of speculations about international society and the Third World, his solidarist ideas on justice and culture, like the realist notions of the earlier phases, were ultimately contained within a rationalist framework.

Despite tensions in his philosophy and changes in his view of international relations, there were both unity and continuity in Hedley Bull's work. The basic reason was his constant preoccupation with the society of states. Surveying the three phases of his writing life distinguished here, one notes, first, a gradual evolution of the concept of international society. In his earliest writings on international security, as shown by Tom Millar's quotations from the article of 1959, there was little attempt to distinguish the societal from the systemic elements. Even in some of his earlier writings on international order, as J. D. B. Miller finds in his analysis of the paper of 1968, there was no significant distinction between the concept of the society and the system of states. Rather, the two ideas were then still merged. In the earlier 1970s, when he was working on *The Anarchical Society*, he separated the two. The system of states was defined in terms of an observable pattern of interaction between the units of a constellation of states, and the society of states in terms of their awareness of common interests and recognition of shared values, rules, and institutions. Secondly, one notes, in the final phase, the beginning of a change in the idea of international society. In pursuit of international justice, Bull tentatively, as we have seen, transcended the traditional state-centric approach. But there was not enough time then for a systematic search for a society which would be both of the states system and of the world beyond it. Had he been able to write the foreshadowed volume on justice in world politics, which would have been a natural complement to his book about order in world politics, he might have based his analysis on a concept of society which represented some combination of his well-established notion of international society and the emerging idea of a world society.

A clearer impression of Hedley Bull's notion of international society may be obtained by first briefly comparing it with Robert Gilpin's views, as expressed in his enquiry above into the old European political order, and then exposing it to J. D. B. Miller's critique. Gilpin's concept of international political order seems to be rather more akin to system than to society, as understood here. He distinguishes three such historical orders, on the basis of the distribution of power between the dominant states in the international system. The multipolar society of states that evolved in Europe in earlier centuries, based as it was on the sovereign state, political realism, and the balance of power, he sees as unique. Having become increasingly anachronistic in the nineteenth century, it eventually collapsed in the twentieth and gave way to the bipolar structure of the superpowers. This now appears to be ending. Through the diffusion of Western techniques to other parts of the world, new centres of power are rising. A pluralistic system characterized by cultural heterogeneity is emerging in the world. What are the prospects for order in such a system, he asks. Will the non-Western powers accept the ordering principles of traditional European statecraft? Or will some other rules provide a basis for global coexistence? Or will there be a return to the inter-civilizational conflicts of the pre-modern era, perhaps eventually leading to the triumph of one civilization over another? Gilpin, it seems, rather fears that the outcome will be an era of inter-civilizational conflict.

Though some of the questions they ask are similar, Bull's approach is different from Gilpin's in several respects. First, Bull tried harder to distinguish between system and society, and focused more clearly on the latter. Second, although he—as his contributions to *The Expansion of International Society*, his last major work, show—in the later years developed a long-standing interest in history, his approach to international society was less historical and much more philosophical. Third, he was probably rather less pessimistic about the future of world politics, noting some signs that non-Western states gradually were accepting basic elements of international society, and finding some grounds for hoping that a degree of cultural consensus, or perhaps simply an awareness of a network of common interests, would develop in the world. The basic difference seems to be that Bull attached rather greater importance to the influence of values and principles in international relations.

The difference between a view which focuses on ideas and one which emphasizes power is brought out rather more poignantly by J. D. B. Miller's critique of Bull's central concept. International society, as used by Bull, is a misleading term, Miller argues, because it does not correspond to the realities of international politics. Even in the period when it supposedly existed in its ideal form, namely the century before the First World War, this society was quite different from what it is assumed to have been. Its so-called rules were broken so frequently that its principles were eventually stretched to the very limit. The rights and interests of its small and weak members were so habitually disregarded at the convenience of the major powers that it could hardly be said to rest on the principle of sovereign equality. On the other hand, the pre-1914 world had the network of economic connections involved in international trade and investment. Regulated by rules and understandings which reflected well-understood common interests, these connections amounted to a very substantial set of societal bonds. This point, Miller explains, is particularly important for the discussion about the relationship between the modern international society and the countries of the Third World. Many of them having in fact been drawn into the world society of commerce long before they gained independence, practically all of them are now through economic interdependence so deeply enmeshed that they are simply in no position to escape. Yet Bull, while devoting much attention to more nebulous elements of international society, had little to say about the very substantial economic component.

Bull's international society, Miller continues, looks at times like a front for the interests of the major powers, or rather for the system of the time. Since its strength rests on power, it is really a power arrangement, which is better characterized as a system or an order (the term Gilpin uses) than as a society. After presenting his own picture of this order, Miller goes on to examine the nature and strength of the social spirit in the system. In economic terms, an international society still exists;

and the operation of diplomatic institutions, particularly of the multilateral kind, has greatly expanded, he finds. But the sense of society, often expressed by the term 'the international community', is now to be found only among some of the second-tier powers and many of the lesser states, not least those of the Third World. The two superpowers do not share the spirit. Each wants to construct the international society in its own image, and exercises its power and influence to that end. Thus the international society that does exist is ultimately subject to the will of the great powers.

Despite marked differences of view between themselves, Gilpin and Miller share certain elements of political philosophy which set them apart from Hedley Bull. Together, Gilpin's implied disagreement with and Miller's explicit criticism of Bull's notion of international society—the latter supplemented by an equally realist critique of the notion of international justice—bring out well the essentially rationalist quality of Bull's philosophy of international relations. Against views which focus on power and accept conflict stands a view which attaches more importance to values and ideas and looks for consensus. On the one hand we have interpretations which are marked by force, clarity, and a measure of confidence, on the other an interpretation which is distinguished more by subtlety and complexity, and ultimate uncertainty.

The most substantial point made by Miller, and supported by other authors of this volume, is that Bull's account of international society does not include a strong economic component. This criticism would hardly have surprised Bull, even though he may not have been fully aware of all the implications of his omission. As convinced as Martin Wight of the primacy of international politics, and always more interested in international law than in international economics, he was little inclined to focus on the economic dimension in his analysis. Perhaps he also liked to leave to others, more qualified, the task of exploring this side of international society. At any rate, the structure that he built does provide a framework within which societal bonds of this nature too could be analysed and assessed. Nor would Bull, one expects, have had much difficulty accepting Stanley Hoffmann's points about unfinished questions. That there is much more to be said about the distinction between society and system in international politics, and about the balance between the factors of society and the elements of anarchy, and that there is important work still to be done in distinguishing and analysing different concrete types of international society shows the richness of the fields of enquiry that Bull opened up. Building on the historical work of Martin Wight and others, he laid the philosophical foundations for such future efforts.

Finally, Bull would certainly have agreed that much theoretical work remains to be done on the fundamental goals of international society, not least on the relationship between the two that preoccupied him at the height of his career, order and justice. His achievement was to build a major structure on the theme of the former and to sketch out another one on the theme of the latter, and to start exploring the possibility of integrating the two. But there is still, and probably always will be, both space and a need for new structures built on the same themes, but of perhaps quite different architecture. By formulating the central questions, defining the relevant concepts, and making concise distinctions, he prepared the way for the next generation of scholars in the field. Thus Bull's study of the nature, foundations, and goals of international society—to use a, characteristically measured, phrase of commendation of his own—constitutes a point of departure.

Some of the qualities that distinguish Hedley Bull's contribution to the study of international relations are particularly evident in his articles and papers on current issues. Moreover, those publications occasionally reveal other qualities which are not so often expressed in his major works. The most influential of this group of writings were probably the more than half a dozen pieces about the foreign and defence policy of Australia written when he was at the Australian National University. As much as any of the more substantial works, they show the author's dissecting and differentiating approach to a topic. They also illustrate well his ability to make trenchant comments on particular issues of national politics while, at the same time, focusing attention on the general goals of international politics, here primarily the construction of a viable international order.

Even more revealing, however, were the papers and articles about the role of the superpowers, the evolution of the central balance, and the future of international society which Bull wrote at Oxford in the late 1970s and early 1980s. Not only do they demonstrate well certain qualities which characterize his work in general, particularly a willingness to take account of new developments, to adopt fresh angles, and to explore novel views. They also show sides of his intellectual style which he usually, though not always, restrained in other kinds of writings but sometimes gave free rein in verbal presentations and academic debate, such as an inclination to state his position in an uncompromising form and to advance his views in a challenging manner. Thus in those writings he presented the superpowers, which in most of the earlier works on international order had appeared largely as would-be managers of international society carrying rights and duties all of their own, rather as 'great irresponsibles' ill-fitted for the traditional role of great powers. Increasingly concerned about the global policies of the United States, he now tended to pin his hopes for mankind on Europe instead. He urged Western Europe to become more self-reliant both militarily and politically, so that it could help balance not only the power of the Soviet Union but also the power of its long-standing ally the United States, as well as take the lead in accommodating the Third World and developing international society. Though clearly constructive in spirit, those articles were strikingly forthright in their criticism and refreshingly challenging in their recommendations.

The authors of this volume have paid tribute to Hedley Bull's sense of morality. More than a factor in international relations to be examined and an element of international society to be analysed, morality was a motivation for his own work. This commitment goes a long way towards explaining two of the most outstanding characteristics of his contribution to the study of international relations, namely courage and integrity: the courage to go against the trend, to tackle the big issues, and to persevere in the search for ultimate foundations; and the integrity to take account of the views of others, to question accepted wisdom, and to admit the shortcomings of his own results. But the sense of moral duty does not by itself explain the tensions in philosophy and changes in views of international politics which also mark his work. They, as well as the occasionally pugnacious quality of his style, may be attributed more to an engaging sense of intellectual adventure, which at times drove him to vary the perspective, explore new territory, and try out extreme positions. Perhaps more than anything else, it was his restless mind and youthful spirit which made Hedley Bull such a stimulating influence on his colleagues, and such good company to his friends.

A Bibliography of
Hedley Bull's Publications

BOOKS

The Anarchical Society: A Study of Order in World Politics (London and Basingstoke: Macmillan, 1977).

Asia and the Western Pacific: Towards a New International Order, ed. (Melbourne: Nelson, 1975).

The Challenge of the Third Reich: The Adam von Trott Memorial Lectures, ed. (Oxford: Clarendon, 1986).

The Control of the Arms Race: Disarmament and Arms Control in the Nuclear Age (London: Weidenfeld & Nicolson for ISS, 1961).

The Expansion of International Society, ed. with Adam Watson (Oxford: Clarendon, 1984).

Intervention in World Politics, ed. (Oxford: Clarendon, 1984).

Power Politics, by Martin Wight, ed. with Carsten Holbraad (Leicester: Leicester University Press for RIIA, 1978). Republished by Penguin Books (London, 1979 and 1986).

The Special Relationship: Anglo-American Relations since 1945, ed. with Wm. Roger Louis (Oxford: Clarendon, 1986).

Systems of States, essays by Martin Wight, ed. with an introduction (Leicester: Leicester University Press for LSE, 1977).

ARTICLES AND PAMPHLETS

'World Opinion and International Organisation', *International Relations,* 1. 9 (Apr. 1958).

'What is the Commonwealth?', *World Politics,* 11. 4 (July 1959; Princeton University, NJ). Reprinted in *International Political Communities: An Anthology* (New York: Anchor Books, Doubleday & Co., 1966); Falk, Richard and Mendlovitz, Saul H., eds., *Regional Politics and World Order* (San Francisco: W. H. Freeman & Co., 1973).

'Disarmament and the International System', *Australian Journal of Politics and History,* 5. 1 (May 1959). Reprinted in Garnett, John, ed., *Theories of Peace and Security: A Reader in Contemporary Strategic Thought* (London: Macmillan, 1970).

'The Arms Race and the Banning of Nuclear Tests', *The Political Quarterly* (Oct.–Dec. 1959).

'Nigeria', *Current Affairs Bulletin*, 25. 7 (8 Feb. 1960; Sydney).

'Systematic Innovation and Social Philosophy', *Inquiry*, 3. 3 (Autumn 1960; Oslo University Press).

'The Many Sides of British Unilateralism', *The Reporter* (16 Mar. 1961).

The Control of the Arms Race (London: Weidenfeld & Nicolson for ISS, 1961); extracts published as 'The Objectives of Arms Control' in Pfaltzgraff, Robert L., Jr., ed., *Politics and the International System* (Philadelphia: J. B. Lippincott Co., 1968) and 'Arms Control and the Balance of Power', in Lefever, Ernest W., ed., *Arms and Arms Control* (New York: Frederick A. Praeger, 1961).

'Cold War Diplomacy', *Current Affairs Bulletin*, 28. 12 (16 Oct. 1961).

'Reports on World Affairs: Strategic and Geographical Aspects', *The Year Book of World Affairs*, 15 (1961; London Institute of World Affairs) and 16 (1962).

'Europe and the Bomb', *The Spectator* (29 June 1962).

'The Spread of Nuclear Weapons', *The Spectator* (12 Oct. 1962).

'Is International Inspection Necessary?', *The Spectator* (30 Nov. 1962).

'Limitations in Strategic Nuclear War', *The Listener* (24 Jan. 1963). Reprinted as 'Limited War and Nuclear War', *Survival* (Mar.-Apr. 1963).

'International Defence Organisations', *The Annual Register of World Events* (1962, 1963).

'Report on the Strategic Aspects of World Affairs' and 'Two Kinds of Arms Control', in *The Year Book of World Affairs* (1963).

'A Comment on the Proposal for a Ban on the First Use of Nuclear Weapons', in Tucker, Robert C., *et al.*, *Proposal for No First Use of Nuclear Weapons: Pros and Cons* (Princeton: Center of International Studies, Princeton University, Policy Memorandum 28, 1963).

'Inconsistent Objectives', *The Spectator* (4 Jan. 1963).

'Thinking about the Unthinkable', *The Spectator* (1 Mar. 1963).

'NATO at Ottawa', *The Spectator* (24 May 1963).

'Strategy and the Atlantic Alliance: A Critique of United States Doctrine' (Princeton: Center of International Studies, Princeton University, Policy Memorandum 29, 1964).

'Pros and Cons of Unilateral Disarmament', *Gandhi Marg*, 8. 1 (Jan. 1964; New Delhi).

'Mr Strachey and World Order', *Political Studies*, 12. 1 (Feb. 1964). (Review of J. Strachey, *On the Prevention of War*.)

'International Order and the Dispersion of Nuclear Weapons', *Science*, 144. 3619 (8 May 1964).

'Arms Control', *Current Affairs Bulletin*, 34. 5 (20 July 1964).

'Disarmament and Arms Control', in *Special Studies Prepared for the*

Special Committee of the House of Commons on Matters Relating to Defence (Ottawa: Roger Duhamel, 1965).

'International Defence Organisations', *The Annual Register of World Events* (1964, 1965).

'Report on Strategic Aspects of World Affairs', *The Year Book of World Affairs*, 19 (1965).

'Disarmament and Arms Control', *The British Survey*, 190 (Jan. 1965; British Society for International Understanding).

'International Theory: The Case for a Classical Approach', *World Politics*, 18. 3 (Apr. 1966). Reprinted in Pfaltzgraff, Robert L, Jr., ed., *Politics and the International System* (Philadelphia: J. B. Lippincott Co., 1968); Knorr, Klaus and Rosenau, James N., eds., *Contending Approaches to International Politics* (Princeton University Press, 1969); Sanders, Bruce L. and Durbin, Alan C., eds., *Contemporary International Politics: Introductory Readings* (New York: John Wiley & Sons, 1971); Hartmann, F. H., ed., *World in Crisis* (New York: Macmillan, 4th ed., 1973).

'Society and Anarchy in International Relations', in Butterfield, Herbert and Wight, Martin, eds., *Diplomatic Investigations* (London: George Allen & Unwin, 1966).

'The Grotian Conception of International Society', in Butterfield, Herbert and Wight, Martin, eds., *Diplomatic Investigations* (London, 1966). Reprinted in Falk, Richard A. and Kim, Samuel, eds., *The War System: An Interdisciplinary Approach* (Boulder, Colorado: Westview Press, 1980).

'Die Ziele der Rüstungskontrolle', in Nerlich, Uwe, ed., *Krieg und Frieden in der modernen Staatenwelt* (Munich: C. Bertelsmann Verlag, 1966).

'Western Policy and Nuclear Proliferation in Asia', *World Review*, 6. 3 (Oct. 1967; Brisbane).

'On the Non-Proliferation Treaty', *Interplay of European/American Affairs* (Nov.–Dec. 1967; New York).

'The Role of the Nuclear Powers in the Management of Nuclear Proliferation', in Dougherty, James E. and Lehman, J. F., Jr., eds., *Arms Control for the Late Sixties* (Princeton, NJ: D. van Nostrand Co., 1968).

'On Non-Proliferation', *Interplay of European/American Affairs*, 1. 6 (Jan. 1968; New York).

'The Strategic Consequences of Britain's Revised Naval Role' (with L. Martin) in Gullion, E. A., ed., *Uses of the Seas* (New York: The American Assembly, Columbia University, 1968).

'Australia, New Zealand and Nuclear Weapons', in Millar, T. B., ed., *Australia–New Zealand Defence Cooporation* (Canberra: Australian National University Press, 1968).

Untitled paper in *Australia's Foreign Policy in the Seventies* (Townsville:

Australian Institute of International Affairs, North Queensland Branch, 1968).

'Strategic Studies and its Critics', *World Politics*, 20. 4 (July 1968). Reprinted in Rosi, Eugene J., ed., *American Defense and Detente* (New York: Dodd, Mead & Co., 1973).

'In Support of the Non-Proliferation Treaty', *Quadrant*, 12. 3 (no. 53) (May–June 1968; Sydney).

'The Non-Proliferation Treaty and its Implications for Australia', *Australian Outlook*, 22. 2 (Aug. 1968).

'The Political and Strategic Background to Australian Defence', in Scott, R. H., ed., *The Economics of Defence* (Economic Papers, 29, Economic Society of Australia & New Zealand, NSW & Victorian Branches; Nov. 1968).

'Problems of Australian Foreign Policy January-June 1968', *Australian Journal of Politics and History*, 14. 1 (Dec. 1968).

'Force in Contemporary International Relations', Review Article, *Survival*, 10. 9 (Sept. 1968).

'Der Indische Ozean-nach dem Rückzug Grossbritanniens', *Moderne Welt*, 3 (1969; Cologne); also printed as 'Security in the Indian Ocean', *Modern World*, 7 (1969; Düsseldorf).

'The Scope for Super-Power Agreements', *Arms Control and National Security: An International Journal*, 1 (1969; New York: Hudson Institute & Pergamon Press); abridged version, 'The Scope for Soviet–American Agreement', in *Soviet-American Relations and World Order: Arms Limitation and Policy*, Adelphi Papers, 65 (Feb. 1970): Paper for ISS conference on 'The Super-Powers: Soviet American Relations and World Order', 1969.

'Arms Control: A Stocktaking and Prospectus', in *Problems of Modern Strategy*, 2, Adelphi Papers, 55 (Mar. 1969); also in Buchan, Alastair, ed., *Problems of Modern Strategy* (London, Chatto & Windus, for ISS, 1970). Reprinted in Rosi, Eugene J., ed., *American Defense and Detente* (New York: Dodd, Mead & Co., 1973).

'*The Twenty Years' Crisis* Thirty Years On', *International Journal*, 24. 4 (Autumn 1969; Canada).

'Prospects for SALT', *Interplay: The Magazine of International Affairs*, 3. 5 (Dec. 1969–Jan. 1970; New York).

'Asia in the Seventies', *New Guinea, Australia and the Pacific*, 5. 2 (June–July 1970; Sydney).

'Chemical and Biological Weapons: The Prospects for Arms Control', *Australian Outlook*, 24. 2 (Aug. 1970).

'Strategic Arms Limitation: The Precedent of the Washington and London Naval Treaties' (Occasional Paper for the Center for Policy Study, University of Chicago, 1971). Reprinted in Kaplan, Morton A., ed., *SALT: Problems and Prospects* (Morristown, NJ: General Learning Press, 1973).

'World Order and the Super Powers', in Holbraad, Carsten, ed., *Super Powers and World Order* (Canberra: ANU Press, 1971).

'The New Balance of Power in Asia and the Pacific', *Foreign Affairs*, 49. 4 (July 1971); abridged version in Lanyi, George A. and McWilliams, Wilkson, eds., *Crisis and Continuity in World Politics: Readings in International Relations* (New York: Random House, 2nd ed., 1973).

'Order vs. Justice in International Society', *Political Studies*, 19. 3 (Sept. 1971).

'Europe and the Wider World', *The Round Table*, 244 (Oct. 1971).

'Civil Violence and International Order', in *Civil Violence and the International System*, p. 2, *Violence and International Security*, Adelphi Papers, 83 (Dec. 1971). (Papers given at thirteenth Annual IISS Conference at Stresa.)

'Nueva Esquema de Poder en el Pacifico', *Revista de Estudios del Pacifico*, 2 (Sept. 1971; Valparaiso, Chile).

'The Theory of International Politics, 1919–1969', in Porter, Brian, ed., *The Aberystwyth Papers: International Politics 1919–1969* (London: Oxford University Press, 1972).

'International Law and International Order', *International Organization*, 26. 3 (Summer 1972).

'The Defence of Australia to the 1980's: The Problem', *United Service*, 26. 2 (Oct. 1972; United Service Institution of NSW, Sydney).

'Ordine e Giustizia Nella Communita Internazionale', *Mercurio*, 10 (Oct. 1972; Bologna).

'International Relations as an Academic Pursuit', *Australian Outlook*, 26. 3 (Dec. 1972).

'Violence and Development', in Hunter, Robert E. and Reilly, John E., eds., *Development Today: A New Look at US Relations with the Poor Countries* (New York: Praeger, 1972).

'Australia's Defence', in Keith, Ken, ed., *Defence Perspectives* (Price Milburn for NZIIA, 1972). (Papers at 1972 Otago Foreign Policy School, New Zealand).

'Australia–New Zealand Defence Cooperation', in Keith, Ken, ed., *Defence Perspectives* (Wellington: Price Milburn for NZIIA, 1972).

'Options for Australia', in McCarthy, Gordon, ed., *Foreign Policy for Australia: Choices for the Seventies* (Sydney: Angus & Robertson, 1973). (Papers of the 39th Summer School of the Australian Institute of Political Science.)

'The Moscow Agreements and Strategic Arms Limitation' (Canberra Papers on Strategy and Defence, 15, ANU, Canberra, 1973).

'War and International Order', in James, Alan, ed., *The Bases of International Order: Essays in Honour of C. A. W. Manning* (Oxford: Oxford University Press, 1973).

'The Indian Ocean as a "Zone of Peace" ', in Poulose, T. T., ed.,

Indian Ocean Power Rivalry (New Delhi: Young Asia Publications, 1974).

'Australia's Involvement in Independent Papua-New Guinea', (fourth Heindorff Memorial Lecture), in *World Review*, 13. 1 (Mar. 1974; Brisbane).

'Australia and the Great Powers in Asia', in Greenwood, Gordon and Harper, Norman, eds., *Australia in World Affairs, 1966–70* (Melbourne: Cheshire for AIIA, 1974).

'The New Strategic Balance in Asia and the Pacific', *Jernal Hubungan Antarabangsa*, 2 (1974–5; University of Malaya, Kuala Lumpur).

'Introduction: Towards a New International Order?' and 'The New Course of Australian Policy', in Bull, Hedley, ed., *Asia and the Western Pacific: Towards a New International Order* (Melbourne: Thomas Nelson with AIIA, 1975).

'New Directions in the Theory of International Relations', *International Studies*, 14. 2 (Apr.–June 1975; New Delhi).

'Rethinking Non-Proliferation', *International Affairs*, 51.2 (Apr. 1975).

'Models of Future World Order', *Indian Quarterly*, 31. 1 (Jan.–Mar. 1975).

'The Whitlam Government's Perceptions of our Role in the World', in Beddie, B. D., ed., *Advance Australia–Where?* (Melbourne: OUP Australia with AIIA, 1975). (Proceedings of June 1974 Conference of AIIA.)

'Wider Still and Wider: Nuclear Proliferation 1950–1975', *International Perspectives* (Nov.–Dec. 1975; Ottawa).

'Australia and the Nuclear Problem: Some Concluding Comments', in O'Neill, Robert J., ed., *The Strategic Nuclear Balance: An Australian Perspective* (Canberra: ANU Strategic and Defence Studies Centre, 1975).

'Sea Power and Political Influence', in *Power at Sea*, 1, *The New Environment*, Adelphi Papers, 122 (Spring 1976).

'The West and the Third World', *Dyason House Papers*, 2. 5 (June 1976; Melbourne).

'Arms Control and World Order', *International Security*, 1. 1 (Summer 1976).

'Martin Wight and the Theory of International Relations', the second Martin Wight Memorial Lecture, in *British Journal of International Studies*, 2. 2 (July 1976).

The Anarchical Society: A Study of Order in World Politics (London and Basingstoke: Macmillan, 1977); extract, 'The Balance of Power and International Order', in Sondermann, F. A., McLellan, D. S., and Olson, W. C., eds., *The Theory and Practice of International Relations* (5th ed., Englewood Cliffs, NJ: Prentice-Hall, 1979); shorter extract of same title in Smith, Michael, Little, Richard, and Shackleton,

Michael, eds., *Perspectives on World Politics* (London: Croom Helm, 1981).

'Neuverteilung von Reichtum oder Neuverteilung von Macht? Der Westen die dritte Welt und die Weltordnung', *Europa Archiv*, 4 (1977; Bonn).

'A View from Abroad: Consistency under Pressure', *Foreign Affairs*, 57. 3 (1979; issue on 'America and the World 1978').

'The Third World and International Society', *The Year Book of World Affairs*, 33 (1979; London Institute of World Affairs).

'Natural Law and International Relations', *British Journal of International Studies*, 5. 2 (July 1979).

'Recapturing the Just War for Political Theory', review article in *World Politics*, 31. 4 (July 1979).

'The Universality of Human Rights', *Millennium*, 8. 2 (Autumn 1979).

'The State's Positive Role in World Affairs', in *Daedalus* 108. 4 (Fall 1979; issue on 'The State'); this issue republished in Graubard, Stephen R., ed., *The State* (New York: W. H. Norton & Co., 1979).

'Human Rights and World Politics', in Pettman, Ralph, ed., *Moral Claims in World Affairs* (London: Croom Helm, 1979).

Review of Suhrke, Astri and Nobel, Lela Garner, eds., *Ethnic Conflict in International Relations*, in *Ethnic and Racial Studies*, 3. 3 (July 1980).

'Kissinger: The Primacy of Geopolitics', *International Affairs*, 56. 3 (Summer 1980). (Review of Henry Kissinger, *The White House Years*.)

'The Great Irresponsibles? The United States, the Soviet Union and World Order', *International Journal*, 35. 3 (Summer 1980; Canada); also in *Europa Archiv*, 18 (25 Sept. 1980; Bonn).

'The Harries Report and the Third World', *Quadrant*, 34. 7 (July 1980; Sydney).

'The Rise of Soviet Naval Power', *Problems of Communism*, 30. 2 (Mar.–Apr. 1981; Washington).

'Hobbes and the International Anarchy', *Social Research*, 48. 4 (Winter 1981; New York).

'Force in International Relations: The Experience of the 1970s and Prospects for the 1980s', in O'Neill, Robert J. and Horner, D. M., eds., *New Directions in Strategic Thinking* (London: George Allen & Unwin, 1981).

'Of Means and Ends', in O'Neill, Robert J, and Horner, D. M., eds., *New Directions in Strategic Thinking*.

'The Revolt against the West', in Rajan, M. S. and Ganguly, Shivaji, eds., *Great Power Relations, World Order and the Third World: Essays in Memory of Sisir Gupta* (New Delhi: Vikas Publishing House, 1981).

'The West and South Africa', *Daedalus*, 111. 2 (Spring 1982).

'Civilian Power Europe: A Contradiction in Terms?', *Journal of Common Market Studies*, 21. 1–2 (Sept.–Dec. 1982); this issue republished as Tsoukalis, Loukas, ed., *The European Community: Past, Present and Future* (Oxford: Basil Blackwell, 1983).

'European Defence: The Political Perspective', in *Thinking Again About European Defence* (London: European Democratic Group, 1982).

'A New Course for Britain and Western Europe', *SAIS Review*, 4 (Summer 1982; John Hopkins University, Washington, DC).

'Die klassische Konzeption der Rüstungskontrolle: Ein Ruckblick nach zwanzig Jahren', in Nerlich, Uwe, ed., *Sowjetische Macht und westliche Verhandlungspolitik im Wandel militärischer Kräfteverhältnisse* (Baden-Baden: Nomos Verlagsgesellschaft, 1982); also published as 'The Classical Approach to Arms Control: Twenty Years After', in Nerlich, Uwe, ed., *Soviet Power and Western Negotiating Policies*, 2, *The Western Panacea: Constraining Soviet Power through Negotiation* (Cambridge, Mass.: Ballinger Publishing Co., 1983).

'Intervention in the Third World', *The Non-Aligned World*, 1. 3 (July–Sept. 1983; New Delhi).

'The International Anarchy in the 1980's', *Australian Outlook*, 37. 3 (Dec. 1983).

Justice in International Relations, the 1983–4 Hagey Lectures (University of Waterloo, Ontario, Oct. 1984).

'European Self-Reliance and the Reform of NATO', *Atlantic Quarterly*, 1. 1 (Spring 1983; Harlow, Essex); also in *Foreign Affairs*, 61. 4 (Spring 1983).

'Die anarchische Gesellschaft', in Kaiser, Karl and Schwarz, Hans-Peter, eds., *Weltpolitik: Strukturen–Akteure–Perspektiven* (Bonn: Bundeszentrale für politische Bildung, 1985).

'The American Presidency Viewed from Britain and Australia', in Thompson, Kenneth W. ed., *The American Presidency: Perspectives from Abroad*, The Miller Center of Public Affairs, University of Virginia (Lanham, MD: University Press of America, 1986).

'Hans Kelsen and International Law', in Tur, Richard and Twining, William, eds., *Essays on Kelsen* (Oxford: Clarendon, 1986).

'Britain and Australia in Foreign Policy', in J. D. B. Miller, ed., *Australians and British: Social and Political Connections* (Sydney: Methuen, 1987).

'Population and the Present World Structure', in William Alonso, ed., *Population in an Interacting World* (Cambridge and London: Harvard University Press, 1987).

EDITED COLLECTION

Hedley Bull on Arms Control, selected and introduced by Robert O'Neill and David W. Schwartz (London: Macmillan and IISS, 1987).

Index

Index compiled by Peva Keane